A Guide to the
Understanding and Practice
of Spiritual Healing

Books by Harry Edwards

SPIRIT HEALING
THE POWER OF SPIRITUAL HEALING
THE HEALING INTELLIGENCE
LIFE IN SPIRIT
THE MEDIUMSHIP OF JACK WEBBER

by Ramus Branch

HARRY EDWARDS
The life story of the great healer

A Guide to the Understanding and Practice of Spiritual Healing

by

HARRY EDWARDS

in collaboration with
RAMUS BRANCH

Published by
Harry Edwards Spiritual Healing Sanctuary
Burrows Lea, Hook Lane, Shere, Guildford, Surrey GU5 9QG

AUTHOR'S NOTE

The original *A Guide to Spirit Healing* was written in 1950. Since then, outstanding progress has been seen in the spirit healing of disease. Ill-conditions which then showed a lack of response now yield more easily, while organic afflictions so often seem to melt away. This progress may well be due to the healing intelligences acquiring greater wisdom and easement in using healers to overcome the causes of sicknesses. Healership, too, has advanced in establishing attunement with the source of healing, in receiving instruction and knowledge from the spirit guides.

This revised book includes this advanced knowledge and tells how healers can establish a closer affinity with Spirit and so understand the basic postulates on which the science of spirit healing depends.

It must be recognised that healing is a natural gift from Spirit, possessed by those of a compassionate nature and who have that deep inner yearning to help the sick. Neither this nor any other book can teach a person how to become a healer, for spiritual healing is an advanced spirit science and not one that can be taught in the way that our other sciences can be taught.

What this book does is simply to offer guidance, as its title implies, and where there is occasional repetition of certain statements and explanations, the author has purposely allowed this not only for emphasis, but to save the reader referring back to previous chapters.

Printed in Great Britain by
the MPG Books Group, Bodmin and King's Lynn

CONTENTS

SECTION I

ABSENT HEALING AND THE SEEKING OF ATTUNEMENT WITH SPIRIT

SECTION II

THE THEORY OF SPIRIT HEALING

Chapter

SECTION III

HEALING PRACTICE

SECTION IV

THE SCIENCE OF SPIRIT HEALING

Chapter

FOREWORD

by the Author

The following question is often asked by people who wish they possessed the gift of healing: "Do you think I could become a healer?"; and, when I speak to gatherings on the subject of spiritual healing, I often ask the audience: "How many of you would like to be the means of healing reaching the sick?" Usually a high percentage will raise their hands.

The answer is: "People who have a deep inner yearning to give of themselves in healing the sick, to take away pain and stress, who possess compassion and sympathy for those who are afflicted and are willing to sacrifice their time without any pecuniary reward; people who are generous in their nature, and who render willing service for good causes, are those who possess the spiritual qualities which mark the healing gift. This healing potential, then, only needs the development of the faculty of attunement with the spirit source of healing and the opportunity to give it practical expression."

It is for such people that this book has primarily been written, to assist them from the earliest stages to acquire the art of attunement and, while this is being developed, to study the postulates and theories which govern spiritual healing. Then, possibly in company with others who are already engaged on their healing mission, to co-operate with Spirit for healing to reach sufferers; and, finally, to receive further thoughts concerning the science of spirit healing and the means whereby healing can reach those suffering not only from all manner of physical diseases but also from ill conditions of the mind.

This book is, therefore, a step by step progression from the initial desire to heal to the more advanced scientific appreciation of the two-dimensional (physical and Spirit) use of energies and thought influences for the healing of mind, body and soul.

Harry Edwards

1974

SECTION I

ABSENT HEALING AND THE SEEKING OF ATTUNEMENT WITH SPIRIT

General Observations

It can be truly said that Absent Healing will become the most potent healing factor for the future. If one accepts the truth that patients suffering from medically incurable conditions can be cured solely through Absent Healing we establish the foundation for a healing revelation of the greatest magnitude.

It is the purpose of this section to examine the postulates which are so far known to govern the process of both Absent and Contact Healing, the implications which arise from them, and how we can develop the healing potential.

The term "Absent Healing" is in itself a misnomer, for the healing cannot be "absent". A truer definition would be "Distant Healing", i.e. healing from a distance as distinct from Contact Healing, where the healer is in actual physical contact with the patient. As the expression "Absent Healing" is so commonly accepted as meaning Distant Healing, we shall continue to use it. Another apt definition, more generally used by religious bodies, is "Divine Healing" or "Prayer Healing" but obviously by whatever name it is called Absent Healing carries out its purpose when conditions are right for its operation and effectiveness.

The efficacy of Absent Healing is proved when there

can be no other possible explanation for a sick person, whether recovering from a physical or mental disorder, making a recovery—partial or complete—from the time the healing intercessions have commenced on that patient's behalf. Consider a typical case of a sufferer of a long-standing disease, who has been under doctors' care and hospitalisation for years and is finally told that medical science can do no more for him and that he must learn to "live with the complaint". No more medical treatment or medicines are given, except possibly a steel-braced corset or pain-killing tablets. It is at this stage that Absent Healing is sought, and within a comparatively short while the symptoms become progressively less, pain dies away, and the ill effects are overcome.

The time period for the healing may be short—a matter of days or weeks, or it may be extended over a period of time, depending upon the patient's condition.

Absent Healing is now becoming a common practice with spiritual healers throughout the world. Distance creates no problems. Churches are taking it up with healing groups, prayer circles and so forth. The Spiritual Healing Sanctuary, Shere, Guildford, Surrey, is the world centre of Absent Healing. The numbers of people who have sought for healing by the Absent Healing method and who have been cured of afflictions are legion. Consistently, the weekly post has been between nine and eleven thousand letters; since 1948 over 14,000,000 healing letters have been received and answered.* Unless there had been a high percentage of success, the inflow of letters would have waned and frittered away. Few people like writing letters, some get tired of doing so; those who get well often just stop writing without telling the healer why. So to maintain a number approaching half a million a year is indeed an eloquent testimony to Absent Healing. This is all the

---

*This was the situation at the time this book was being written by Harry Edwards in 1974.

more significant when it is remembered that people seldom write for minor complaints, but rather when they are not responding to medical treatment, or have been declared to be "incurable" or in cases of emergency such as severe injuries suffered in an accident. Absent Healing is often considered to be the Cinderella of the healing movement, simply because it is intangible and impersonal, in so far as the healer may not know the patient or even see him at any time. In Contact Healing the body and faculties of the healer are used. He is a knowledgeable instrument or co-operator with the healing guides. The flow of healing energy to the patient is sensed; the reduction of affliction is seen, movements are easier, pain is less, minds are less harassed, weak sight and hearing are strengthened, wastage is overcome, and so on and so on. The benefit is tangible. None of these things are personally experienced by the healer with Absent Healing. He never (or rarely) sees his patient. Sometimes he only knows his patient through a third person. All he has to go upon is a verbal message, a letter or a telephone call.

Patients, too, do not have the psychological advantage of being physically treated; of meeting the healer and hearing his words, of feeling the flow of healing energy from the healer into themselves. Thus patients sometimes are unable to appreciate the value of Absent Healing in the early stages until they begin to feel benefit. Others only consent to give Absent Healing a trial as a last despairing hope.

Another attitude encountered is that when a busy healer is asked to help yet another sufferer, possibly entailing a visit to the patient's home some distance away, the healer might well suggest that "he will place the patient on his Absent Healing list" and as far as the enquirer is concerned that is the end of the matter and the request disposed of. We have to face the situation in which the ordinary person does not place much reliance on the efficacy of intercession whether it is given by a healer or a priest. It has become a kind of expression of sympathy and disposal of the subject. Absent Healing is much, much more than this. It is an *advanced spirit science*, more evolved than the wonder of Contact Spirit Healing. To attain mastery over the cause of a disease and the disposal of the ill-effects, without the presence of the healer to act as a communicating transformer for the corrective healing energies, indicates that Absent Healing is a superior science.

It is the way of thought today, to consider the Absent Healer as being less developed than a Contact Healer, a kind of Grade 2. In the development of the healing gift, the Absent Healing process is often used as a preliminary training for Contact Healing, and this is so because the beginner establishes the art of attunement by this method—and attunement is the fundamental essential for Spiritual Healing in all its branches.

It will be explained later why Absent Healing is a more evolved science than any other human or known spirit science. As Absent Healing and its implications become more fully appreciated and understood, so in future years this form of healing will assume ascendancy over other methods, and be a major factor for the prevention of disease.

The Qualifications for an Absent Healer

Many people wish to know if they possess the healing gift and how they can develop it. Healing is a natural talent, and generally speaking all those who inwardly feel for those who are sick and in pain and have that deep inner yearning to heal may well possess the healing potential, which only needs developing and the opportu-

nity for expression. Absent Healing is often the way
through which the gift is awakened and developed.

Those people of good will who feel love and compassion for those who are unwell and whose natural desire
and inclination is to awaken their latent gift of healing,
can find no better way of arousing this than by the Absent Healing method. It cannot help but encourage the
faculty of attunement that is so necessary for any phase
of spiritual healing.

Thus the seeking of the ability to become an Absent
Healer can serve as an introductory method for the development of psychic potentials generally; but I must
stress that it is not merely an introduction, for Absent
Healing is the most enlightened method of healing the
sick. It is indeed an evolved spirit science, in spite of its
intangibility and abstract nature, as far as the employment of the human effort is concerned. By its very nature,
it helps more than in any other way to bring about that
affinity with the spirit realm in a free and natural
manner.

Before we come to the way to develop the healing gift,
it is necessary to appreciate a number of primary postulates, that is, if the development is to be conducted in an
intelligent manner. The more we comprehend the basis
upon which the science rests, then we can co-operate with
the healing purpose more intelligently rather than being
inanimate instruments.

Spirit Healing Uses Thought Energies

Spirit healing is a thought process. The healing is set
into motion from the mental request from the healer to
the healing guides for help to reach a given patient.

Divine or spirit healing is common to all religions and
it has been known throughout time past with all peoples,
civilised and primitive. It is a law that there must be a

directive given in the form of a thought request before any healing can take place. In religious circles it takes the form of prayers to God, whether the god be the Christian God, or the God of any other religion. The incantations of the medicine man fall within this meaning. With the spiritual healer the motivating thoughts are directed through attunement during intercession.

The Physical Mind

Man is both a physical and a spirit being *now*. He has a physical and a spirit body and a physical and a spirit mind.

The physical mind is concerned with bodily conditions and sensations; it registers when we are cold, hungry, tired, or in discomfort from physical disorders. It registers experience, it collects information and has the ability of relating one piece of knowledge to another and arriving at a conclusion. Its servant is the brain, a wonderful computer.

All these qualities are received by the conscious mind. It is the conscious mind which directs the brain computer to act. For example, the sensory nerves report through the brain to the conscious mind that the body is very cold; the conscious mind then seeks the means to protect the body from further cold, and through the brain we are informed where our overcoat is, and with further direction from the conscious mind, the brain instructs the nerves to work the legs and so take the person to where the overcoat is, and so on. The physical mind is in tune with the material or earthly realm.

The Spirit Mind

The spirit mind is also a reasoning mind. It is concerned with emotions: love, hate, kindness, sadism, good and evil, ambition, and it is largely influenced by the character genes in the human make-up. It inspires us to seek high ideals; it is the conscience; and it provides the motive for soul progression and the awakening of the spiritual consciousness.

The Thought Process

The two minds, physical and spirit, are intimate one with the other, and they are both able to register on the consciousness. This is an elementary but important fact to keep in mind when considering the mechanics of Absent Healing. The spirit mind is in tune with the spirit realm.

The healer's physical mind receives the information concerning the patient. It appreciates the nature of the ill condition, e.g., if there is mental stress and/or physical pain, etc. It assesses the mental picture of the healing needed and this is passed on to the conscious mind, from whence it is conveyed to the spirit mind, where it can be received by the spirit guide who is in attunement with the healer.

So when it is said that "Absent Healing" is a "thought process" we can begin to see the general manner of its operation.

Another vital implication arises from this conclusion. It proves "that man is part Spirit and akin to Spirit in this life **now**". If this were not so, then no act of spiritual healing could take place. Moreover, it is provable by the study of the laws which govern life and healing.

It is an established law that there must exist a state of harmony between the emission and reception of any force. There would be anarchy in the world of science if this were not true. Therefore, for any person to be used as a healing intermediary or for any patient to benefit from a spirit healing force proves that that person is in harmony with the source of healing energies, which come from Spirit.

Let us approach this conclusion from a different angle:

The Postulates which Govern Healing

We have already established that to initiate a healing there must be the emission of a purposeful thought force.

Everything which takes place, every movement, every change in the state of matter, is the result of law-governed forces applied to the subject. There is no exception. We witness this in the evolution of matter, the courses of the stars, germination, birth, death, the atomic formation of an element, the operation of the known forces of electricity, gravity and so on. Physical science is based upon the application of certain laws, otherwise there would be chaos.

The same ruling must apply to spirit healing. So often a chemical change has to take place to overcome the affliction. With every spirit healing, law-governed forces are put into operation; therefore, within this universal principle, healings must be the result of law-governed forces applied to the given condition.

This conclusion introduces one of the limiting factors in healing, which is that no healing can take place if it is contrary to the law. For example, if a finger is amputated, a new one cannot be grown; or if advanced age has brought senility, then healing cannot restore juvenility. While the causes of disease are maintained, then the ill-effects will be maintained. At the same time, the healing will maintain the patient in as happy and strengthened a condition as is possible. Consider the common case of weakening eyesight due to undue strain imposed by close and exacting work. If the latter is persisted in, recovery is unlikely, for the healing result is negatived. If a sufferer receiving healing from arthritis lives in a damp house and sleeps in a damp bed, then the arthritis will be maintained in spite of the healing. This need not imply that the healing effort will be entirely negatived for it will maintain the ill-condition in as good a state as can be induced, and uphold the general health tone of the patient.

Just as the physical realm is controlled by physical laws, so it is logical that the spirit realm is likewise law-governed, too, for such must exist wherever there is order. In spirit healing there is every reason to believe that the healing intelligences (or healing guides) are able to direct the spirit law-governed forces or energies to effect a change for the better in the total self of the patient.

Combining these first two conclusions we see that **spirit healings result from law-governed forces being put into operation following the emission of a thought directive.**

The records of healing successes denote a further common factor. We see healings take place of very diverse kinds through the instrumentality of one healer. For example, (a) the restoring of an unbalanced mind, (b) the removal of a malignant growth, (c) the restoration of sight or other sense, (d) the change in the blood content in leukaemia. This means that there is no one healing force, but that a different character of force is necessary for the treatment of each individual complaint.

So it follows that to create the right quality of healing energy to overcome the respective human affliction indicates the ability of diagnosis and discrimination. To achieve this there must be a directing and discriminating intelligence.

When a sick person is deemed to be incurable it means that human wisdom has become exhausted; medical science can do no more. When, through spiritual healing, the "incurable" recovers and is restored to health, it must mean that a superior intelligence has intervened. As this intelligence is not human, it must come from Spirit.

To those critics who say that healing knowledge comes from the human subconscious mind, the reply is that there is no evidence that mankind possesses today, or ever has possessed, the detailed knowledge to carry out a planned act of healing when human skill can do no more. Therefore, there has been no human experience from which the subconscious mind can draw such precise and profound knowledge.

It follows that the spirit guides have been able to acquire this wider knowledge. It also implies that to carry out a healing of the mind and body this wisdom must not only include the ordered employment of the spirit forces but the knowledge to combine them with the physical forces which govern our bodies and at some stage to transform a spirit force into a physical effect. This transformation may be effected in Contact Healing through the healer or through the spirit body of the patient. In Absent Healing the spirit body of the patient is most probably used as the transformer.

Every healing must be a planned act, having both intention and direction. Thus for the desired result to be attained there exists the knowledge of the administration of the corrective forces to produce the desired chemical or functional changes in the patient.

There must be intelligent direction to achieve any planned act, even though it may only be the building of a rabbit hutch; and intelligent direction is used to employ the law-governed forces to bring about the result. For example, to use a force such as electricity we must understand the laws which govern it and its potentials, and then we can administer them to obtain the results we are seeking.

The acquiring of wisdom by the human faculty has always been through the slow and laborious process of trial and error. It is a logical assumption that the mind of a spirit guide does not suddenly become the possessor of infinite wisdom but that it, too, has to travel the same road, acquiring step by step its greater comprehension of the spirit law-governed forces and how they can be applied to, and co-operate with, the physical forces to produce a forseeable beneficial change in the state of a sick person. Some evidence for this is seen in the greater ease with which certain diseases yield to spirit healing today than they did in years past.

So now we can add a third summary to our two previous conclusions:

That consequent upon the emission of a thought appeal by a human mind in attunement with a spirit intelligence, the spirit guide is able to receive the request and to administer the correct quality of force to heal the particular disharmony in the body of the patient.

Absent Healing is intangible, imponderable, not clear or definite to the mind. Yet it is proven by the inexhaustible mass of evidence which is being added to every day. Having arrived at an appreciation of the fundamental conclusions just set out, then Absent Healing begins to take form with a precise structure to support it.

The Seeking of Attunement

Let us return to our first conclusion: that an emission of a thought directive is the first necessary act in seeking a healing. It follows that the beginner should first try to establish that happy condition when his thought requests can best be received by the healing guide who is "listening in". This "happy condition" is termed "attunement" or "affinity". We prefer the word "attunement".

Reflect for a moment on the two states of mind: (a) the physical mind and (b) the spirit mind. It must be quite clear that to bring about attunement with Spirit, the physical mind goes into the descendant while the spirit mind becomes more ascendant. Interpreting this in practical terms, it means that the mind allows thoughts of a material and physical nature to give way to thoughts of an idealistic and spiritual nature. For this the beginner makes himself as comfortable as possible so that there is no bodily stress. He does not think of next Saturday's football match, or his dinner, or what work he has to do in the morning, for these are occupations of the physical mind. Instead he allows other thought pictures of a spiritual nature to occupy the consciousness.

Let us give closer consideration to this process of attunement, for the better one appreciates the truths which underlie the healing process, the easier will the early stages of development become.

The Simplicity of Healing

The more we study healership, the more experience we gain in being used as instruments of healing, so we learn that the part the healer plays is one of **simplicity** and this applies to both Contact as well as Absent Healing. The healer does not heal of himself, healing comes **through** him and is not **of** him. The healer does not ‚possess the knowledge to eradicate the causes of disease which defy the experience of our medical scientists. Every healing must be a planned act, with purpose and the knowledge for the plan to be put into effect. Every healing is individual according to the nature and the severity of the disease and its causes. In Contact Healing the healer is the instrument through whom the corrective healing forces are administered. In Absent Healing the healing forces reach the patient direct, for just as the healer possesses a spirit-self, so the patient has a spirit-self, too.

The Way of Attunement

The development of the healing gift is the seeking of a state of affinity or attunement between the healer and the spirit guides or spirit doctors.

Many healers obtain their preliminary development in a home or church healing circle under the guidance of an experienced healer. Others have developed their healership while sitting in a circle for other psychic gifts including trance control by a guide. This serves a useful purpose in so far that the sitter becomes conscious of the personality of the guide which gives him assurance and confidence that what takes place in trance is not the result of any conscious effort on the sitter's part. In Absent Healing there is no need for trance; indeed it could be an encumbrance. Also in Absent Healing there is no cause for self-consciousness.

This book is designed to help the person who does not wish to join any established circle or indeed is unable to do so, but who wishes to encourage his healing ability quietly at home.

In healing nothing is casual, there must be purpose at **all** times, and therefore the beginner should look ahead to the occasions for meditation with a quiet anticipation and happiness. In the early days, twice a week should be sufficient, although as time goes on experienced healers give some time each day to attunement with Spirit for those who are in need.

For the reason that Absent Healing is a thought process the more contented and happy our minds can become the better it is, and we should psychologically encourage that. Looking forward to the time of meditation is part of this preparation, and it is good, for example, to refresh oneself and so prepare for the very important purpose of establishing attunement with Spirit.

The beginner should be unconcerned with the individuality of the names or personalities of his healing guides—that might come later with Contact Healing. He should find a corner of his room or house where he feels quiet and comfortable. Should he be able to reserve this corner as a hallowed place, with fresh flowers, etc., then this helps not only psychologically but spiritually, too.

He should make himself comfortable in an upright armchair as this helps to maintain a good posture and the chair arms on which his arms rest help the body to be thoroughly relaxed.

The light should be lowered to avoid any glare and so help the eyes and the mind to be relaxed and easy. There is no special reason for using coloured bulbs, unless one wishes to do so.

Those seeking spiritual attunement often mistakenly feel that deep "concentration" is necessary; but this is a word of the worst meaning to employ. It is not mental concentration that is needed, but rather the abandonment of the mind to spiritual things. One should not try to make the mind a blank, for this is not possible.

The ideal to be looked for is a state of gentle meditation. When one is quietly alone and can meditate on many things, mundane and otherwise, thinking about prospects, holidays, wishes, happy memories, etc., there exists a condition of mind known as "day-dreaming", when thoughts wander, oblivious of other things. This is an illustration of the state of mind to induce during the early stages of meditative contemplation. As the physical mind surrenders itself to this and the spirit mind becomes ascendant, so the guide will be able to "listen in" to the healer's thought directives. Later on, with the healer's greater degree and ease of attunement, so the guide is able to influence thought directives.

It is important to have the purpose of the meditation as a sort of background thought, as this helps to establish a state of communication with Spirit by means of attunement.

The first thoughts on each occasion should be prayerful ones addressed to God, the Father of all mankind. Try to avoid set prayers for they tend to become mechanical and meaningless. Speak to God in simple thought, in a perfectly natural way. Express in these thoughts that you desire to serve Him for all that is good and perfect; to restore happiness and remove disharmony, whether it be of the mind or body. Ask that His ministers in Spirit will give you guidance and protection during your meditation and thus have the utmost confidence that Divine strength and good influences will be with you.

Then let the mind dwell gently upon some spiritual symbol; the glory of a flower; the wonder of the universe; or perhaps float in your imagination down a peaceful river, being conscious of the slow motion and the passing scene. Let your mind imagine all the colour and beauty of a sunset; or think of the healing work of Jesus, recalling mental pictures of Him healing the leper, the lame man, the crippled, and the various healings He accomplished. (Remember it was by the employment of the Absent Healing directive, with which we are now concerned, that He healed the daughter of Jairus.) These are only suggestions but they indicate the way to free the physical mind from the prosaic things of everyday life, thus giving the spirit mind the opportunity to become ascendant on the consciousness.

It is unlikely at first that any difference will be felt within oneself. You will be quite normal. Have no fear of any kind, for if one is fearful it is best not to continue.

This is not sitting for trance, for one should never sit alone for trance development.
After the meditation has been taking place for a while let your thoughts turn towards a friend or relative who is unwell; you will probably know the character of the symptoms of the illness. Spend a few moments recalling to your mind the sick one, his or her personality and the nature of the sickness. Do this as if you are telling your thoughts to someone who is "listening in". **That is all.** Do not complicate the situation by addressing the spirit guide in any way—keep the purpose simple. Just believe for the time being that a spirit guide is listening in and receiving the thoughts you are expressing, wishing, for example that healing may reach your neighbour Mr. Brown who is suffering from influenza with a high temperature, a tight chest and headache.

Your previous meditation on peaceful things and healing purpose will have brought ascendant the feelings of love and compassion for those who are unhappy through illness. Your spirit mind will be in the ascendant and so create the condition in which attunement between Spirit and yourself is established. When this is so, the simple request for the sick one is all that is necessary. You have fulfilled the first essential step of sending out a purposeful thought message to set the wheels of spirit healing in motion.

Do not stress the situation by fervently and emotionally imploring God or the spirit guide to heal your patient. This is the worst thing to do, for it stresses the mind, creates confusion, and ends the attunement.

Do not dwell upon the situation too long, for this will only be occupying your mind with your own thoughts and again hamper or end the attunement. The purpose of intercession is simply to convey to Spirit the request for healing to reach a certain person suffering from a certain malady, and that is all.

Simply try to project the picture outwards for the guide to receive it. As this is done through your spirit mind, so it will be received by the spirit guide. One can add to the request the hope that those who are listening in may be able to take away the pain or to ease the stiffness, relieve the stress or whatever it may be, so that comfort and harmony may return to the sick one.

Do not try to do too much at first or prolong each situation. After the intercessions for the sick, let the mind continue its relaxation. If you wish, hum a favourite hymn then give prayerful thanks to God for the opportunity of helping someone and so lead the mind back to the return of normal activity.

If one is receptive to music, one can employ this either as a prelude to meditation or to conclude it. Indeed there is no reason why music that one is sympathetic to cannot be played softly all the time if this is helpful.

There is no set time for how long a sitting should continue. At first the minutes may seem long ones, but as they continue the time so spent will become a real pleasure and be looked forward to.

When it is necessary, the sitter can also request help for himself, or herself, as needed.

It is considered best to hold the sittings for a limited number of days a week, say two or three times, and if possible on regular days. This is not imperative, but it does assist to introduce a kind of order into the development which is better than casual or spasmodic sittings being held at any time. At the same time habitual rigidity is not good. Wait until the daily tasks have been comfortably finished and do not rush them to be ready by a set time. The spirit people are not regimented by time as we so often are. See happiness in doing those things that have to be done and then, when you are ready and have the desire to sit for communication with Spirit, that is the right time.

Do not impose upon yourself any penances or other peculiarities, such as fasting, sitting with bare feet, periods of silence, etc. One should just be natural, with the body comfortable to help relaxation come in a simple, easy way.

There is an important ideal to be woven into your way of life, and that is to seek to live by a code of true values. You will do no harm to anyone, and will always seek to serve. You will be tolerant and generous in all things, and will not allow temper, ill-will, or thoughts of revenge to follow any act which has displeased you. This does not mean that you should feel spiritually superior to other people although you will certainly feel more buoyant, and will convey through your eyes, smile and demeanour, that you are feeling good. But avoid setting yourself up on a pedestal of your own making. You should still be able to enjoy a saucy story with a friend—so be natural! If, during the day, you see someone suffering in any way, retain the healing need in your mind, so that later in the quietness, you can ask help for him. You will probably never know whether any healing reached the sufferer, but that does not matter; what is important is that you have made the effort to seek the overcoming of the evil of disease.

Some people will be able to establish attunement with Spirit more quickly than others. No time can be laid down for this to take place. Each person is a law unto himself and in fact the perfecting of attunement is never finished, for it becomes stronger and more intimate as long as there is purpose in seeking it. As the practice of sitting is continued and experience gained, the art of attuning will become very much easier and eventually will be as "second nature", enabling the healer to establish a state of rapport with Spirit as easily as holding

HARRY EDWARDS

Harry Edwards, seen above in his world famous Spiritual Healing Sanctuary as thousands of those whom he helped with his superb gift of healing will remember him, was acknowledged to have been the greatest healer the world has seen since the time of Christ. His passing in 1976 at the age of 83 saw the earthly end of one of the best loved men of our time.

For over 40 years he devoted his life to the healing of the sick in body and mind, easing pain, correcting deformities, overcoming ill conditions of all sorts and generally bringing about restoration of health to countless thousands of sufferers the world over, from the humblest of citizens to royalty.

Apart from his continuous work of contact and absent healing at his Healing Sanctuary at Shere in the heart of Surrey, his memorable public healing demonstrations, lectures, books, and numerous articles on healing made him the world's leading authority on spiritual healing, a field in which he still has no equal.

BURROWS LEA

Home of the world renowned Harry Edwards Spiritual Healing Sanctuary. Below:
The front of the house. On the extreme right is the Healing Sanctuary.

a normal conversation with a friend. Moreover he will be assisting his own spiritual progress.

The difficulty many people find in the early days is to know when attunement has been effected. This is not easy to describe in words, for physically one does not feel any different. It is more a sense of "inner knowing", a subtle condition of "awareness"; there may be a feeling of inner strength and happiness or contentment. It is more easy to understand this, when one's mind returns to a normal outlook. One feels "different", as though one has passed from a phase of "knowing" back into ordinary life. The more tangible proof will come when you find that those who are ill and for whom you have interceded get well far more quickly than might otherwise have been expected, and contrary to medical expectations.

Cosmic Breathing

The next phase of development is the encouraging of the self to receive cosmic strength through characterised breathing. The beginner need not do this, for it is not an essential for attunement. What has already been proposed can be all that is needed. Nevertheless, beginners are strongly advised to encourage cosmic breathing because it can aid development and be of tremendous help in maintaining bodily health and reserves of inner vitality and strength.

What is "cosmic breathing"? Cosmic energies exist for our well-being and their presence can be simply explained by the analogy of a tree. The tree does not live by the nutriment it absorbs through its roots alone. (Such nutriment is akin to the food and drink we consume.) Its vitality and full health depend upon the cosmic forces it absorbs in breathing, through its leaves. Chlorophyll is created in this way. The tree absorbs the solar rays and other health-giving forces which eddy about it. It lives in a "sea" of nutritive forces. We also live within a sea of vitalising forces which in ordinary life we take into ourselves to maintain our reserves of inner and bodily strength. So when we **consciously** take in these vitalising cosmic forces with our breathing, we take in an abundance of energy, thus building up our reservoir of strength to the full.

A further illustration is when we go to the seaside and sense the ozone, for we do not need to be told to take in deep breaths of this vitalising air; we do it naturally because we inwardly know that it is strengthening and good for us.

When a person possessing abundant energy visits a sick one, he transmits this energy to the patient. Indeed this does not only apply to healers, for how common it is when after an invalid has been visited by one who has an abundance of cosmic energy, he says "how much better he feels for the visit". The visitor is not conscious of giving of his strength but through his compassion and sympathy for the invalid it flows from him to the sick one. This is called Magnetic Healing and a healer can **purposefully** direct a flow of these energies into the patient. When he does this more than he should at one time, he feels depleted and tired, and remains so until he again builds up his reservoir of energy. Characterised breathing is the way of doing this.

There is a reason for everything, and on those occasions when one feels "on top of the world" and can jump for joy, etc., it is simply that the reservoir of cosmic strength is full to overflowing.

The sitter should enter into meditation as outlined and then, after a while, having established "peace within", he should become consciously aware of his breathing. Then he should inhale very gently and slowly through the nose, filling the lungs, and, after a pause to give time for the blood to receive oxygen and strength, breathe out the used air just as slowly.

As the inhalations take place the sitter should in all confidence be conscious of taking in with the air, inner strength and vitality to supply his body with cleansing and invigorating forces. As he exhales he should also feel conscious of exuding waste.

The normal healthy body naturally absorbs a blending of all the cosmic forces necessary to maintain a good health balance, but by purposefully characterising the inhalations one strengthens and invigorates oneself and fills up the reservoir of inner strength.

This practice, when sitting for Absent Healing, should be a prelude to the time when the sitter intercedes for the sick. Cosmic forces are pertinent to the physical realm, but are more closely in tune with the spirit healing forces. Therefore, as the sitter builds up his reserves of energy and he feels this new strength, his inner mind can be more attuned to Spirit and his intercessory thoughts for healing to reach a sick one will be better received.

This kind of characterised breathing must not be confused with stressful, forced and rapid breathing sometimes observed in a developing circle for psychic gifts. The breathing I have in mind is gentle, stimulating and satisfying, so that as the characterised breathing blends into normal healing practice one feels inwardly strengthened but at peace with everything. That, then, is the time to turn the thoughts gently towards healing for the sick.

Incidentally, this characterised breathing need not be limited to the time set for attunement. It can profitably take place at **any** time of the day, before or on rising, waiting for the kettle to boil, when going out to business or shopping, and again on retiring before sleep comes. If you are in the vicinity of trees with bright foliage, like the birch and oak, or some kinds of hedge plants, be conscious of taking into yourself the strengthening emanation which flows from them, just like the ozone at the seaside. Sanatoria are built in pine country because it is known medically that the sick ones who need strength for their breathing, blood and general recuperation can obtain this from pine trees.

How Patients are Contacted in Absent Healing

We are only paddling on the foreshore of spirit science. Some of the results we see cannot be explained in physical terms, but we know they happen and we must therefore accept the fact that they are true. Those who have given little or no thought to spirit science cannot be blamed if they think it fantastic for anyone to believe that a person can seek help through a spiritual healer for someone who is, for example, suffering from an incurable disease and who may be some considerable distance from the healer; and then for the disease to be overcome and the patient restored to health. Even healers find it difficult to appreciate the means by which the spirit guides are able to make contact through Absent Healing with a patient in a distant place, even on the other side of the world.

We have to accept the fact that this contact is made, for otherwise Absent Healing could not take place at all.

The difficulty arises in assessing the means by which this contact is established through judgment based on the physical dimensions of time, distance and location that we have to employ in earthly life. Such limitations are related to physical existence, but they need not necessarily exist within the dimension of Spirit.

Some comparison can be made when one considers someone in London wishing to speak to a friend in New York whose telephone number is not known. All that is needed is to give the London telephone operator the

name and other available information. The New York
people will find him and arrange a time for you to converse. When this takes place the sound vibrations of your
voice are transformed into electrical impulses which
travel along the telephone wires. Then these impulses
are converted into beamed radio waves and in this form
they travel in space over the Atlantic in distortion. These
distorted radionic impulses are received in New York,
where the distortion is removed, and converted into
another form of energy so that they can be received by
the telephone receiver where the friend in New York is
listening.

If, therefore, man can do this in such an involved way,
cannot we give credit to the spirit guides—who possess
advanced wisdom and are masters in manipulating
etheric energies—to contact a patient wherever he may
be?

It is now accepted that every thought is a form of
characterised energy. We also know that thought communication between the spirit and physical realms is
clearly proven and is accepted as factual. So we link
these two facts together and arrive at the obvious
conclusion that a purposeful thought force can be
received in Spirit. Such a terminal is established when
the application for healing is made to the healer by the
patient, or by a friend on his behalf. The healer is in
tune with the spirit doctor to whom is conveyed the
picture of the healing need, and as this is another terminal link between the healer and Spirit, so all that is
needed is to connect the two terminals in Spirit for the
guide to contact the patient, irrespective of time, distance
or location. Having made this contact the spirit doctor
is able to "see" the sick one and arrive at his diagnosis
for the remedial treatment to be given.

This explanation cannot, as yet, be proven, but it
possesses elementary logic, and whatever ideas we may

have on this subject, the fact is that the healing guides **do** make contact with the patient sufficiently clearly to determine the character and strength of the healing forces needed to master the sickness.

As a final explanation, the author and other healers have, at times, through astral travelling, found themselves in the presence of a patient and the subsequent accuracy of descriptive detail of the patient's surroundings has shown that the healer's consciousness was present on that occasion.

The author has known of occasions when he has been at home in intercession for a patient and, within a moment—with no conscious experience of travelling— he has found himself in the sick room where the patient is. Every time an effort has been made to verify the description of the patient and the furnishing details of the room, as well as the presence of other people at that precise moment of time, so it has been found to be factually correct.

Sometimes the healing is more direct, i.e. between the patient himself and Spirit. I recall that in the past I would occasionally meet the relative of someone who was very sick. I had heard the details of the illness and in all sincerity had promised to place the sick one within my intercessions that evening—but had forgotten to do so. Then it would transpire a day or so later that the relative would come to me in gratitude for the healing which had taken place . . . yet, in fact, I had done nothing more than listen in sympathy (and thereby attunement) to the details of the patient's illness.

When I spoke of this experience to the assembled healers at a Summer School I asked how many of them had a similar story to tell, and a forest of hands went up. So this is a common experience in healing and there is a lesson to be learned from it. It is, that at the time the healer was being told the details of the sickness his spirit healing guide was listening in, and so was able to contact the patient right away and proceed to heal him. This is Absent Healing in its simplicity.

But perhaps even more direct and simple is the following common experience: A patient or friend of a sick person sits down to write to a healer for Absent Healing. The details are set down and the letter is posted next day. This means that two days pass before the healer receives the request. In the meantime the patient's trouble goes. If it is a lump, there is dispersal; if it is a ˷tiffened joint, misty vision, bodily sickness, whatever it is, the trouble improves before the healer gets the letter. The lesson from this is that at the time of writing the letter, the writer was tuned in to Spirit, and the healing request was received and acted upon. There can be no other possible explanation.

It should be remembered that people do not usually ask for spiritual healing unless a condition is very severe and is not yielding to medical treatment. So that we can be supremely confident in saying that spirit doctors are easily able to contact a sick person wherever he or she may be.

Diagnosis

The Absent Healer is not responsible in any way for diagnosing the nature of the sickness. This is the responsibility of the spirit doctor. When the Absent Healer makes his first appeal for healing he gives all the information he has, i.e. "Mr. Brown in Blackpool is suffering from diabetes, and arthritis in his knees and elbows, is finding sleep difficult and awakens with head pains described as a circle of pain around the upper part of the head." The spirit doctor, receiving this knowledge of the symptoms, will form his own conclusions as to the basic causes of the complaints and do all that can be done to master the causes and then to overcome the symptoms.

As in all things experience counts. The beginner is content to seek attunement and pass on details of sick people. Later on he may well find that after passing information on to the guide he will be conscious of receiving thought impressions about the case. The healer is not looking for any information but finds that a flow of thought is coming to his consciousness. This is intuitive, and at times the information given tells how the patient can better co-operate with the healing by doing this or that, having massage, avoiding fats and certain foods, and so on.

In this way the healer becomes an interested partner in the healing process; he is informed of what is taking place and how he can advise the patient or his people of any way to ease and help the sick one.

In this connection the healer is urged not to discount any thought impressions he may receive on the grounds that his imagination has been active. It is not easy at first to distinguish between a physical thought and a spirit-directed one, but this improves with experience. As a rule, during the meditation the thoughts that are received may well be directed from the guide. It is however wise to review all such information in the light of reason and common sense, and if there is any doubt, do not reject it completely but place it in reserve within the mind.

When advice is received suggesting some form of treatment and the healer feels it is good, then he can pass it on to the relatives to act upon or not, as they decide. The patient will, most likely, be under medical care and it is a wise policy for the healer to suggest to the relatives that they ask for the doctor's consideration for the proposed treatment to be given. If this is done, the healer will have fulfilled his duty to the patient without incurring any personal responsibility.

Absent Healing is not Casual

From the descriptions so far given it would be a great mistake if the beginner receives the impression that Absent Healing is a casual thing, that a sufferer's sickness has only to be mentioned to be healed. Casualness is the enemy of Absent Healing. Remember it is an advanced spirit science. Every healing effort on our part must be purposeful and directive. At the same time we need to avoid the other extreme, of emotionalism, and stressful mind concentration.

Are Repeat Intercessions Necessary?

NOTE. This section and the one which follows should be considered together for so much depends upon the individual development and outlook.

Two questions are often asked: (i) How long should a healer intercede for one patient? (ii) How often are intercessions needed for a patient? It has already been said that intercession for a sick one should only be for the time necessary to pass on to the spirit doctor the request and known details of the diagnosis and/or symptoms and need. If one tries to do more, one is actively employing one's mind and so hampering attunement.

The second question is more easily answered. When an Absent Healer has made contact with the spirit guide and conveyed the healing request, he should have confidence in knowing that the spirit people are already actively engaged in doing everything possible to restore the patient's health. If we have to go to a doctor, it is not necessary to see him every day to implore him to make us better. The doctor has diagnosed our trouble and has prescribed the treatment he thinks best for us.

We do not go to him every day, tell him our symptoms all over again, and ask for further treatment. On the same reasoning it should not be necessary to repeat every day the same healing request, once we are aware that through our attunement the guide knows about it. This applies more to the experienced healer.

With healers who are not experienced in Absent Healing, and are therefore not confident that they have reached a stage of development where they can be sure of having achieved attunement, it is good to devote a little more time to each patient when sitting for intercessionary attunement.

When Constant Intercession is Helpful

People who are gravely ill need particular attention, and constant intercession is needed for them, especially when it can be arranged for a daily report to be given to the healer, either by a verbal message when the sick one is nearby, or by telephone. In this way the healer is kept in close touch with the patient's condition and healing needs, and is then able to transmit the necessary information to the spirit healing guide.

In the Absent Healing practice at Shere, for certain very serious cases we arrange for the relatives to telephone each day to give the latest information. This forms the basis for further purposeful intercession, thus enabling the healing guide to have the latest possible picture of the patient's condition and need. This practice is continued until the crisis has passed. When we have this daily contact we seek all the pertinent information which can be given, i.e., the patient's temperature; whether he is taking nourishment; sleeping well; the extent of pain and stress, and so on, so that all information possible is conveyed to the guide. When the next daily report is received it is noted whether there has come relief from any particular symptom or whether any new ones may have arisen. By this means we are able to let the guide know of the patient's **physical** reaction to the healing effort, for his information and guidance.

There are often many questions arising from the foregoing, as sometimes statements made seem to contradict one another. For example, it may well be asked that if the healing guide is able to make his own true diagnosis of a complaint and its symptoms, why is it necessary to furnish reports of progress to the guide by intercession? Experience shows us that when during the course of a healing a symptom arises, such as a swelling, a new pain, sleeplessness, sickness and so on, and this new information is conveyed in attunement to the guide, it so often follows that within a very short time the symptom is mastered and no longer troubles the patient.

Another explanation rests upon our not knowing exactly in what way the spirit guide "sees" us. Is he able to see us as we are, physically, or does he see us through our spirit mind and body? We are not able to see the spirit people in the form they see each other; likewise the spirit people do not see us in physical form, therefore they would not be able to observe functional symptoms. It is best to proceed by a known way until a better way is discovered, and therefore Absent Healing intercessions should continue for a sufferer whenever there is news to convey to the guide.

With certain diseases only gradual progress can be expected. For instance, where wastage has affected the muscles, sapped the patient's strength and impoverished the tissues, it will take some time to restore the muscular action and build up the patient's strength and vitality. With forms of paralysis, time is necessary to induce a return of co-ordination; with certain mind obsessions, again time may be needed to subjugate them. Therefore, it is good policy for the healer to arrange for a regular weekly report to maintain the continuity of the healing purpose and let the guide know if the patient is responding or not. Negative reports are equally as important as those telling of steady progress.

Healing Letters

As will be observed, Absent Healing is not an abstract academical exercise. It has a planned purpose and any plan needs not only intelligence to carry it out but organisation, too, and for our part we must employ a system to enable the healing to function. We have referred to "reports". These are given either by word of mouth, by telephone, or by letter. The great majority of people send in their reports by way of a letter. Except for very urgent and grave cases, when hourly or daily reports are encouraged, the healer needs frequent and regular reports. Some healers ask for them monthly, others weekly. Here again, it is wise to be flexible and to consider each case separately. For example, if a healer is seeking help to reach what may be termed a slow yielding condition such as a "club-foot" then a monthly report may be adequate; but for illnesses in general, a weekly report is suggested. Of course much may depend upon the healer's available time to reply to patients' letters, and the number of patients interceded for. One will need to adjust the method to what is practical.

It is held that as it is important for the healer to receive reports, so it is just as important that he should answer them—and without undue delay, for remember that the sick person is invariably very anxious to hear from his healer. Those patients who are recovering very well need only write occasionally, for the healing is continuing successfully with them. Even when a patient has fully recovered, it is helpful to keep in touch with the healer from time to time, as this assists in consolidating and maintaining the happy result.

Let us consider what happens when healing letters are written. Whilst the letter is in the process of being written the thoughts of the writer are focused upon his particular healing need; and when the healer replies, his thoughts are directed to the healing purpose. These thought directives bring into operation the healing processes, which are discussed in Section IV, "The Science of Spirit Healing", but for now it can be said that the act of directing healing thoughts of a spiritual nature helps to strengthen the faculty of attunement.

As the patient or his friend writes, so the emission of a thought request is sustained, and when a condition of affinity exists between the healing guide and the patient then this is strengthened and possibly used directively by the guide.

When the healer reads the report and as he replies, so his spirit mind becomes conscious of the details of the patient's situation and a state of intercession naturally and purposefully takes place.

When the patient receives the healer's reply, the healing purpose is conveyed to his mind and so new courage is given, the "bodily healing intelligence" is activated (see Section IV, "The Science of Spirit Healing") and progress is made. These letters are as links between healer, patient, and spirit doctor.

Method of Letter Writing

It will have been observed that to maintain the Absent Healing directive successfully involves a good deal of correspondence, and this may, in the beginning, deter some people who dislike letter writing from becoming Absent Healers; but this need not be.

The patient or his relatives are not seeking a learned

letter or a treatise on disease in medical terms. Most of
them are ordinary folk who only wish to have a friendly
letter in straightforward terms, simply expressed, and
one that they can easily understand.

There is little doubt that the healer would be able to
talk to the patient about the healing need and intention,
so all he has to do is to simply write just what he would
say were he actually talking to his patient.

Avoid clichés, obscure terms and high sounding
phrases. A friendly little letter expressing a hopeful
sympathetic view, just as if one were writing to one's
sister or brother about their health problems, and telling
of the healing intention to soothe the fears and tensions,
pain and stresses; to overcome weakness by giving
strength and vitality; to seek freedom and looseness of
movement; to restore co-ordination and control, and so
on, according to what the healing is required to do in
that particular case.

Write just as if you were talking to the patient or his
people then the reader will feel that the letter comes
from the heart and not from a book. There will be no
sensing of artificiality and you will enjoy your letter
writing, for you will feel that it is a part of you; that you
are blending in with the patient and achieving good in
so doing.

Just one more word on this. Do not write your letters
on cheap note paper. Your letters are worth while.
They should convey a dignified appearance and a note-
paper of reasonable quality, with a printed address on it,
carries with it a sense of respect and distinction.

It is just as well for the correspondent to be asked to
enclose a stamped addressed envelope, for this is a
reasonable request. It saves the healer's time and makes
sure the reply reaches the correspondent; it also saves
the healer the expense of postage, which in the aggregate
can become considerable.

Letters Act as Interviews

Absent Healing to be carried out as it should entails an amount of correspondence, but it would be a mistake to value this simply as "correspondence". Every letter is a human document with a human story of pain and affliction, and of unhappiness; but it is also one of hope based on healing of which the healer is the centre. Each letter giving a report should be to the healer the same as an interview (similar to a patient seeing his doctor in the consulting room). The reply should be in natural language as if the healer is talking to his patient or to the patient's friend.

How to Answer Letters

These letters are of tremendous importance—both ways. They not only serve as a link between healer and patient but also between themselves and the healing guide. In reading them they should not be glossed over, but read with a sensing of the patient's condition and the symptoms of the trouble they depict. Later in the day the healer may hold a special intercession with the letters before him, when he will again recall the individual healing needs, and, if necessary, re-read the letters and so convey the information to the guide. It may be that with experience, when attunement is more easily established, this conveying of the information will be transmitted to the healing guide **during the reading and the answering of the letter.** The condition is subtle, and only comes with experience and therefore the period of purposeful intercession should preferably still take place in the quiet of the evening's meditation.

The healing need as described in each report should be the subject for the intercessionary period in the days that follow, until the patient's next letter is received.

Think of the healing guides as if they are your own special friends, and as the reports tell that certain symptoms have yielded during the past days, express your thanks and pleasure in your thoughts to the guide.

Encourage patients to write briefly of the healing need, outlining the prevailing symptoms at the time of writing, to say if the ill-conditions are better or not. The healer wants a concise "word picture" of the healing need. Some sufferers will write long, very long, letters which may try the healer's patience. Bear with these, for most likely the patient has experienced relief in writing at length. He may be suffering from mental tension and the letters are a means of relieving these tensions, giving a chance for him to unburden his troubles to the healer. Other sufferers may be leading lonely lives and the coming of the healer's letter heralds a red letter day for them. They may have no one who has time to converse with them, so relief is found in writing down their thoughts to their understanding friend, the healer.

The Need to Maintain Intercession

If the Absent Healer does not receive reports of a regular nature, either by telephone, orally, or in writing, the healing as far as the healer is concerned naturally becomes unsatisfying, for unless the healer is kept informed of the patient's progress, he is in the dark and his interest will be inclined to wane. If no letters or reports are received, then the healer should continue to retain the patient within his intercession for a period of time; but cannot be expected to continue indefinitely, for after a while the intercession becomes repetitive and there is no constructive purpose in this.

Generally speaking, however, the time comes when all who engage in Absent Healing are told how greatly a person has been helped (often when doctors have given him up) but who has failed to report to the healer after the first letter or so. The reason is, of course, that once the healing had commenced it was carried through from Spirit, even though the link between healer and patient had not been maintained. We also need to remember human frailty, for as the patient loses discomfort and feels better, the incentive to write to the healer falls away—even at times to the point of failing to give a word of acknowledgement or thanks to the healer. This is just one of those things that the healer has to accept philosophically.

Precautions to be Taken in Correspondence

The healer's replies should always be carefully worded. They should maintain a positive outlook, but avoid giving any definite promise or undertaking—even though the healer may have intuitive knowledge that the patient will get well. No one can foresee what intervening circumstances may upset progress. Patients often place great importance on the healer's words, and may sometimes misconstrue them through their own wishful thinking, interpreting them in a way that is not intended.

Remember this: the patient writes (or goes) to a healer because he "expects to get better". He goes to his doctor "to get treatment". There is all the world of difference in this approach. This especially applies to Absent Healing. Often Absent Healing is the "last hope". The patient or his people are looking for comfort and assurance in the reply the healer sends and it is good to maintain the confidence in the healing, but at the same time to avoid any definite promise that a recovery will take place, or that it will do so within a specified time. The reason for this is, that even if a healing is well on its way, other factors can intervene, such as the patient catching an infection, a cold or influenza, receiving a mental shock or having a fall and so on, which according to natural law, may prejudice for the time being the effective healing result.

Replies Should be Positive

Healers' replies should not be negative, they should convey that confident and positive outlook that healing is bringing, or is SEEKING to bring about a recovery. Healers are—indeed they must be—optimists. They should always look for improvement and tell their patients that they expect this to take place.

There are certain occasions when it is better to use general terms in a letter rather than to be specific, for it is so easy for statements to be misconstrued. Sometimes "hopes" for recoveries become firm promises, and exaggerated values are placed upon expressions of opinion.

Patients will sometimes ask a healer for a diagnosis of their trouble, or ask how it was caused. Such requests should be answered in general and not specific terms. It is wisest to avoid any direct diagnosing. There is good reason for this. There are those patients to whom a diagnosis would produce a depressing effect, as it would weigh on their minds, cause anxiety, and help to negative the healing effort. In Absent Healing it is best to avoid putting into writing any cause or diagnosis of a patient's trouble and furthermore avoid the pitfall of any "guesswork" on the part of the healer.

Letters in Cases of Extreme Sickness

There are two types of letter that are not easy to answer, and there is no set way of doing so. The healer has to rely upon his sympathy and understanding at how to write them.

The first kind is the application for healing at the

eleventh hour, as a last hope. It tells of the very serious condition of the sick one when the doctors give no hope at all. For example, it may be one of cancer where an exploratory operation has disclosed an inoperable state; the relatives are informed that the passing can only be a matter of time. Knowing that the doctors can do no more, the relatives turn to spiritual healing hoping for a miracle.

The healer shares the concern of the relatives, and whilst he will not limit within his mind the power of the Spirit to heal, he is also aware that healings can only take place within the laws governing life. It may be that the patient is so weak that he is unable to take any nourishment to maintain his physical strength, and the time is too short for the ill-effects of the disease to be overcome. It may be that the disease has gained such a strong hold on the sufferer that a recovery is not possible within the scheme of things.

The healer's reply to such letters, therefore, should be carefully worded to avoid arousing undue hopes or expectancy of a recovery, but at the same time to give an assurance that everything possible will be done. He will, in his letter, express sympathy in knowing of the grave nature of the sickness, and will assure the writer that he will immediately enter into prayerful intercession for the sick one, to seek, through the healing, for inner peace and comfort to reach him, and that he may be granted strength, fortitude and healing in every way that is still possible.

We know that in such extreme cases the healing can indeed grant much help, for should a passing take place, pain is eased, sleep is given, and the transition into spirit life comes without stress. Therefore, when the application indicates that the sick one's condition is so very serious that a continuance of life cannot reasonably be expected, the healer can say in his letter that "if it should not be within the scheme of things for a recovery to take place, the sick one will receive the companionship of Spirit to grant that inner comfort and peacefulness which will help the sufferer in every way that can be."

This kind of wording will give assurance to the relatives that everything possible will be done, and so comfort them; but the healer during his intercession will not allow limiting thoughts to be with him, for he will seek through Spirit for healing to reach the patient in every way that is possible.

Letters When a Passing Has Occurred

This is the second kind of letter most difficult to write. Yet one must be written for the good purpose of giving a degree of understanding and comfort to the bereaved.

After expressing sympathy in the healer's own words he can say something to the effect that: "It will comfort you to know that 'X' is now free from all pain and stress on his entry into his greater and fuller life. That his love for you will endure, and he would not have you grieve for him. He has been received into arms of loving kindness, and in the fullness of time there will come a reunion."

Sometimes the relative's letter will be a very distressed one, and may ask "Why God made him suffer?" and "Why has He taken him away?" The letter may also say that the writer has now lost all faith in a loving God, and similar things. It is the healer's duty to help to steady the distressed mind, and wordings like that suggested above will not only help to give consolation but help to lead the mind towards a right perspective. The healer should also put into his letter that he will continue to intercede that inner strength and comfort shall be with the bereaved during the days of sadness.

He will say that it is not God's will for anyone to suffer

—that our infirmities do not come from God, but through earthly causes, and so on. Intercession will then follow to grant comfort to those who mourn, to ease their sufferings and restore serenity to their minds.

How to Advise with Regard to Operations

Healers will also be asked to advise whether an operation recommended by the doctor should be carried out. It is not within the province of any healer to reply "Yes" or "No". Generally speaking, the healer will not know the purpose or character of the surgery, and cannot be held responsible for what the surgeon may do. It must be assumed that the medical men have good reason for deciding to operate, and that they consider it necessary for the patient's welfare. This is the responsibility of the doctor and not the healer. Should a healer advise a patient in a letter not to undergo surgery, and it then transpires that the patient gets worse or even passes on, then the healer will be blamed for advising wrongly.

While it is the intention of Absent Healing to avoid the need for surgery, it is the best plan to tell the patient that the responsibility for agreeing to an operation must be that of the patient or his people. The healer should at the same time tell the patient that if the operation does take place then the healer will intercede for strength and vitality to reach the patient to bring him through it as speedily and as well as can be, helping to avoid operational shock.

Advice to Seek Medical Opinion

There are those patients who place all their reliance on Absent Healing and refuse to consult a doctor. This is often seen with ladies who have the symptoms of a growth in the breast. They are afraid of disclosing their condition to the doctor, for fear they will have to undergo surgery. These people place an unfair burden upon the healer, for if it should be that the breast trouble becomes worse, it may come to pass that the trouble will develop into a chronic state, and the healer will be blamed accordingly.

Therefore, when a patient's letter discloses trouble of a serious nature, and the writer does not indicate that he or she is receiving medical attention, the healer in his reply should advise the patient to obtain a medical opinion. Once the patient has seen the doctor, then the healer is safeguarded.

It should be pointed out to patients that it is common sense to take advantage of medical knowledge, and that spiritual healing and medical practice are complementary to each other. It is wise to avoid any criticism of doctors in replies to patients' letters, and to encourage patients to co-operate with their doctor's advice and treatment.

In Absent Healing, the patient may not understand the limitations of healing (Please see paragraph in this section "Why Some Healings Fail") so the healer's reply should be worded in such a way as to maintain the patient's morale and expectancy of improvement but avoiding raising undue hopes for a complete recovery which may not be possible.

The Joy of Absent Healing

While the Absent Healer is concerned with unhappiness and sickness, pain and mental upsets, there is a great joy in seeing these troubles overcome, and receiving the reports and letters to tell of it.

It will give the healer great happiness to read in the letters of easement and improvement being progressively made until a full recovery comes. It will give him a sense of satisfaction and fulfilment in the healing when he observes that the particular symptoms for which he interceded have yielded, and that he has been the instrument through which this has been attained.

But there are occasions of sadness, too, when one does not see the progress wished for, and on other special occasions. These are dealt with a little later on.

The Absent Healer will not judge the effectiveness of the healing by non-success, but by success. It will be remembered that as a rule people do not apply for Absent Healing except for very obstinate conditions, often deep seated, and for which medical treatment can do little or even nothing at all. Under these circumstances even one triumph is an occasion for rejoicing, so I venture to repeat that it is reasonable to judge Absent Healing by its successes.

If there is no apparent success with any one particular case there is reason for it. This reason may not be obvious to either healer or patient, and this aspect of healing is also dealt with later on. In such cases, however, the healer should not doubt the efficacy of Absent Healing, or blame himself for being an unworthy or not sufficiently experienced instrument; nor should he think the guides have failed, or seek any other excuse, or try to put the blame upon anyone or anything.

With success or even non-success it is only right that the healer should send out his mental thanks to the healing guides for all that they have done.

The Psychological Approach

I have heard it said that Absent Healing is just psychology and suggestion, and it might be thought from what I have written concerning letters to patients that this is so. It is true that psychology plays an important part in all healing. Doctors recognise this in their efforts to maintain morale and the will to get better. In our endeavours it is psychology **plus** the healing.

After all, when so much trouble has its causation in mental stress, it is only what we expect to hear soon after the patient's first letters that the writer is conscious of "inner upliftment", "new strength and vitality" and "feeling generally better". This surely indicates that the first step has taken effect in the healing, namely to calm nervous and mind tensions, and to uplift the outlook, thus leading the way to the re-establishing of a better health tone. For the reason that this is a common expectancy with Absent Healing, there is no harm in telling the patient in the first letter to look forward to, and anticipate this. It may be a psychological suggestion, but all the suggestion in the world cannot produce the effect of improved health unless it actually comes.

This is the preliminary phase of the healing; it indicates that the cause is being overcome and with this the physical ill-effects are enabled to yield. These good signs are seen particularly with Absent Healing—even more so than with Contact Healing, when direction is often more concentrated upon the physical ill-effects.

When a person is so sick that he is urged to write for Absent Healing, his "condition" is often low, with a depressed outlook. To encourage the state of being "on top of the world" is surely a good thing, and is an introduction to the fulfilment of the healing purpose, namely to overcome the particular stress, pain or disease.

Is Absent Healing Limited?

The question is often asked "Can 'X' disease be healed through Absent Healing?" The Absent Healer should never impose within his mind any limit to the power of Spirit to heal, whatever the trouble may be. At the same time it is not within our province to say which condition can be healed or not. We have the postulate that healing operates within the total laws that govern us, and within this undefined scope there can be no limitation. Every case is individual, and the cause of the trouble has its individual origin, too; therefore, the successful healing of one patient cannot be taken as a precedent for another, even though apparently suffering from an identical complaint.

Sometimes the healer is presented with a tragic case in which the continuance of life has been despaired of by the doctors and the patient's passing is considered to be imminent. The normal reasoning may be that such a case is hopeless and nothing can be done, yet the healer will seek spirit healing for the sick one in all ways that can be.

There are the occasions when a seeming miracle takes place, the patient gathers strength, the pains go, the appetite returns, and before long he is well again. If the healer has thought there was no hope and had not interceded in a positive manner, it is unlikely that any recovery would have followed.

The removal of the cause of disharmony and its physical ill-effects is the task of the spirit guides. From the records at Shere, and with others who conduct Absent Healing on a measurable scale, the percentage of betterment is in the region of 80%, and of these a third report complete recovery. The applications for Absent Healing cover the whole realm of disease and affliction, therefore the figures show that no limitation can be imposed on the good that healing can do.

Even when we may not see all the progress we would wish for with very deep-seated troubles, the help that is given in many ways, such as restoring the good health tone of the patient, relief from nervous and mind stresses, the easement from pain, the checking of any further advance of the disease and so on, makes the healing effort worth while. Indeed it is the author's opinion that whatever the ill-condition may be, the patient is helped in some measurable way.

It is well for the reader to consider the following section dealing with the 20% who do not respond, and so appreciate further this aspect of our healing ministry.

Those Who Fail to Respond

This is a most important matter which concerns every healer. Just as there is a reasoned process behind every healing, so must there be reasons to account for non-success. There is no general answer, for every case is individual and needs to be studied separately. I am, therefore, reproducing here the full chapter on this subject from my book *Spirit Healing*, which was first published in 1960.

Why Some Healings Fail

One day a mother brought her few months' old baby to me. The little one was perfect in every way except that the feet were noticeably contorted with an inward turn. The balls of the feet and the toes were stretched downwards. The doctors had told the mother that it would be advisable to postpone any surgical or manipulative treatment until the child was a little older. The point of this story is that to me, both feet were affected in an identical manner. I took one foot in my hands, sought for healing aid, and ever so gently moved the foot up and round. Within my hand I could feel the changing in position taking place. When I took my hands away the foot was facing forward and could move up and down in a normal manner. So next came the other foot, but with this I was unable to discern any change at all. It remained contorted and restricted in movement. This greatly intrigued me. I saw the baby on two further occasions, without obtaining any response. It was on the fourth visit, when the baby was nearly one year old, that the foot responded and the child could begin to stand squarely on both feet. The problem in this case was: Why, with seemingly two identical conditions with the same baby, had one foot yielded immediately to the healing, and the other did not respond until some six months afterwards in spite of repeated efforts being made?

The second case concerns the passing of my friend Jack Webber, who in the 1940's was one of the outstanding physical mediums. We had been daily companions for over two years. There had not been one ill-thought between us as I sponsored his mediumship and looked after his interests. Suddenly he became ill. I knew intuitively the illness was very serious. I felt so acutely for him that I was willing to draw the trouble from him into myself. Now I know that I should not have sought to do this, nor could it have been possible, but I mention the fact to indicate the depth of affection that I had for him. He passed into spirit life some three days later, when it was pathologically established that Jack had contracted a virulent form of spinal meningitis. It is noteworthy to recall that at no time did he suffer any bodily stress. Usually with this disease, the days previous to a passing in normal cases are most distressful and agonising ones. My last memory of him was on the evening before his release from earth life. I was sitting on his bed and together we were singing his favourite song, "Danny Boy" During the night he lost consciousness. His body stiffened and he was taken to hospital, where the final change shortly took place. The importance of this story is in the sequel.

The following week brought into my shop a mother and father who had specially broken their journey from the North of England to Portsmouth to see if I could obtain spirit healing for their son who was dying from spinal meningitis. They had been urgently asked to go down to Portsmouth in view of the seriousness of their son's condition. Indeed they expected to find him dead by the time they reached the hospital and so had made the break in their journey as a last hope.

With the recent memory of Jack and spinal meningitis in my mind, I felt very sorry for the parents. I went into the quiet and sought help for the lad. When the parents arrived at the hospital and entered their son's ward they were astonished to find him sitting up in bed, with four doctors in conference around him, studying what to them, was nothing more than a "miracle". All trace of the disease had left him. The doctors "wondered where he had got his strength from", and in a few days he was home. It transpired that the patient was a soldier belonging to the Hussar Regiment. So complete was his recovery that he was able to return to full duty. This fact makes the healing all the more remarkable when it is remembered the complications that so often follow in the train of this disease.

Thus I was faced with a problem that did little to ease my mind of the sadness of the passing of Jack and actually made me feel a little bitter about things. Why was it that my dearest friend, with his close attunement to his own spirit guides, and who had so often been the means of healing the sick, plus the help from my healing guides from whom I so dearly sought help, should not have been helped to recover, while a perfect stranger, one I had never seen before or since, should be helped so much? It was very hard to understand.

From these experiences I learned the lesson that no one case can be taken as a precedent for another, not even with one foot as to the other.

With this conclusion we have a position that may

create some difficulty in obtaining medical co-operation
for doctors are accustomed to expecting predetermined
results from definite treatments. They rely on their
knowledge of anatomy and the chemistry of the body, so
that when they administer a specific medicine they
should see the anticipated change take place. With
spiritual healing this is not so. We cannot give any
promise or undertaking in advance for any person that
a healing result will occur. We cannot call for healing
"on demand", even though we can visualise the postulates that bring it into being.

In our analyses of healing results there appears to be
approximately twenty per cent. who do not record
improvement. As a rule all those who request spiritual
healing do so because they have lost their faith in doctors
or are afraid of what the medical diagnosis and treatment
may be; or in the great majority of cases because the
trouble does not yield to medical treatment, or the doctors have said they are "incurable". Considering these
factors twenty per cent lack of beneficial result is a very
favourable figure, yet we must be concerned with it.
Just as there must be a reasoned process behind every
healing, so there must also exist reasons why no response
is apparently seen, all other contingencies being equal.

It has already been shown that the limit that governs
healing is the total laws that control our well-being, from
conception (and even before conception) to passing.
One of these limitations is that, in time, the energies
comprising the atomic structures of matter begin to lose
their force. With all animal life this limitation is very
much more marked, and deterioration in function as age
advances is just one of the penalties of being born. Perhaps it is not a penalty, for it is doubtful if one would
wish to live forever. In the greater scheme of things it
would prevent our enjoyment of the Spiritual heritage
that we enter after this phase of life has ended. Just as

the metamorphosis of the caterpillar into the chrysalis state and thence into the final butterfly stage to carry on the species is a law of life, so our metamorphosis is likewise the law. Thus it may often be that when healing does not appear to take place it can well be for the reason that the time has come for the change to take place.

It is also the law that "effects follow causes". Should it be that the physical cause of a complaint is persisted in then a healing cannot be fulfilled. To prove this point, the examples of waning eyesight and arthritis have been mentioned earlier in this book. To recapitulate: if a person's sight is weakening through eye strain induced by close work in daily employment, and this is persisted in, then the return of full sight is prevented, although the healing will maintain it in as good a condition as the circumstances allow. If a patient suffering from rheumatism, arthritis or fibrositis has to work outside in inclement weather or sleeps in a damp bed, the healing effort must be largely negatived. Thus in a number of cases the full healing depends upon obeying the laws of health.

I recall one patient who was suffering badly from arthritis. I noticed that she had a number of badly decayed teeth. It seemed probable that the teeth were causing toxic conditions that interfered with the health of the bloodstream. I ventured to suggest that she had all these bad teeth out, which she would not do, because she had a fear of dental treatment. Her arthritis was eased but did not clear, and she would have been registered as a "failure". Eventually she plucked up courage and had her mouth attended to and dentures supplied. From this date her arthritis progressively disappeared until she was free of the trouble.

When the cause of the disease has its root in mental and inner-self disharmony, the progress of the healing will depend upon the rapidity with which corrective influencing from Spirit is able to soothe and calm the upsets. With some people the inner frustration has become so deep-seated that it has become ever present in the pattern of daily life. It may be with such people that the progress of the healing is far from what we would wish to see.

Many times the help of spirit healing is enlisted during the critical days before a passing. The doctors have said that the person is unlikely to live more than a few days. The distressed relatives in a last act of desperation come to a healer. While occasionally recoveries from such chronic states do take place they are not the general rule. The healing is said to have failed. In this respect, when a recovery is not within the scheme of things, there is no question that help from Spirit is given. Instead of a troubled and painful passing, the patient loses the sense of pain. Comfort, inner strength and peacefulness come to the mind. The patient sleeps without the need for drugs and the passing is free from stress. While such a case is listed as a failure, it is questionable whether it really comes within that category.

In this connection I would like to tell of my mother's health history. Some years ago she was sadly troubled with attacks of giddiness and heart weaknesses. Her doctor expressed the opinion that she might pass away at any time from a heart attack. Naturally we sought healing aid for her, and not only did the giddy attacks completely vanish but so did all the symptoms of heart strain. My mother in her ninety-second year, is in full possession of all her functions except hearing. She is robust and in reasonably good health. As her hearing waned so came the distress of head noises. I tried to seek their removal but without result. Then one day, my mother thought of asking the wife of one of my collaborators at that time if she would seek help to overcome the noises. This extra help was sought, and shortly afterwards, the noises ceased and for some years she has not been troubled in this way. Yet the deafness continues, and in spite of all our seeking it does not diminish. The reason probably is that with her advanced age the faculty of hearing has deteriorated into a senile state. It may be said that the healing has failed to restore her hearing and she should be registered as a "failure", but in view of the many other ways she has been healed this would surely be a wrong description.*

There is another factor to consider in the discussion of "failures". It has been previously pointed out that every healing must result from an intelligent administration of corrective healing forces within the law. By "intelligent administration" is meant the extent of the wisdom of the spirit guides to produce a satisfactory change. We should be in error if we ascribed to the intelligences, who are the healing guides, all wisdom and omnipotent power. They, too, have need to acquire knowledge through experience. This takes place progressively as they study more closely our needs and the potentials within the healing forces. Evidence of this has been seen with the healing of certain troubles, as with poker-back spines. Today, this condition yields far more easily and quickly than it did, say, ten years ago, establishing the evidence that the guides have advanced in their knowledge and ability to cope with this particular trouble. A similar story can be related to the dispersal of cataracts and growths, etc. Thus spirit healing is ever progressing. Conditions that do not appear to respond readily today may do so in the future.

In the endeavour to assess the reasons for non-success there are other factors to be taken into consideration besides those already mentioned.

One of these is that the patient has become so used to

---

*Author's Note: The foregoing was written in 1960.

THE HARRY EDWARDS SPIRITUAL HEALING SANCTUARY

Founded by Harry Edwards in 1946, this world famous healing sanctuary has been a haven for thousands suffering from all manner of human ills and who have found relief from their troubles, very often in situations where medical science has been unable to help them further.

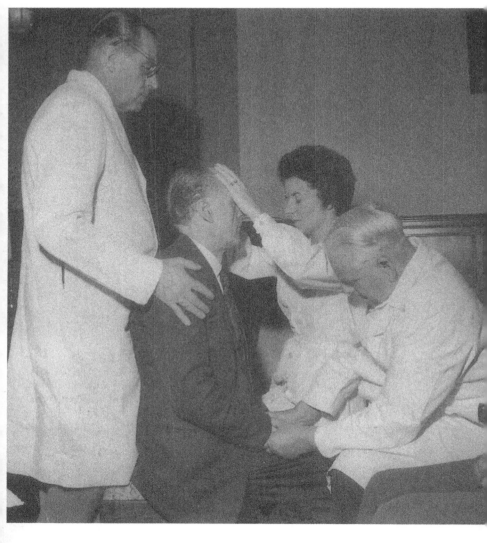

Harry Edwards with Olive and George Burton giving healing to a patient.

the adverse effects produced by the disease that the perpetuation of the symptoms has become a fixed habit of the body. If we assume that a hip or knee joint has suffered for a number of years from pain or locking, the patient has got into the firm habit of walking with the leg stiff, and possibly swinging it from the pelvis. With the healing, the disability is removed and under the healer's direction the patient is able to circulate the joints freely and normally without any pain at all. He is shown that he can now walk properly, but even with this object lesson it will at times be seen that as a matter of habit he returns to the former method of walking with the leg stiff. So, it might be said he is no better for the healing. If the cause of the immobility is arthritis and no advantage is taken to sustain the restored loose movement, then it is likely that the joint will stiffen once again.

Fear is another cause of patients refusing to acknowledge the healing result. They are afraid that if they continue to take advantage of the healing benefit the pains will return. They take refuge in returning to the limiting conditions to which they have become accustomed as being bearable.

Then the healer has to meet those whose minds are firmly fixed on their infirmity; it has become part of their way of living. The words, "I cannot do that" have become so deep-rooted that they will not on any account use their bodies more freely, even though the healing has removed the weakness and stress.

There is also that class of people who would not be happy unless they have the infirmity perpetuated, so that they can receive sympathy from others. Even though they seek the good that spirit healing can do for them they do not really want to respond.

Healers also have to deal with hypochondriacs who maintain a list of imaginary complaints. With these healing is said to fail because the patients persist in believing themselves to be ill when they are not.

When all these factors are considered it will be seen that the twenty per cent for whom a good report cannot be given would be greatly reduced.

The healer has to learn that he should not blame himself or his healing gift for any lack of success. There is good reason for it. Neither should he blame the patient, and definitely not the healing guides.

Now that man understands a little of the nature of energies locked in the atom, spiritual healing comes within the rational field. It can be explained in terms of laws parallel to those which rule healing success and non-success. The power to repair wasted tissue, to restore nervous force, to cleanse the physical body from disease, to repair broken minds, to bring new light to darkened intelligence, is the result of applied energy in a planned way.

Only because we are more scientific in our approach to these matters can we become more spiritual. That is to say: only as we increase our real knowledge of the forces of nature and the spirit can we align our moralities and lives to come within the borders of these truths. Only because we have come slowly upward from a pit of deep ignorance dug by priests and others throughout the ages can we understand now that the healing miracles of Jesus were manifestations of the same knowledge to use the power as we are witnessing today. That mankind did not learn from Christ's teachings is not the fault of God who sent Him or His disciples. They did all they could. Nearly two thousand years have had to elapse before we have been able to learn sufficient to appreciate the nature of matter and the existence and co-operation of Spirit.

It may seem a long way from the understanding of both success and non-success in the healing of a broken body to the secrets within the atomic energies, but all is interwoven for good in the end. Without our modern knowledge of radio, radar and atomic energy it would be harder to explain the wonder and existence of the soul and spirit healing. Perhaps that is why true religion has languished for so long; there was not enough knowledge to make spirit healing credible. The Church in the past, as well as ignorant men greedy for power, created dictatorships for the enslavement of the un-informed. The only outpourings of the Spirit were in the realms of the arts and in the slow and painful march of reform and tolerance.

Now that we have more knowledge to comprehend the capabilities and limitations of healing, the work of the Spirit can go ahead. In the healing effort, even though unsuccessful, good work is done. In healing there is ordered progress. It works from good to better and thence to greater good, until one day, in some far distant time, man will truly heal himself since he will fully know himself and his spirit-self.

Instantaneous Healings

While instantaneous healings are not infrequent, they are not the rule. No healing can take place until the cause is first overcome. If it should be that the cause is simply organic, the healers in Spirit are often able to deal with it quickly, removing the symptoms so that an immediate healing is seen. Generally speaking, it takes time to overcome the cause, especially if it originates in some form of inner-self frustration or long-standing fear. Then time is necessary to induce the corrective changes, especially with functional troubles. If there is wastage, such as with paralysis, it takes time to replace the lost tissues and stimulate cellular reproduction. Thus heal-ings as a rule, progress gradually. Everything depends upon the cause and nature of the sickness, and receptivity to healing is particular to each patient.

Two examples can be offered to illustrate the above paragraph. They are both extreme cases. The healer is asked to intercede for the removal of a growth. It is a purely organic one, capable of dispersal by the direct methods of breaking up the atomic structure of the growth; and so it is seen to disappear within hours. The second example is that of a backward child with whom there is little or no co-ordination, the mind and senses are dormant. In such a case it needs continuous and untiring effort first to arouse the awareness of the mind, and, when this comes, to encourage nerve co-ordination. The latter is likely to be a gradual process, but once it has begun progressive improvement can be anticipated.

Therefore, in Absent Healing the healer must be patient and content to witness a gradual recovery. Fluctuations may be liable during the period of treatment, but these are invariably overcome as the healing fulfils its purpose.

Tolerance

At times the Absent Healer will have to face opposition from those who write to him on religious grounds. They may discover that the healer is a Spiritualist, and therefore be unwilling to continue to seek his services. In these cases it is wise for the healer to be tolerant and not to "answer back". Every person has a right to his opinions, religious or otherwise, and we should respect them just as much as we hope those who disagree with us will respect ours.

When replying to such objections it is as well just to point out gently that all healing comes from God, and is a Divine intention; that spiritual healing is God's gift to **all** His people, irrespective of race or religion. The healer's answer should always be very courteous, for no good will be served in being otherwise.

If a person asks the healer to discontinue intercession on the grounds of a contrary religious belief, then he should do so—for we should respect the wishes of others, and not attempt to interfere with their "free will". The responsibility then rests with the other person and not the healer.

Incidentally, it is a matter for conjecture whether once the healing guides have commenced their healing treatment for a sick one, that they would discontinue their beneficial work for so trivial a human weakness.

In this connection, the writer has had instances where the near relative has said words to the effect that: "I would sooner see my dear one suffer and die rather than receive healing from a Spiritualist source." Any attempt to reason with such an obdurate opinion is a waste of time, but it is good to reply and say that the healer will follow out the wishes expressed, and then add the points mentioned above and conclude by saying, "that if in future he can be of service, the writer has only to ask for it". This will leave the door open, create a good impression and possibly give the writer further food for thought.

Donations

Healers give of their service without any desire for financial reward. They heal through their love and compassion for the sick. They know that healing cannot be "bought", and that is why no fees, as such, are generally charged for spiritual healing.

There are many healers, too, who refuse to take any pecuniary rewards for their healing, as a matter of principle.

There are, however, some factors that need consideration. Perhaps the most common of these is that the patients or their people feel that they would like to express their gratitude in some tangible form, and if this is denied to them they feel under an obligation. It may give them some pleasure in sending a free-will offering to show their appreciation. Then there are those people too, who are unwilling to accept any service of any kind without feeling they should give some return. There are the Absent Healer's expenses, too, if only those entailed in the use of good stationery and postage.

It is suggested that there can be nothing wrong in the healer accepting free-will donations that are sent to him in gratitude. If the healer does not wish to take any personal advantage from such offering, or to repay his expenses, he can put them aside and from time to time donate them to any good cause that he favours.

Advice to Patients

It is commonsense that if a patient can be advised to live rightly, and to take simple measures to help himself, much can be done to make the patient an ally of the healing purpose. It would take too much time to write in a letter all that the healer would like to say about this, therefore it is a good plan to have duplicated or printed statements concerning the particular ways in which a patient can help himself, these to be enclosed in the healer's reply where necessary.

In Conclusion

It is hoped that this section will be a means of helping all those good people who wish to serve the sick in a practical manner, and to see that Absent Healing is not just an abstract practice, but a spirit science; to give the Absent Healer an awareness of perspective and confidence, opening the way to fuller understanding of the spirit healing potential, and so advance our usage by those grand personalities, the spirit healing guides, who are God's Ministers carrying out the Divine intention and awakening the consciousness of man to realise he is part Spirit now, with an infinite heritage of spiritual progression before him.

SECTION II

THE THEORY OF SPIRIT HEALING

Note:—As this study of healing proceeds it will be seen that there is repetition. This is to allow for additional explanations and to save referring back to previous chapters. An example of this follows in this section, where a more detailed explanation is given of the postulates which govern healing.

Chapter 1

THE HEALING SPIRIT

Many people wish to know how they can become healers. Those who have succeeded in developing the gift desire to know how they can become **better** channels, and it is the purpose of this section to show how this can be achieved.

Spiritual healing is God's gift to all His children, irrespective of race or creed. It is the Divine Plan to foster the spiritual progress of the human family. Healership is not only an integral part of this Plan but forms the very spearhead of it. Healing is the greatest gift that can be bestowed, and it is certainly the most spiritual one.

We enjoy the co-operation of those wise ones in spirit life whom we call our healing guides or healing doctors.

They, too, are part of the Divine Plan, inspired to further its purpose by demonstrating through healership that all people are akin to Spirit and thereby to God.

The reason why healers give so willingly of their time and service for the sick is that they possess the Divine attributes of love and compassion for those who are in misery and in pain and yearn to restore them to health and happiness.

In order to co-operate intelligently with the healing process, healers need to appreciate the fundamental postulates and laws which govern it. These were included in the Report of the Healing Methods Committee and are as under:

The Fundamental Postulates That Govern Spirit Healing

The source of spiritual healing is God, Who created the perfect laws that govern life. Sickness follows the transgression of these laws.

The purpose of spiritual healing is to stimulate man's latent divinity, so that he lives in harmony with God's laws and, automatically reaping the result, fulfils the reason for earthly life.

Spiritual healing, therefore, helps to accomplish the Divine intention for man's spiritual progress.

The postulates which follow are concerned with the fulfilment of the Divine purpose

Every change in the universe is the result of law-governed forces. Nothing takes place by chance or without a reason. Thus our bodies are subject to definite laws which control our health from birth to the grave.

Spiritual healing is the result of law-governed healing forces that induce change.

For any state of change to be **purposefully** effected, intelligent direction is needed to administer the law-governed forces to the subject.

Example:—Man must direct the force of electricity to produce a **given** result within the laws which govern that force.

The effective administering of a healing force requires intelligent direction.

Through spiritual healing, "incurable" patients are cured. The term "incurable" signifies that medicine can do no more, that earthly wisdom is exhausted, and the patient is condemned to suffer without hope of recovery. Thus when a spiritual healing succeeds with an "incurable" it denotes that a wiser intelligence than that of man is responsible for the law-governed, ordered change. If this intelligence is not earthly, then it must be of the Spirit.

The intelligent direction of a healing force originates from the spirit realm.

A diversity of human ills, from mental sickness to cancer, from nervous breakdowns to cataract, from blue babies to arthritis, are successfully treated by spiritual healing. This denotes that the directing intelligence is able to diagnose the cause of the affliction and to determine the correct character and strength of the healing force needed to remedy each given condition.

In a successful healing, the directing intelligence is able to ascertain the cause of disease and knows how to administer the remedial force to induce a state of beneficial change within the patient.

The Laws That Govern Spirit Healing

There are some physical laws which control the material world. As there must be order in spirit life there are spirit laws. The administering of a spirit healing force must conform to its laws, just as physical laws govern physical forces.

The physical and spirit laws combined come within the definition of the total law.

No healing is possible outside the confines of the total law.

Harmony between Spirit, healer and patient. It is a law that harmony must exist between the transmission of a force and its conscious, or unconscious, reception. Furthermore, the receiver must be in attunement with the transmitter.

The intelligently directed healing forces emanate from a non-physical realm, but through healership such non-physical forces are transformed into physical effects.

In Contact Healing, the healer is the attuned receiver through whom the spirit healing forces are received for transmission to the patient.

One function of the healer is to be the means, where necessary, for non-physical energy to be made physical.

The patient's spirit-self can act as a receiver and transformer of healing force, in Contact Healing as well as in Absent Healing.

Absent Healing: When Absent Healing is effective, attunement is established between the healing intelligence and the patient.

The healer's function is to be the communicative link between the absent patient and the healing source.

Every person has a spirit-self which can be in attunement with spirit intelligence. He is therefore able to receive spirit direction and healing forces.

In Absent Healing, the patient's spirit-self acts as the transformer, and receiver of healing forces.

The patient's spirit-self is able to receive corrective thoughts and directives from the healing intelligence to influence him rightly and so overcome primary causes of disease.

The Healing Forces

For the alleviation and healing of physical ill-effects the healing forces produce a changed chemical effect in the patient's body. This implies a profound spirit knowledge of chemistry and energies.

The spirit healing forces, producing a planned chemical change, must, before the act of transformation, be synonymous with the energy-formations comprising physical matter.

These healing forces are able to create chemical changes through the application of one given form of energy to another.

Beneficial chemical changes are also induced through the bodily intelligence.

The healing forces possess individual, particularised characteristics to effect beneficial change through introducing new factors that alter or disperse the harmful conditions.

In cases of direct dispersal or induced chemical change, the effects are directed to the disharmony alone, and there is no interference with the healthy tissue or structure.

This implies that the spirit intelligence performs an exact process, influencing only diseased cells or structures, without disturbing the healthy ones.

The establishing of this state of harmony is called "attunement".

When a healer is in an attuned condition for healing he is in a state of harmony with the healing guide, who is able to receive thought impressions from the healer and to give thought impressions to the healer's consciousness. This can be likened to a very slight degree of trance. It is through attunement that the healer becomes "conditioned" to be a channel through whom the healing energies flow.

Some healers are accustomed to heal under an advanced state of trance control, when the presence of the healing guide is invited strongly within the orbit of the healer's personality to attain a dominant influence over the mind.

Some healers have commenced their healing ministry in this way, but as their experience in healing practice has progressed they have found it unnecessary to invite the condition of trance control.

When a healer is working under the close control of one guide, then the scope of the healing is limited to that which is within the knowledge of the guide. No matter how wise a guide may be, it is unlikely that he possesses all the knowledge necessary for the healing of the wide range of afflictions the human mind and body can contract.

As no human mind can contain all the knowledge within medical science, there is need for specialisation, so it is logical to assume that the same applies in spirit life, too.

When a healer is not possessed by the personality of the guide, but is simply in a condition of attunement with him, then he is free to be used by any other spirit doctor who is better qualified to treat a specific disease.

There are further advantages in healing through attunement, rather than under guide control. Firstly, the healer becomes a more conscious part of the healing act; secondly, his intuitive awareness is cultivated; thirdly, he becomes a knowledgeable partner (to some extent) in the healing purpose; and finally, he is able to sense that "knowing" when symptoms are yielding.

Furthermore, attunement will enable the healer to achieve a responsible level of spirit communication, showing him, intuitively, the cause and symptoms of a patient's trouble.

As the healer's ability to attune becomes more of "second nature" through usage and experience, so will he receive more freely and simply, an understanding of the healing need, and counsel for the patient in the ways to co-operate with the healing purpose. Healership is, as has already been stated, a part of the Divine Plan. It is truly spiritual and therefore healers should try to adopt a spiritual code of values in the conduct of their lives. This does not mean that they should adopt the artificial guise of being "Holier than thou". They should enjoy a sense of humour and just be natural, having a song in the heart, with a smile for themselves as well as for all others whom they meet on the path of life. They should not bear resentment and do no hurt to anyone; they should enjoy rendering service to those in need, to their neighbours and the aged, and generally serve good causes. They should take no part in hurtful gossip . . . and, what is also important, they should respect and care for all living creatures, protecting them from cruelty and recognising them as our "lesser brethren" and part of God's creation. These are the ways in which the healer's countenance will naturally radiate goodness and to be seen by all as reflecting and possessing the Gift of the Spirit.

Chapter 2

THE ART OF ATTUNEMENT

Let us first consider some basic generalisations upon which every act of healing must rest. We must acknowledge the truth that every change in life is the result of law-governed forces acting upon the subject. Therefore, when a spirit healing takes place this, too, must be the result of the application of law-governed force, for in healing we are still, in part, dealing with the world of matter. There is, however, a vital difference between the functioning of the physical and spirit laws.

As man can direct a physical force, so it requires a spirit mind to direct a spirit force, for the latter belongs to the spirit realm and not to earth. So it is with the spirit healing forces, every act of healing demands independent, intelligent direction.

This is easily demonstrated. With an individual healer, one witnesses healings of a widely divergent character, the restoring of an unbalanced mind, the dispersal of a growth and the correction of sight or hearing. Obviously a different quality of healing force is necessary for the three examples just mentioned.

The act of healing, which produces a change within the physical body, demands not only knowledge of the manipulation of spirit forces but also their co-ordination with the physical forces that govern the human anatomy.

We are, therefore, forced to the conclusion that the

Harry Edwards checks over some patients' letters with his colleagues, Joan and Ray Branch. As in Harry Edwards' time, absent healing has remained the major part of the extensive healing work of The Sanctuary at Shere.

The vital role of attunement in spiritual healing is captured in this splendid study of Harry Edwards at one of his major public healing demonstrations.

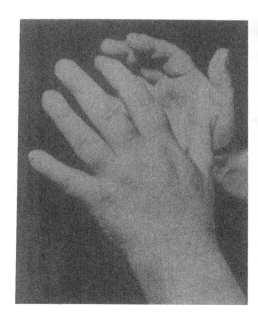

"We use our hands as part of our minds to express the healing intention".
Harry Edwards.

Right: the expressive hands of the author.

operating mind must be a non-physical one; a spirit mind that has acquired greater wisdom than man possesses. These spirit operators we call the "healing guides".

To develop the ability to act as a receiver, it becomes our primary purpose to prepare ourselves by cultivating the art of attunement with the healing guides and the healing forces.

When any transmission is received, there must be attunement between transmitter and receiver. If we are to act as transmitters for the spirit forces, we must possess some spirit quality to enable us to do so. This affinity is a quality of the spirit mind. Healing is a natural act and it is obvious that healers are used for the transmission of healing power.

It is natural that healers are not content with being used so simply for healing. They want to do something more themselves and it is difficult for them to realise that further personal effort is not necessary. This is, perhaps, one of the hardest lessons the healer has to learn, to be satisfied that he can be the means of healing the sick in such a simple way.

What we can do, and this is of primary importance, is to train ourselves to attune to Spirit and so become more useful instruments of the spirit healing operators. The healing power comes *through* us and it is not *of* us.

Attunement means establishing a state of affinity with the spirit guides. For the beginner this is often a problem, but with experienced healers it is not difficult; indeed, no healing could have taken place if attunement had not been achieved.

With continued experience attunement comes as second nature, but even with the most advanced healership it can always be further strengthened to advantage.

It is good to seek purposefully and regularly to attain a more perfect state of affinity with Spirit. Apart from the healing purpose, it enables the healer to obtain spiritual relaxation and this is good for all of us. There is no one way of achieving this, but the following suggestions may prove to be helpful.

We should remember that the attaining of attunement is a simple, natural act. All sense of "performance" should be avoided. It is almost like dozing but with the consciousness of inner-mind awareness.

The healer should retire to a place where he will be quiet and undisturbed for twenty to thirty minutes. This period can be extended as time goes on. In the beginning, half an hour two or three times a week will suffice.

He should make himself comfortable, with the body upright. A Windsor armchair is ideal for the purpose. He has the chair to rest his arms on and to facilitate complete relaxation of the body. The light should be dimmed. A low light prevents the optic nerves being impressed and so disturbing the consciousness.

The word "concentration" is commonly used in association with spiritual development, but from the healing point of view *it is the very opposite* of the mind state required, for we are not seeking mental concentration but mental *abandonment*. Do not, however, try to make your mind a blank for you will not succeed. One cannot divorce all thought from one's mind by mental effort or concentration, but one can, however, let the mind be gently contemplative, thinking of contact with the spirit people and of the purpose for which the attunement is intended, i.e. to heal the sick, to take away pain and to remove causes of disease. By letting one's thoughts dwell lightly upon these associated ideas so the mind becomes amenable to intuitive thought through the spirit-self. Do not keep up any thought flow for long, or the mind will become tense. Tenseness is always to be avoided. For a change let your mind dwell on beautiful things. Take a mental holiday into a garden of beauty, envisaging the glory of the flowers with all their colour and scent; or contemplate the idealism portrayed in the scriptures. These are only suggestions, but they indicate the way to rest the mind from the prosaic things of everyday life.

We possess a physical mind that is concerned with daily detail, but we also possess a spirit mind, and it is the latter that we desire to bring into a superior state.

It is unlikely at first that any difference will be felt within oneself. **You are not sitting for trance or for any spirit entity to take possession of your faculties. This would be most unwise, for one should never sit solo for this purpose but only in a well-conducted developing circle under the guidance of a qualified leader.**

You are sitting for meditation and for your mind to attune with Spirit rather than the attracting of spirit entities to you.

On each occasion that you sit your first thoughts should be prayerful ones addressed to God. Set prayers are of little use for they become recitations. Your simple thoughts are best and they should be quite natural, as if you are talking to God. Avoid high-sounding phrases and unnatural ones; for example, ask for help "this evening" rather than "this eventide". Express your desire to serve Him for all that is righteous; to remove disharmony and evil, whether it be of the mind or of the flesh. Ask that His ministers in Spirit will give you guidance and protection while you mediate, and then have every confidence that only good influences will be with you.

Be comfortable in your body and easy in your mind, and then when you feel you have reached a state of

attunement, consider a patient that you know is unwell.
You will probably know the character of the illness. If
you do, then spend a few moments in allowing your
mind to picture the patient, dwelling upon his personality, where he is, and the nature of the distress causing
the illness.

As you do this, let it be done as if you are communicating these thoughts to "someone" who is "listening in" to you. Let it be simple and natural. Do not stress
the situation. Try to project the mental picture outwards,
linking up with the spirit mind that is receiving it.
Because your spirit-self is open to Spirit so it will be
received by those who are associating with you.

Then follow this up with your mental request, again
gently and naturally made to those who are "listening
in", that they may be able to take away the pain, stiffness, stress, or whatever it may be, so that comfort and
perfection may return to the sick one. Let these thoughts
be purposeful and directive as distinct from a casual
application for help. For example, if the patient has a
painful arm, let the outgoing thought be that the pain
may be taken away from the arm and easement given.

This is, of course, the way to develop the gift of Absent
Healing. After seeking help for one patient, allow that
line of thought to cease and then proceed to seek help
for the next patient. Know within yourself that the
healing guides are there "listening in". The time necessary for each patient should only be that of the thought-
time to cover the ill-conditions and the healing need;
lengthy intercession will not add to the efficacy of the
healing.

When a healer has taken part in a Contact Healing
session, or he has given treatment to one or more
patients, he can, in meditation or Absent Healing go over
again in his mind his patients' needs and renew his
memories of the trouble with each of them and the heal-

ing purpose. Generally speaking, the healer will find the next time he gives Contact Healing the act of healing will be easier, the patient responds more readily, and the attunement both with the patient and Spirit will be more close.

After you have made this intercession, let the mind relax. Hum to yourself a hymn or tune that appeals to you during your break in contemplation. Let your mind swing with the rhythm of the melody, and meditate on some peaceful, happy situation. Picture in your mind a pleasant landscape, with water, trees and hills, etc., and enjoy the contemplation of this. Other suggestions are to think of your favourite flower, picturise its form, petals, colour and scent. Imagine you are strolling through a peaceful wood and watching the rays of the sun as they filter through the trees. Picture within your mind how you would like to render greater service to humanity by healing or in any other way. And by so doing naturally encourage the spiritual aspect of your nature by thoughts that possess grace and beauty and virtue.

There is a condition of mind known as "day-dreaming", when thoughts are wandering oblivious of all else; this is the state of mind to be arrived at during the periods of contemplation.

There is no set time as to how long a sitting should continue. At first the minutes will seem to be long, but as the sittings continue the time so spent will be a real pleasure and quickly go, and will be joyfully anticipated during the day.

It is further suggested that you do not discipline yourself by fixing a definite time to start the sittings. Let them take place after the daily tasks have been comfortably finished. Do not hurry these, but rather see happiness in their accomplishment. Then when you feel the desire to sit for communion with the spirit people, that is the time to do it.

The impression may have been given that night is the only time when this may be done. This is not so. With many people who are employed during the day, evening time is best when the day's work has been ended and there is the opportunity for peace and relaxation. To those who have opportunities at other periods of the day, any time is suitable, so long as the desire is there. If you are out for a walk by yourself, and conditions are quiet and you can saunter slowly along, you can again let your thoughts turn to spiritual things.

There is another important ideal to be woven into the way of life, and that is to live by a code of true values. You will not do harm to anyone, you will always seek to serve. You will be tolerant in all things, and not allow temper or ill-will to follow an act that may not please you. As you place any displeasing act in its true perspective to life, its relative unimportance will be seen and that it is not worthy of causing disharmony of mind.

Help your neighbours by any act of kindness, especially those who are sick and need a word of comfort or an errand undertaken. If during the day you see a sufferer, hold him in reserve in your mind, and then, later, in the quietness, you will ask for healing to reach him.

If the healer has knowledge of the spirit guide associated with him, then his thoughts will be tuned to him at the start of his period of sitting. He may well picture to himself the personality of the guide as he knows him. Then when the sitter feels he is attuned to the guide, he should convey the thought directive for the sick. This should take place as freely and as naturally as if the sitter were "talking to him by thought".

To those who do not know of the personality of their guides this need not worry them. Just be assured that "someone" is there and that your inner thoughts are received. Hold this knowledge with supreme confidence that it is so. It is quite straightforward, for as you are using your spirit mind so the spirit guides can, and do, listen in.

You will not be doing this unless you have the desire to establish a close affinity with Spirit. That of itself is a product of your spirit mind. It is a spiritual desire. Therefore, as you sit for this purpose, you can have the fullest confidence that you will be able to tune in with Spirit and that your spirit mentors are anxious for you to do so.

This, then, is your mental preparation to establish attunement and the first steps in your further development as a healer. Do not be in a hurry—a slow but sure development is stronger than a quick growth. The time spent in this way will never be regretted. It will give serenity of mind and happiness within. As the healing gift develops, and you become a finer instrument of the Spirit to heal the sick, it will be a reward that cannot be measured in material terms.

Attunement is a subtle state between consciousness and spirit awareness, very difficult to describe in words. There is a word common to teenagers, that is somewhat near an explanation, applying to one who is in a state of "far away" ecstasy known as being "sent".

Attunement is so natural that there are rarely any physical symptoms by which to recognise it. One does not get hot or cold, or feel any physical sensation. There should however be consciousness of a feeling different from normality, which is often more readily appreciated when returning to normal full consciousness after emerging from the state of attunement.

Healers are more aware of the attuned condition when engaged in Contact Healing and a sign of this is the great joy, inwardly felt, when pain has been relieved or an affliction lessened or overcome. This feeling of inner ecstasy transcends all other experiences of happiness. It is joy of the spirit-self, and this could not be felt unless an attuned condition had been established.

Before engaging in Contact Healing, the healer sits quietly for a few moments to attain affinity with Spirit, and in spite of other activities that may be going on at the time and the changing of one patient for another, the attuned condition will, with experience, remain with the healer.

Some healers stand to do their work before the seated patient. There is no reason for this. The healer must be relaxed himself; he must attain the condition of attunement, and this is far more easily obtained seated than standing.

As a patient comes before him for healing, the healer feels a sympathy for him, or her, and then seeks to attune or "blend in" with the patient.

After inducing in the patient a relaxed state, it is well for the healer to spend just a moment or two to deepen his attunement both with Spirit and the patient. By this we have the perfect state: healer attuned to Spirit and to the patient, bringing about a state of "oneness" between all three. The need for establishing attunement with the patient cannot be too strongly stressed. The reason for this is that healing is not achieved by the healer's body. He is only the instrument through whom the healing forces are passed. Like can only contact with like. The spirit force flows through the healer's spirit organisation, so closely allied to his physical body, and through him to the patient's spirit body and then to the patient's physical body.

Therefore, the first contact with the patient is to obtain harmony in the fullest sense between the healer and the patient.

Attunement is an art, it is a quality. It is the essential factor a healer needs to establish rapport with the source of the healing and the recipient. Healers possess the high motives of love and compassion for the sick. Healing from Spirit also has these two great qualities. Thus it is, that through love and compassion from Spirit, blending in with the same qualities in the healer that the attunement is brought into being. Such attunement is a natural act requiring no technique.

Nothing is attained unless it is sought for. The guides render service to further the Divine Plan to overcome the evil of disease and so make manifest to mankind its kinship with Spirit and Divinity. The healer also serves in the same way, thus there is a primary unity of purpose. Spirit mind links with the healer's spirit mind, and as they become akin to each other, so attunement comes.

The desire for attunement by Spirit is ever present, but it is necessary for the human instrument to seek the linking-up with Spirit as an intention. The more this intention is sought for, the easier will attunement become, until it is "second nature" as soon as healing thoughts become a directive.

Chapter 3

DIAGNOSIS

Every healing is a planned act, needing particularised individual treatment for each patient.

Obviously a different kind of healing energy is required for the healing of different diseases. There will be dispersing energies for arthritic deposits and growths; others for stimulation to provide forces for balancing the blood content; soothing influences for nervous tensions and so on. It is logical to assume that the healing energies will vary in composition and strength according to the nature and severity of the sickness. This is elaborated in Section IV, Chapter 2.

The healing guides alone are the administrators of the healing energies. Therefore, it is the guide who is able to make a correct diagnosis in order to know the character of the healing energies the patient needs. Thus the diagnosis is the responsibility of the guide and not the healer.

This leads to the view, that it is not essential for the healer to make a diagnosis. At the same time the healer wishes to play an intelligent part in the healing, and the suggestions that follow may provide the means of attaining this.

The means by which healers receive knowledge of the cause and nature of the sickness will vary according to the manner in which the guides can use the healer. A common form of diagnosing the area of trouble is when the healer places his hand over the affected part, both the healer and the patient becoming aware of a strong heat emanating from the healer's hands and which appears to penetrate into the patient's body.

If the hand is moved away from the affected area the sensation of heat dies away, only to return as the hand comes back to that part. If the hand is withdrawn a short distance from the affected part the heat can still be felt by both healer and patient.

It is interesting to note that this heat is not clinical— that is, if a thermometer is placed between the healer's hand and the patient, there is no rise in the recorded temperature, though the heat sensation still exists. No person is able to induce this heat by will-power or desire. Place the hand over any other part of the body and no sensation will come. This is an elementary proof of the gift of healing.

Study of this leads to the conclusion that the heat is not a physical heat at all. It does not arise from additional circulatory activity in the healer's body. It follows that the heat is **an expression of healing energy** directed from Spirit, through the healer. Therefore when this heat is experienced, it is logical to allow the hand to dwell over the affected part for a time.

With many healers this heat comes to aid specific conditions where **dispersal** is needed, such as in dealing with arthritis or rheumatic adhesions, with fibrositis and growths, etc. It is rarely felt with heart or digestive treatments unless there is a need for dispersal.

Some healers are able to sense coldness instead of heat, or both; others may not experience any such sensations.

Let us remember that all sensation is a mental experience, i.e. hunger, pain, tiredness, etc. Therefore this heat sensation is a mental experience and as the heat is not a physical heat (though it is felt physically)

it is likely to be a mental experience of a force arising
from a healing directive.

Another, and perhaps the best form of diagnosis, is that
received "intuitively". Such diagnoses are received
when a state of attunement is established. The healer's
mind receives a thought impression of the cause of the
trouble and where it lies. Being human, there is always
the risk that such impressions may not be from Spirit
but from the imaginative qualities of the healer's
mind. Only experience can differentiate between them.
Healers can, however, put intuitive impressions to the
test.

As a general rule the healer should not offer diagnosis.
Firstly, he may be wrong—as medical diagnoses can also
be wrong. Secondly, the patient may be over-impressed
by the healer's comments, and so induce a state of
anxiety. Thirdly, when a healing is successful, it may
appear to discredit the diagnosis. Therefore, the less
the healer says in this connection the better, and no
prognosis, or prophesying future outcome, should ever
be given.

One way in which the healer can prove whether the
intuitive impressions he receives are factual is when he is
impressed that the centre of the pain is at a certain place.
Then there is no harm in asking the patient whether this
is so or not. Remember that intuitive thought from Spirit
comes as naturally as normal thought does.

It is good to convey to the guide all the information
the patient can give. It is questionable whether guides
are able to "see" patients **physically,** any more than
we can see the spirit people in spirit form. The guides
have the means of knowing the cause and nature of the
disease or trouble, otherwise they could not receive
their diagnosis, to transmit healing energies. How they
attain this we do not positively know. It may be they
perceive disharmonies through their awareness with the

patient's mind which records all sensation and receives messages from the bodily system of communication. They may be able to observe the character of disease, etc., through the auric emanations.

It is helpful for the healer to ask the patient to describe his symptoms and get him to speak of his trouble. As the healer's mind learns of this so the guide, in attunement and "listening in", will receive the information, and so give him the knowledge of the physical conditions which may assist the guide in his diagnosis.

Similarly with Absent Healing, it is helpful to know the nature of the sickness, and from regular reports a description of the progress being made (or otherwise) so that this information can be passed on to the guides. Thus it will be seen that "attunement" and "diagnosis" are intimately linked together.

There is another aspect that can be associated with "diagnosis". This is when healers appear to "take on within themselves" the conditions of patients. This does not usually affect an established healership, it is more often seen with those who are entering into the healing ministry. A satisfactory conclusion which arises from this is that the healer has established a condition of attunement with the patient.

All sensations are mind experiences. The patient's mind receives the strong impression of his pain and upset. When the healer's mind is attuned to that of the patient these same impressions are received by him. Sometimes, they are so real and strong that it appears the healer is actually suffering from the trouble—such as severe gastric pains—and he feels he has "taken on" the sickness. Of course this is not so. They are simply "mental impressions" alone.

As the development of the healer advances, so the guides use the healership better and any such impressions are avoided. When the healer is able to appreciate the character of the feelings he receives, then his mind places them in their correct perspective and they do not register as stressful impressions.

Some healers claim to possess "clairvoyant diagnosis", that is, they say they are able to see inside the patient where the trouble is located. For example, they may "see" stones in the gall bladder. Others say they are shown a "light" on the patient's body over the troublesome area, and so on. These are personal impressions, and there is no purpose in commenting on them here. They are very exceptional.

If a healer is unable to get any mind impressions or unable to perceive the cause or nature of the trouble, he should not be dismayed. If, in a state of attunement, he lets his guide know of the symptoms he can leave the actual diagnosis to him.

Of course, the nature of many diseases is self-evident, such as with arthritis, and paralysis, spinal conditions, etc.; anaemia is another, as are some mental stresses, so easily discerned in the patient's drawn face and tired and "hurt" eyes. The practised healer is often quickly aware of a patient's need by visual observation.

Even so, it is suggested that the healer, after receiving his patient with sympathy and putting him or her in a relaxed state, should first of all ask the patient to say what is wrong and describe the symptoms. These will usually confirm the healer's impressions.

Furthermore it is good to seek from the patient at the outset the full story of the healing need. This is better than treating a patient "piecemeal". So often troubles in other parts of the body are "effects" from the main cause, and are part of the full picture. A typical example of this is that there is invariably mental tension linked with gastric ulcers, etc.

A healer need not be reticent in asking gently any

question he is impressed to ask to add to his knowledge of the patient's condition. Such questions can arise from his healing experience or can be an intuitively received request from the guide.

Chapter 4

HEALING ENERGIES

This chapter is concerned with the healing of organic conditions rather than with psychosomatic diseases.

In the healing movement much is said about "vibrations" and "rays" even to the extent of such descriptions as the "blue ray" or "golden ray", etc. Instead of using these words we employ the word "energy" as being a truer description of the "healing power".

Every healing of a physical weakness or disease promotes a chemical change in the patient. The dispersal of arthritic substances or a growth, etc., is a chemical change. We need to view spiritual healing not merely as a magical abstract act from Spirit but the employment of spirit science.

Let us consider a simple case common in healing—that of freeing a joint locked by arthritis. The joint cannot move, or only partially move, because arthritic deposits have "cemented" it up or contracted the ligaments and tendons. No physical forcefulness can get the joint to move freely while it is in this state. When doctors do a forceful manipulation an anaesthetic has usually to be given because of the pain caused. The healing of arthritis is not "manipulation". The arthritic deposits must first be removed. This is the chemical change.

To understand "energies" we must first briefly study the composition of matter itself.

All physical matter is composed of atoms, and each atom is a form of characterised energy. Each element is constructed in an identical way.

When one form of atomic energy is associated with another it produces a third substance, and so on. In this way, chemical changes are brought about.

To bring about a change in the existing state of specified matter, additional energies have to be applied to it, for example we apply heat energy to boil water. Under spiritual healing when we see arthritic deposits dispersed, it must follow that some other energies have had to be applied to them to induce a chemical change in their structure, and so bring about their dispersal. In medical science this is the basis of clinical treatment, of which deep ray therapy is an example.

Arthritis is medically incurable, and medical scientists have not yet been able to discover any form of force or energy to dissolve the crippling adhesions.

Scientists are now able to split the atom, change its structure, and break up the characterised energies that comprise it.

The healing guides do the same, but with their advanced wisdom and knowledge of both spirit formed energies and their physical counterparts, they are able to direct to the patient's joints energies that have the quality of inducing a chemical change in the state of the deposits, thus "splitting the atoms" comprising the arthritic adhesions and dispersing them into their original primal energy. Thus, in the successful healing of arthritis, the guides apply remedial energies to break-up and disperse the chemicals cementing a joint.

The same principle applies in all healing of physical trouble, but with different characters of energy according to the patient's need.

So it is, that when a healer places his hand upon say, a shoulder joint locked by arthritis, the specially selected characterised energies from Spirit are directed to disperse those particular arthritic substances which will yield to the spirit energy forces without harming any other tissues in the shoulder.

Such a change can take place in a matter of seconds, and it is obvious that for a joint to be so freed, the cementing deposits must first be dispersed. One cannot open a screwed-up door until the screws have been withdrawn.

The spirit guides must be masters in the art of manipulating energies, because they use them to overcome many different causes of disease and to remove the physical ill-effects.

These dispersing forces must necessarily be of various kinds, for there are those which are used for breaking up the cellular formations in a growth; for dissolving cataracts; or dispersing structures where there are malformations and so on.

There must also be other forms of energies for other purposes, for example, for stimulation. How often do we hear in the healing of sick ones, often near to death, who regain strength and vitality to such a marked degree that doctors are amazed and cannot understand how it has come about? Why is it, that the greater percentage of patients feel all the better in a general way for healing treatment? Simply because they have received vitalising energies (and spiritual upliftment as well).

When a person is suffering from cellular malnutrition, resulting in the wastage of tissue or the malfunctioning of some vital organ, it means that the patient's digestion, circulation, or breathing, is not providing the particular chemical foods the cells need. Some groups of cells require different nourishment from others, needing specific nourishment in the form of special energy for their particular function in the body.

Because we see such patients get well, often dated by

the commencement of the healing treatment, and when medical science is helpless to aid them further, it follows that the guides, knowing of the deficiency, have been able to direct to the patient the qualitative energies the cells need to restore them to a healthy condition.

All this should emphasise the simple part the healer plays, for he has neither the knowledge nor the ability to manipulate these spirit energies; he is simply the channel through whom the healing energies flow to the patient.

[*The healing of cellular and other energy deficiencies is dealt with in detail in Section IV.*]

How does this take place? Let us examine in more detail the function of the healer himself.

Spirit-directed energies come from a non-physical dimension, and whilst they are the precise counterparts of the physical energies, they are in a non-physical form.

The time must come when these energies are transformed from their non-physical state into their physical counterparts. Such changes can only take place where there is a merging of Spirit with physical conditions. Thus it seems a logical assumption that through the healer's faculty of attunement with Spirit he is used as a transformer for the change, becoming like a laboratory, where the spirit forces are converted into their physical counterpart through him and are directed by the guides to the site of the healing need.

Hard and fast ideas should be avoided. It need not be the healer's hand that is the terminal for the flow of healing energies to the patient. They may flow to the patient direct. The fact is, that a chemical change is induced within the patient as a result of the attunement between the healer, guide and patient.

In Absent Healing, when the healer is not in close proximity to the patient, a similar process of transformation takes place through the spirit-self of the patient.

It is good to remember that there is no rigid dividing line between any state of being, between the physical forces, classifications of life, or anything else. Therefore, there is no rigid division separating the spirit realm from our own physical realm, in energies; or indeed within any part of living creation.

As healers accept this postulate, so they become better instruments of the Spirit, acting simply, without trying to "heal of themselves". It is only natural that a healer wishes, through his love and compassion for the sick, to play a greater part in the healing than he does. Thus we are learning to abandon all those unnecessary techniques and rituals of the past, for instead of assisting the healer's usage by the guides they tend to hamper the good effort, which is different from the healer being satisfied at being used as a passive instrument by the guides.

Chapter 5

"THE GIVING OF POWER"

It is contended that our hands possess no healing
qualities of themselves, and that we use our hands as
part of our minds to express the healing intention.

For example, if a patient has pain and we seek easement for this, then our hands will move in a soothing
movement as if to take it away, the hands thus expressing
the healing intention. If we touch a lovely piece of wood
carving or a piece of soft material, we use the sense of
touch to convey to the mind our appreciation of the
beauty of the handicraft and the texture. We love to feel
the hands of our dear ones, or to touch the face as an
act of endearment, showing that our hands possess a
sensitivity that is very intimately associated with our
mental processes.

Thus as the sensitivity of the hands is an aid to mental
appreciation, they are indeed servants of the mind. It is
as if our brains are in our fingers. It is difficult to imagine
any other activity where the intimacy between the hand
and mind is stronger than in the act of healing.

In considering these things, it is fundamental to remember that it is neither through the hands nor the mind
that healing takes place. Every healing is a planned act,
needing the intelligent application of the particular
corrective healing energy to master the given ill-
condition.

Thus, when a healer seeks healing for a patient, his

hands naturally become part of the healing intention, to soothe away pain and to make contact with the patient in order that the healing energies may be directed to that part of the body where the affliction lies.

When a healer is supporting another healer in a healing circle, he instinctively blends in, co-operating with the healing purpose. It naturally follows, as he does this, that his hands become part of the mental directive, and they are extended forward with the fingers opened towards the healer and patient, expressing the act of "giving help".

It will be observed that the holding out of the hands is **not** an act of healing but simply a subconscious indication of co-operation on the part of the supporting healer.

Healers need to be reasonably strong in character and it is hoped that as they realise the holding out of the hands **in a noticeable manner** does not contribute to the healing, execpt as a subconscious extension of the desire to co-operate, **then they will realise it is not necessary at all.**

The logic of it is this: to heal a **given** condition, a given quality of characterised healing force or energy is necessary. For example, if a patient is suffering from arthritis and the joints are calcified, then a particular healing energy is needed to disperse the calcium adhesions. Therefore when healers sit to "give power" they do not, **of themselves,** direct qualitative healing energies to overcome the patient's disease. However, there are other important factors to be taken into consideration when supporting healers sit to "give power".

Through their desire to see the sick made well, they give their love and sympathy, thus helping to create the right "conditions" to assist the healing. Before we go further it is well to understand what is meant by the word "conditions". In ordinary life we appreciate good conditions, we like to be warm and comfortable; if we are engaged in writing we like to be quiet and undisturbed, and so on. These are physical conditions. In the healing circle the conditions that help are those of love, compassion and the healing intention, for there is no doubt that these qualities are as real as warmth, comfort and quietness. Thus when supporting healers sit to "give power" they are actually giving their love and sympathy, providing a radiating force thus creating conditions in which the healing can take place more easily and happily.

There is another factor that can come into the picture. With the sympathetic attunement of all the healers present with that of the patient's spirit-self, the latter becomes aware of the help that is so willingly being given and is thus able to receive strength and assurance from this. The spirit-self of the sufferer can be comforted and reassured, through the affinity of the spirit-selves of the co-operating healers.

The spirit guides associated with the co-operating healers are present too, and this is important, though an aspect often lost sight of during the period of "giving power".

Thus in the healing circle we have (i) the patient, (ii) the executive healer and his spirit doctors and (iii) the co-operating healers with their spirit doctors. Thus we visualise a picture of mutual co-operation by a number of personalities, seen and unseen, who have come together for a healing purpose. In public healing services, with many supporting healers, this creates a wonderful picture if we could but see it.

It is surely right to assume that as we gather together to help the sick, so the spirit guides assemble, too. It is also logical to assume that in the essentials of the actual healing effort the direction is under one spirit doctor. This spirit doctor is likely to be the healing guide of the executive healer. Let us recall that a healing needs a given force, intelligently directed, to overcome a given condition; and therefore it is likely to be that the actual healing effort is administered by **one spirit doctor.**

It is not unreasonable to assume that the degree of knowledge and experience possessed by the spirit doctors is variable. Some may possess a wider knowledge than others in the treatment of specific diseases—in other words, there may be "specialists" on the Spirit side as well as on the human side. If this is so, then the situation may arise where the spirit doctor of a co-operating healer may become the one who deals with the problem at the time.

Note:—While reference has been made to a "healer's spirit guide", it is of course known that a number of spirit doctors or guides are associated with most healers, with the exception of the healer who works alone only under the trance control of one guide. It follows that the guide may be less qualified to diagnose and treat a patient's disease than another spirit doctor who is associated with the healer.

Every healer is justifiably proud of his healing guides, and while we may be weak enough to wish a healing to be administered by one's own spirit guide, particularly if one is the executive healer, we can be sure that no such weakness exists in Spirit. It may be another guide who assumes the healing directive.

To sum up, therefore, when we co-operate with each other in a healing effort, we do not personally send out individual healing energies from our hands. The help so given is conditional and not executive. As healers accept this, so will the co-operation be given with reason and in a true perspective.

Chapter 6

THE USE OF THE HANDS IN HEALING

It has been shown how the hands of a healer can be used for diagnosis; the methods by which healing energies are transformed and transmitted through them; and to explain the use of the hands by co-operating healers in the healing clinic. It has also been shown how the hands may sometimes be used as transformers of spirit healing energy into a physical corrective force, remembering that the hands are used as extensions of the mind.

It can be well argued that it is not necessary for the healer to place his hands upon a patient for the healing to take place. Consideration of Absent Healing supports this view.

In the paragraphs that follow dealing with "Healing Treatments" the healer should not limit within his mind that the hand is necessarily the instrument through which the healing energy flows. This may well be true but it is not necessarily so at all times.

The hands serve as the focal point for the healing intention.

We also have to consider the mental attitude of the patient. He will naturally look for the healer to direct his attention to where the symptoms of trouble lie. If the healing need is wanted for the eyes, then the patient will look for treatment being given to the eyes by having the healer's fingers touching the eyes.

It is essential to maintain the patient's confidence in the healer and in the treatment, so it is desirable that the healer's hand rests where the seat of the sickness is and this has psychological benefit also.

We have the picture now of the healer in attunement with his spirit guide or spirit doctor, blended in with the patient. Either from the information the patient has given and/or by the diagnosis received.

The spirit doctor has learned through his "listening-in" to the healer's mind the physical nature of the trouble from which the patient is suffering. He has in the ways known to him "seen" the cause of the illness and the symptoms, thus arriving at his own diagnosis, and determining the right quality of healing energy needed to overcome them. The time has now come for the act of healing.

It may well be that if the healer's hands are resting near the affected part of the patient's body, they will be used as the terminal for the transmission of the healing force. If, for example, it is the shoulder joint locked by arthritis, the healer will let his hand rest upon it, and being inwardly attuned to the healing purpose "that the shoulder joint may be freed from adhesions", he will allow the healing forces to flow through to disperse the "cementing" matter.

This seeking of the healing intention need not be prolonged. As a rule the extent of the dispersal possible at the time will take no more than a moment or two. Then the healer, still blended in with the patient, will look to see the extent of the betterment by gently moving the upper arm to observe the looseness of movement now possible. Further details on the healing of arthritis, etc., are the subject of a later chapter.

The same method is applied generally to the healing of most physical troubles. First, the healing intention and next, to assess the result. In the movement of the shoulder joint **no force of any kind is used.** The hands are but an extension of the attuned mind and with experience the healer will be able to sense inwardly what movement is possible. Of course, the healer looks for the joint to be freed and it may well be that using gradual movement in getting the joint to circulate, the arm can be stretched upwards without pain. If the patient shows any sign of pain then the healer is going too far, and if the joint is not fully freed at the time, the healer must learn to be satisfied for the time being, and not to pursue further movement on his own. It cannot be overstressed that in seeking the looser movements the healer's hands continue to be as part of his mind, as indeed they are.

The art of blending in with a patient can be greatly helped by the use of the hands. The healer is making contact with the patient, the latter preferably being seated before him. He will take the patient's hands within his own, and hold them gently but firmly, while he talks to the patient to put him at ease and learn of the healing need. This will establish attunement with the patient.

The healer, either from his knowledge of the trouble and where it is sited, or from his intuitively received spirit diagnosis, then purposefully joins in with the healing intention to secure betterment. For example, if the trouble be a goitre or a growth, the healer will allow his hand or hands to rest lightly where it is located and seek within his mind for dispersal to take place. It may be the healer will wish his fingers to move in a gentle erasing movement over the goitre as if to soften and disperse it. He must allow his hand to be used for the healing dispersing forces to flow through it. The spirit doctor is in close affinity with the healer and the latter may intuitively receive the healing direction, although he may not be particularly conscious of this. Next will follow the observation to see the result. If the growth is visible, as with a goitre, it can be seen whether there is any reduction in its size, or whether its consistency has noticeably softened.

The healing act is simple as far as we are concerned, but often healers are not content with its simplicity and wish to do more themselves. It is in this way that healing passes and other elaborations have arisen. It is only natural for the healer to wish to continue the treatment himself if the total result has not been all that he has wished for and as the healer still has the healing intention in his mind, so his hands may move in a "taking away" gesture to soothe the trouble further.

From what we have already observed no physical movement of the hands can constitute an act of healing. With some healers the practice of passes has become an established technique. It is not denied that healings do take place through this method and the reason for this is that the healing intention has been present so the healing has taken place—not because of the passes, but because of the **intention.**

It has also been seen that in addition to such passes there has followed the desire to cleanse the hands, thus leading to a "throwing-off" movement. Exaggeration leads to exaggeration and so, unfortunately, it has been observed on past occasions violent and eccentric "throwing-off" movements of the hands as if the healer was throwing traces of disease onto the floor. This of course is absurd; and it has even been known for some healers to warn those present not to stand too close, as otherwise they may become infected and contract the disease! This is even more absurd.

If a patient is nervous or tense, then the hands can be used in soothing passes to induce a relaxed condition. If there are head pains, the fingers used in a gentle smoothing way over the forehead can often be a means of taking away the head pains as part of the healing intention to do so.

The purpose of this chapter is to indicate how the hands of a healer can be used in a reasoned way to act as extensions of the healer's mind by the spirit doctors. Spiritual healing by contact must be a thought process— it is not haphazard. The healer possesses the art of attunement between his spirit mind and his conscious mind thus becoming an instrument to be used by the spirit guides. The guide is able to direct the healing purpose to the physical mind via the spirit mind, and so **with experience** to become a conscious instrument in the act of healing. The hands are used as terminal points whereby the healing energies are transformed and transmitted to the patient, generally in a very short time— perhaps in a matter of seconds.

The use of the hands in any other way, such as making passes down the patient, are but expressions of the healer's desire to heal, but they of themselves possess no healing virtue.

Chapter 7

HEALING ETHICS

Almost all the material in this section is already understood and observed by practising healers. The reason for its inclusion here, is that no book dealing with spiritual healing could possibly be complete without some reference to this most vital facet. All full members of the National Federation of Spiritual Healers, when they sign their membership form endorse their acceptance of the Hippocratic oath, which is as follows:

THE OATH OF HIPPOCRATES: The regimen I adopt shall be for the benefit of my patients according to my ability and judgment, and not for their hurt or for any wrong. I will give no deadly drug to any, though it be asked of me, nor will I counsel such, and especially I will not aid a woman to procure abortion. Whatsoever house I enter, there will I go for the benefit of the sick, refraining from all wrong-doing or corruption, and especially from any act of seduction, of male or female, of bond or free. Whatsoever things I see or hear, concerning the life of men, in my attendance on the sick, or even apart therefrom, which ought not to be noised abroad, I will keep silence thereon, counting such things to be as sacred secrets.

Embodied within this ancient and solemn dedication is a standard of conduct upon which any healer may safely base a life of healing service.

In general the ethics relating to healing divide into three categories.

1. **The relationship of the healer to his patient.**
2. **The relationship of the healer to doctors and other practitioners.**
3. **The responsibility of the healer to his gift.**

It would perhaps, therefore, be simplest to consider them in this order.

Healer-Patient Relationship

Any information conveyed to a healer by a patient is a sacred trust that must not **under any circumstances** be broken. In this respect a healer is in the same position as a doctor or priest. In the course of a treatment, for instance, a patient may mention to the healer an indiscretion or even a criminal act that is troubling him. Whilst the healer may be guided to suggest the course of action that might correct the problem he must not divulge to any other person the information that he has been given. Especially where other members of the same family are being treated, the greatest care must be taken not to pass on information that has been received by the healer in his position of trust.

Healers may often find themselves tempted to advise their patients outside their normal capacity as spiritual healers. This can be an extremely dangerous practice. Healers must constantly examine themselves to be sure that they are not giving advice which stems purely from their own ego rather than from some outside source. Even where the healer is quite sure that such advice he is giving has been given to him directly by the spirit guide or doctor working with him he should still be quite certain that he is not, by passing it on, attempting to live the patient's life or solve problems that are in fact the direct responsibility of the patient. In general it might be said that as far as advising the patient is concerned the principal purpose of the healer should be to cause the patient to seek for the solution to solve his own material or spiritual problems. The great asset which spiritual healing has above all other therapies is that it works at a depth beyond words and does not necessarily require, as with for instance psychiatric therapy, the involvement of the therapist in the direct problem of the patient.

Healing Protocol

There is no reason whatsoever why any healer, at any time, should ask for the removal of the clothing of his patient. Quite obviously for the sake of comfort, a man may remove his jacket or a lady her top coat, but beyond this there is no need for undressing. In the past, even where healers have quite innocently sought the removal of patients' clothing, complications have on occasions arisen. It is, therefore, advisable that the healer should avoid this practice at all costs.

Where healers are treating patients of the opposite sex it is desirable that a chaperon should be present. There are, of course, times when this is impossible but there should always be someone close at hand in case they are required. This applies particularly to the visiting of patients in their own homes. It may occasionally be necessary for a male healer to treat a lady in bed or in her bedroom, and in such cases it is essential that her husband or some female relative or friend should be present. It is as well to remember that even a qualified medical practitioner treating a patient in a hospital will call for a nurse to be present before carrying out an examination. These are not rigid and inflexible rules but a code of conduct that will be advantageous to the healer in protecting his own good name and position.

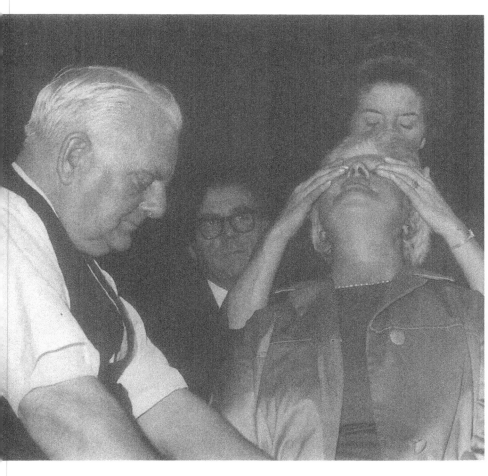

Harry Edwards with George and Olive Burton at a public
demonstration of spiritual healing.

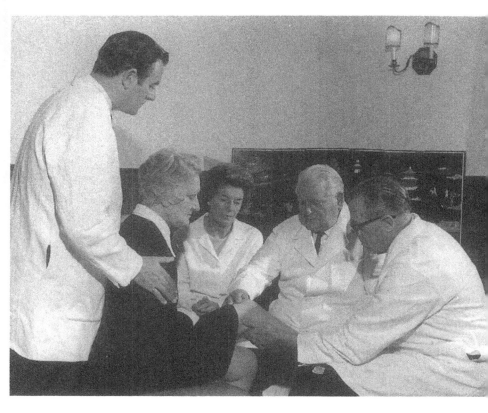

Harry Edwards with his colleagues Olive and George Burton and Ray Branch.

Healer-Doctor Relationship

It would of course be a completely desirable state if there was complete co-operation and understanding between all practitioners treating the sick. Healers must remember that from the point of view of the qualified medical practitioner they are unqualified and, to use a harsh word, are "quacks". Many doctors now understand the work that healers are doing and do honestly attempt to give reasonable co-operation; but to others the position is still one of grave suspicion. Doctors spend a minimum period of six years in training to become qualified. It is understandable that some of them should feel as they do. It is the duty of every healer to do all that is within his power to seek fair and honest co-operation with all other practitioners. By so doing he will greatly further the work of healing and he will make it possible for more and more people to have the benefit of the combination of both spiritual and physical therapy.

An increasing number of doctors are sending their patients, or giving their approval for them to visit healers; hospitals are also sending their patients in hospital ambulances to receive healing at healing sanctuaries, and healer members of the National Federation of Spiritual Healers have permission to treat patients (with the physician's consent) in over 1,500 of our national hospitals.

A healer should always be certain that he is never overstepping his position as a spiritual healer by attempting to take the place of the medical practitioner. It is not the healer's province to advise the patient in relation to drugs or medicaments; neither is it his responsibility to interfere with any medical advice the patient has already been given by his doctor. Such conduct might well bring the healer into conflict with other practitioners.

Advice Concerning Drugs and Surgery.

A healer may often feel that a drug that has been recommended is harmful to his patient. He may equally well feel that an operation that has been suggested by a doctor will ultimately be harmful or even fatal to the p tient. In such circumstances there is a tremendous temptation for the healer to give contrary advice, but this must be avoided under all circumstances. The healer may treat the patient by spiritual healing and then advise him to visit his doctor and show the doctor the change which has taken place in his condition. The healer should ask the patient to tell the doctor what has taken place and to seek the doctor's co-operation in allowing more time before such physical remedies are sought. Such a course of conduct will frequently succeed and may add another doctor to those who are already co-operative and understanding as to the purpose of healership. There will, however, be times when such co-operation will not be given, and it then becomes a matter for the direct decision of the patient, and much as the healer may feel inclined to intervene, he must allow the patient to reach his own decision as to what course he is going to follow. (*See also Section III, Chapter 7, p. 183.*)

Healing of Children

Particular care must be taken in the treatment of children below the age of 16 years. **It is illegal for an unqualified practitioner to be the cause of a child not receiving full medical attention should it be necessary.** A healer should, therefore, always advise parents that they should seek the advice of their doctor in relation to the child, and where the parents refuse to do this, particularly where the child is suffering from a terminal disease, the healer must ask them to commit to writing the fact that he has asked them to seek medical advice.

There are two golden rules which it is well worth remembering. One is for the healer in all cases to suggest to the patient that it would be as well to consult his doctor as well as to receive spiritual healing. The second is that it is better to avoid giving advice in relation to drastic dietary change or physical remedy where the healer is not directly qualified to give such advice. By following such a course of action the healer will make the co-operation of other practitioners far more readily available and will be adding to the ultimate complete co-operation of all practitioners. Spiritual healers are able to treat cases of every description. Their therapy is a spiritual one, operating at a spiritual level. As long as they remember the predominant nature of Spirit over physical matter then they will realise that such a course of conduct will in no way limit what they are doing, but that it will, in the course of time, bring their therapy into a true perspective within the whole scheme of remedial treatment.

Responsibility of the Healer to his Gift

Spiritual healing is a gift of God and should be available to all who seek it. The healer has a great responsibility to be certain that he is providing a clean, alert and intelligent vehicle through which it may operate, free from any prejudice of race, colour, or creed. As long as the healer remembers that he is the channel through which the love of God may flow and keeps in mind a humility and dedication to the service of all mankind, then he will in every way be fulfilling the responsibility to his gift.

THE MEANING OF OUR SYMBOL

Healing is God's gift to all His children, irrespective of race or creed. It cannot be the prerogative of any religion. Thus, the circle represents the whole of the human family, and the cross indicates the influence of the Christ spirit within it.

HARRY EDWARDS
SPIRITUAL HEALING SANCTUARY
BURROWS LEA, HOOK LANE, SHERE
GUILDFORD, SURREY GU5 9QG

HEALING IS A GIFT

Chapter 8

THE CONDUCT OF A HEALING CLINIC

As with healing methods there are no fixed rules, nor is there any one way to conduct a healing clinic. There are, however, pitfalls that can be avoided and general practices which it may well be helpful to adopt. Wherever the clinic may be, whether it is in a room specially kept for this purpose in a healer's home or in some public place, it is always best to adopt procedures that are simple and uncomplicated. It should be remembered at all times that the clinic is conducted for the welfare of the patients rather than for the aggrandisement of the healer.

The following ideas may be regarded as generally applicable, but of course, modification and alteration would depend entirely on the special needs of the clinic and the personal tastes and ideas of the healers.

The Decoration and Furnishings of the Healing Clinic

This is entirely a matter of personal taste. In general, it must be remembered that simplicity is always the most effective. There is always a danger of accumulating too many trappings and ornaments, which may well detract from the emphasis on healership and raise difficulties in the mind of the patient. Many healers have found that surroundings which emphasise peace, light and cleanliness are most likely to induce the best frame of mind in the patient. The old idea of treating patients in heavily curtained dark rooms or in red light is no longer seen.

White coats: Some healers wear white coats whilst healing, and whereas a fresh clean crisp coat may induce a sense of confidence in the patient, a dirty, crumpled drab one will have just the opposite effect. It should be remembered that the mere wearing of a white coat does not turn a person into a healer. The purpose of the coat is that of hygiene, not of creating a uniform.

Washing of hands: The act of washing the hands between attending patients was at one time believed to serve the purpose of cleansing the hands psychically of diseased conditions that might adhere to them. In all probability this derived from the healing passes which were once commonly used in healing. These were believed to "cleanse the aura". These practices are today far less common and generally believed to be unnecessary. From the point of cleanliness, however, it is desirable that facilities for washing should always be readily available to the healer.

Case Cards: The keeping of case cards has a double purpose. They serve to remind healers of details concerning their patients and to add materially to the body of evidence as to the effectiveness of spiritual healing.

Reception: When it is possible to have a receptionist this will greatly assist in the keeping of case records. The receptionist should be a quiet, reliable person who will give the patients a feeling of confidence and clear away any doubts or problems that they may have before receiving healing. It has often been said that "Healing commences in the waiting room". With a really good receptionist this is unquestionably true.

The Organisation of a Healing Group: This will of course, follow a prearranged agreement between the healers concerned. Most healing groups have a leader who receives all new patients and allocates them to the healers most suited to treat their condition. It is of paramount importance that there should be harmony between healers working together and where a healer finds it impossible to co-operate harmoniously with the group he is in, it is better that he should transfer his services elsewhere than allow his feelings to disrupt the healing purpose.

Advertising a Clinic: Although there is nothing wrong in doing so, generally speaking, it is not desirable that healers should advertise their services. When sick people are ready to receive healing, they will either seek it themselves or be led to it. Some healers do, however, find it necessary to advertise, and indeed, particularly at the commencement of a new clinic, it may be found necessary. Healers' advertisements should not contain promises as to the results that will be achieved, and advertisements for healing best serve their purpose when they reflect the dignity of healership. The best advertisement of all is the recommendation of a satisfied patient to others. Where healership is getting results it will soon be found that people will flock in for treatment and thus render advertising unnecessary.

Dealing with the Press: Occasionally healers may be approached by representatives of the press or television. All too frequently it is the job of these people to report the sensational. In endeavouring to do so, they may attempt to lead the healer into making generalised claims for healership. It should always be remembered that healers interviewed in this way are not speaking for themselves alone, but for all their fellow healers as well. Exaggeration should be avoided at all costs, and the greatest care should be exercised to avoid the presentation of an image of healership that will appear to the public at large as spurious or "cranky".

Under no circumstances should the names or addresses of patients be given to reporters without their prior permission. A healer's patients are entitled to the same protection and privacy as that afforded to the patients of a medical doctor.

The Sale of Medicaments: It is illegal for a healer to offer for sale at his clinic medicaments of any description. This includes herbal or homeopathic remedies.

Concluding thoughts: If we make sure that in our clinics we are presenting only the best which dedicated healership has to offer, then we will be ensuring that healing clinics of the future will take their rightful place in the general practice of treating the sick. The healing clinic is the place where healership is presented, and it is our duty as healers to make sure that we offer our patients only the very best in comfortable and sympathetic surroundings.

Chapter 9

HOW PATIENTS CAN HELP
THEIR HEALING

In discussing how a patient can directly assist the
healing effort, one cannot be personal, nor can one lay
down any set of rules because each patient is a case unto
himself, requiring individual healing according to the
nature of the cause and the symptoms of the trouble.
But there are some general directions that can be of
mutual help to both patient and healer.

Before a cure is effected the cause must be discovered.
Now most of our afflictions have their cause in some form
of mental or nervous unrest and very often the patient
may be unaware of this.

Some patients possess a happy nature and their domestic life is such that there is little or no cause for worry
or anxiety. It may well be thought that surely in these
cases the cause of the affliction is not that of mental stress.
The patient is generous and open-hearted—a good
person. We find that through his very generosity and
sympathy with others he may take other people's
burdens to heart and that unconsciously allows his mind
to be troubled. This is but an example of a form of mind
stress that can, when persisted in, lead to physical
disharmony.

The first essential for a patient to become fully
receptive to the healing forces is that of a tranquil and
serene outlook—of being happy within oneself and looking

forward to being fully well. One of the first effects seen to come with spiritual healing is a sense of "inner upliftment". This is the result of the happy influencing of the patient's mind from Spirit—so often the first phase of the healing effort.

This lighter and uplifted feeling should be anticipated, enjoyed, and encouraged, and be shown outwardly in the demeanour and expression. This enables the spirit doctors to establish a serenity of the mind and nervous system. It helps to create that "happier condition" that is obviously so good in all healing, whether Spirit or medical.

The second rule is that the body hygiene must be looked after. How many of our blood and abdominal troubles are the result of constipation! Here the toxic poisons enter into the bloodstream, preventing the blood from doing its invigorating and cleansing work. Patients should always see that constipation is held off by taking whatever laxative is found to suit them.

Bad or decayed teeth are a constant source of distributing poison into the system and may well be the cause of rheumatism, arthritis and digestive unbalance. They should be removed.

Some people think, and we agree, that cosmic energy can be absorbed consciously with breathing. The patient should study his breathing to see if he is inhaling as fully as he can, or whether his inhalations have degenerated into small intakes of air with its limited supply of oxygen. The blood comes to the lungs to discharge its waste gases and to take in oxygen that the blood and cells so vitally need. Encourage the patient to cultivate this full energy-giving breathing, not merely for a few minutes in the day, but constantly.

Another good healing help is in general massage. Do not think this is only necessary when one has a pain or stiffness. A general rubbing, using any oil or cream, helps the blood to flow more freely, it loosens up the tissues, helps to disperse waste that has been left by the blood in the fibres of the muscles, etc. Massage is a stimulation. No elaborate technique is needed—just a gentle rubbing, not too vigorous like "scrubbing" but firm and smoothing, will do wonders to assist the bloodstream and the tissues. On retiring, the patient should place a pillow under his knees and knead and massage the abdomen—this will often help to overcome any tendency to constipation.

He should drink plenty to keep the body well flushed; a glass of warm water last thing at night and first thing in the morning is excellent (prepare a thermos flask overnight for this).

Again, the patient should avoid overeating, and an excess of fatty and fried foods. If he is in robust health then he can eat "anything", but if he is "sluggish" in any way, excess fat should be avoided. He should take plenty of fresh salads, sweet fruits and "sun" foods in general. Orange and blackcurrant juices are rich in vitamins. Above all, he should not let meals become a dull routine, but should enjoy the act of eating and drinking, having in his mind "this will do me good". Of course, if his disability needs a special diet then that should be followed.

When he goes to bed, he should go to sleep; that is what beds are for. He should get into the habit of relaxing and looking gently for sleep to come right through the hours of darkness to waking-up time. He should not imagine he cannot sleep, or dwell on last night's restlessness or unhappy things of the past. That is futile and only does harm. He should not anticipate future troubles either, they may never happen and, if they do, brooding on them will not help. By going to sleep and so renewing his strength, it will enable the patient to meet trouble much more easily should it come. The imagination can easily exaggerate a molehill into a mountain, so tell the patient that if he must think, then contemplate some happy thing, and enjoy doing it.

Some people call all this "natural healing", and so it is; but what can be better to help spiritual healing than natural healing?

These are some of the practices I recommend all patients to follow. It may be easier to read them than to put them into effect. But some can be applied without any great effort—massaging, breathing, etc. If your patient will start, he will soon find that the others will follow and he will feel all the better for it; and will be materially assisting the spirit doctors to remove the major troubles.

Chapter 10

THE SOURCE OF ALL HEALING

Here is a question that I am so often asked by clergy-men and church people:

"Healers state they communicate with spirit doctors and the like. Why not communicate with God himself—and why does a spirit person need to be called in?"

First and foremost in healing our prayers are to God—we do not *pray* to the spirit people.

When we attune to Spirit for healing we are not praying to God—it is quite a distinct and different process.

We believe that the source of all healing comes from God and is therefore divine.

We believe that the healing doctors in Spirit are God's ministers, just as much, if not more so, than the ordained priest.

When God has work to be done, the scriptures tell how God sent His angels to do the work. It is exactly the same with spiritual healing.

The spirit healing doctors are God's angels or ministers. It is they who, in His name, use their wisdom and the forces at their command to heal the sick.

Thus the part we play in the healing effort is through our faculty of attunement with those spirit doctors to whom we convey the need for help to be given to any individual for his, or her, given complaint. This is what we mean by "directive intercession".

The Church believes in the "Communion of Saints". In what way can this differ with our "Communion with Spirit?" Who made the personalities into "Saints"? Man has done so, not God.

What is the qualification for a "Saint"? It can be summed up in the word "spirituality". Therefore cannot those who through their nearness to God and their knowledge of His laws who heal the sick also qualify for "Sainthood"? And while we are on this subject, we believe there are many unknown humble people, mothers, and others, who by their unprofessed spirituality may be more entitled to "sainthood" than some who have been so honoured because of their work for the Church, and building up its power and resources.

We believe that all positive thought is a "recorded experience" and prayers come within this category; so does "directive intercessionary thought" for the sick.

It may well be, we believe it is, that when prayers are given and with these the request for healing of one's self or another, that these thoughts (being recorded experiences) can be received by God's healing ministers in Spirit, and are acted upon in all ways that are possible.

To those who may think it is incorrect to receive healing through spiritual healing because we can attune with God's healing ministers, the question is asked "Would they refuse help from the Saints or God's angels?" We suggest the help so given is the same.

Because of its very nature, spiritual healing is divine. Its source is divine and its application must necessarily bring into the picture divine agencies —and these are our spirit doctors, guides and helpers.

Chapter 11

AT WHAT TIME DOES THE HEALING REACH THE SICK?

In our work at The Spiritual Healing Sanctuary at Shere the question, "At what time does the healing reach the sick?" often arises in the minds of those in need of healing. It has become a little complicated to understand by the introduction of the Healing Minute at 10 o'clock.

We are also asked at what time do we intercede for a particular patient so that he can "link up" with us in thought for the healing effort at that time. Sometimes we are asked if we will intercede at a special time in order to co-operate with other good efforts.

Let me answer these questions first by telling a story. Before the advent of the V.1 bombs in the last war, it was my practice, in accordance with general custom of those days, to make a separate time appointment with each patient, so that the sick one or his people could also link-in with the effort during that special time. We were getting good healing results.

Then one day a V.1 bomb destroyed my house and all my healing records and appointments. I felt as if the bottom had dropped out of life, for no longer had I the schedule of time appointments, and all that I could do was to engage in intercession in an unorganised way. I expected to hear in the letters and reports of a dropping down in the good healing results. To my surprise they not only continued but greatly improved . . . and this made me think.

I realised two things. The first was that healing from the realm of Spirit is not governed by clocks; that we had imposed upon the healing the limitation of time factors, following the custom of our own earthly way of existence. I recalled that in Spirit there is no time as such.

Secondly, my attention was focused upon the essential but simple need to establish attunement with the higher forces, and that is, that one's mind must not be occupied with normal thinking about everyday affairs but that it has to recede to allow the mind of the inner-self to become ascendant—in other words, to bring about a state of attunement, or one-ness with Spirit.

I began to see that keeping a time-table did not encourage this, and for the patient it was still more difficult. It takes a long time, years in fact, to develop the fine art of attunement, and it is upon this that our healership rests. How, therefore, could I expect ordinary folk, who knew little or nothing of this, to allow their minds to become quiet, suspended from normal thinking (especially if they were in pain and looking for relief) to permit them to tune in with the healing effort? I saw that they were not likely to do so.

I realised that it was quite wrong to impose any time on spiritual healing, and that those in spirit life who conducted the healing act would do so whenever conditions were favourable and indeed probably **all the time**.

It may well be that in some cases it was found best to direct the healing forces when the patient was asleep and his mind at rest, providing the best opportunity to restore strength and vitality and overcome the cause of the trouble, and so we engaged in intercession for the sick late at night until the small hours of the morning.

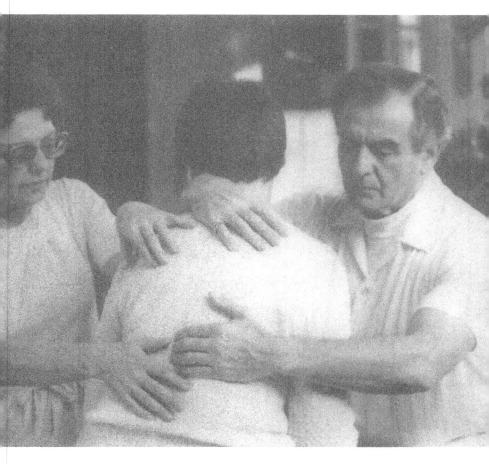

Joan and Ray Branch at work in The Sanctuary.

Harry Edwards and Olive Burton in the early days dealing with some of the many thousands of letters that arrived weekly at The Sanctuary.

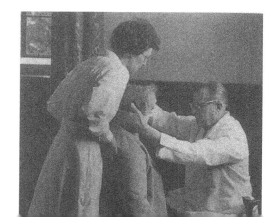

George Burton with Joan
Branch giving healing to a

With others whose minds were distressed and fearful, so promoting the bodily ills, there was a constant need to soothe and calm the nervous and mind tensions during the waking hours when the outlook was disturbed. Another thought I accepted was that it was in daily active life that the spirit doctors could enlist the aid of the bodily intelligence to ally it to the healing effort through directive influencing and so quicken the overcoming of weaknesses, disease, etc.

So it has been that since the V.1 bomb incident we have never at any time made appointments for healing (except in exceptional circumstances, as during times of surgery). The healing has not suffered, indeed the contrary has been seen with the greater ease with which healings have taken place.

Therefore, the answer to the question is that the healing is being directed to the sick ALL THE TIME.

Healing is not time-governed by our standards at all. It is not as if the healing is like medicine that has to be taken every four hours; it is continuous according to the patient's needs and opportunity.

There is never any one set answer to any question concerning spiritual healing. There have been the many occasions when a telephone or special request has been made to overcome a particular condition—to bring down a temperature, to ease a painful state, to enable nourishment to be accepted and so on. These requests then become part of a special intercession, and it so often follows that immediate relief is timed by the moments of such intercession, of which the patient has had no knowledge at all.

The observance of the Healing Minute has a quite different application. This is the joining together at one time of many people for the purpose of directing outwards a unified thought force to widen the channel through which the Christ-spirit can reach all who suffer, and for the peace of the world.

It is true, and admissible, that during the Minute a sufferer can seek help from Spirit to aid him, or for the relatives of a sick one to seek healing for him. Again evidence has often been supplied to show that the help so sought by this means is effective. In general the Healing Minute is a time for giving of one's self for good purposes, and only good can come from this.

The Healing Minute Observance is, however, different from our intercessionary times for those who are sick. In intercession we do not seek for the balm of healing in a general way, but in a directive form for individuals and the overcoming of their particular symptoms.

We, too, link up with the Healing Minute, thus joining in with everyone else for the common purpose. and it may well be in this way that individual patients are helped who also happen to be tuned in to the Observance.

So I return to the question about the time when the healing takes place for a particular patient. My answer is there is no special time as, say, "five minutes to eight". With many, the healing reaches them effectively during the hours of sleep; with others, all the time—every minute of the day, sustaining, strengthening, alleviating, soothing, correcting, inducing good changes, calming troubled minds, allaying fears, dispersing unwanted matter, giving comfort, and in all the other ways that are required to master the cause of the trouble, removing the ill-effects, and so restoring the sick one to perfect health and happier days.

Chapter 12

HAVE I ENOUGH FAITH?

A vital question frequently asked by patients with whom the healing is not making the rapid progress wished for, is: "Is this because I have not enough faith?"

I am going to link with this two further questions that are asked for the same reason. The first is "How can I have faith in God when he makes me suffer so?" and the other is "Why should I have faith in healing when I am suffering from my Karmic Debt?"

These three questions have a common answer and a simple one, it is this:

Sickness and disease result from transgressing the laws of health.

Spiritual healing endeavours to overcome the effects of these transgressions by, firstly, removing the cause and, secondly, mastering the symptoms.

Thus "faith" in any direction is **not** an essential for a healing to take place.

True it is that if a person has belief and faith in the goodness of the treatment, it is a very great help. This uplifts the whole mental outlook, the patient avoids pessimism, which is depressing—and depression blankets any treatment, whether medical or spiritual.

God does not inflict disease on anyone. How absurd this idea is! How mean a conception of the Deity. Any person who thinks God so mean and revengeful that

He would inflict pain and torture in an effort to "get His own back" for some sin or the other, falls into the error of thinking he is so important that God takes this special notice of him. If this were so, then God must have a very busy time in noting all the sins of His children and serving out punishment. Of course, this idea is pure nonsense!

Then just as God does not (I repeat **not**) inflict disease on us, then neither should we expect Him to discriminate in favouring anyone more than another by over-riding the laws that govern health to restore a sufferer by divine dispensation.

Let us come down to earth, to plain reasoning and logic. If I put my finger in the fire it will be burnt. If I go out in the cold with little on and get soaked with rain and chilled, I shall get a severe cold. If I worry continuously, I shall get headaches and eventually a gastric ulcer. If I live in dampness I shall probably get rheumatism or arthritis. If my teeth are decayed, or I take no steps to overcome constipation, then my blood system will be poisoned and I shall suffer in some way ... and so it goes on. **Ill-health is the result of transgressing the laws of health.**

By the same logic, the theory of Karmic Debt falls to the ground.

Spiritual healing is not an act of magic, it is a spirit science. Medical science is based upon knowledge of the physical laws that govern our bodies and their functioning; there is no magic in this either. It is simply a study of cause and effect.

Just as there is the framework of the physical laws that the doctor must work within, so there is the framework of the spirit laws that the spirit doctors must work within. Thus with these two sets of laws we have the *total law*. Every act of spiritual healing must come within the framework of this total law. This is the only limitation that applies to spiritual healing. It is also easily seen that when healing forces are directed from spirit sources in some form of radiation they must be transformed into a physical state to promote a beneficial change in the patient's condition.

Having said all this, the question still remains why in some cases the healing does not seem to succeed as it does with the great majority of patients. If it is not anything to do with God or Karmic Debt or personal faith, then what is it?

Apart from the basic answer that healing can operate only within the possibilities allowed within the total law, it is necessary to judge each case upon its individual merits to provide the subsidiary answers. I will give a few illustrations.

Firstly we must recall the essential for all healing, that the cause must first be overcome. If the primary causation lies within disharmony, frustration, anguish, etc., of the inner mind, then that must first be eased and removed. This can come only within the sphere of influence of Spirit—it cannot be overcome by taking medicine. With its overcoming, then the symptoms of the disease are soon mastered, provided the bodily state is not too weak to respond.

For example, if the help of spiritual healing is asked for in a case of advanced cancer, it may be that the physical resistance of the patient has become so weak, that in the time available it is not possible to re-stimulate the resources of the body sufficiently to fight the effects. Help is given in other ways, by granting comfort and peace to the mind and the dispersal of pain, but the patient is not cured.

If arthritis has deposited a bony substance around a joint then freedom of movement cannot come until that mass is removed, and this does not always seem possible in chronic cases. If tendons have contracted and knotted up, then again, joint movements cannot become free until they are loosened at source. This is the law.

If there is a weakening of the senses, nervous system, etc., due to advancing age, the healing cannot overcome this law and make the patient young again, but compensation is given by maintaining virility and strength in every way possible and so checking the advancement of weakness.

Another important factor is that patients sometimes maintain the causes of sickness. They "hold on" to grievances of the past, and so continue the disharmony within the mind. They may continue to live in damp conditions which sustain rheumatism. They may be receiving wrong treatment that perpetuates the disease. There are many, many causes that are responsible for preventing the healing being as successful as it might be, if those causes were removed.

Spiritual healing can and does reduce the symptoms or effects of disease, even though the cause persists, and temporary benefit is experienced; possibly with the complete removal of the pain or stress. In these cases, the healing cannot be blamed if later on there is a recurrence of the trouble, for the cause is still there.

If we view sickness, and the good that spiritual healing brings, on the basis of what I have said in this book, we bring them into correct perspective; based on logic and common sense.

No good purpose is served by "escape arguments", by blaming non-success on lack of faith, or trying to put the responsibility on God.

Spiritual healing is in an immeasurably strong position, based on the uncountable number of cures that have taken place, and which are being seen every day. In this we recognise the good work of those wiser minds in Spirit who have acquired that extensive knowledge to employ the law-governed forces of healing and do so as part of God's divine plan. If it were not for the existence of these laws, life would be chaotic for there could be no reason or security in any form.

As we understand a little about these things so do we marvel at the wonderful plan with all its infinite possibilities that is our heritage, granted to us by God, the Creator.

Chapter 13

OTHER ASPECTS OF HEALING

In this chapter, I wish to deal with various aspects of healing which may help to clarify a number of points, either by way of definition or observations which I think will be of guidance to both the beginner and the experienced healer.

Magnetic Healing. Magnetic healing is a direct inheritance from Mesmer. It is the ability to direct to a patient some of the healer's own abundance of natural vitality or cosmic strength. The word "magnetic" may be a poor description to apply to this gift, but it has become a common definition now. Other terms which have described it are "Magnetic Force", "Odic Force" and "X Force".

A healer who possesses this excess of energy is able by holding a patient's hands to direct into the patient some of his strength. It is not essential for the patient's hands to be held, for a patient will often feel all the better through being visited by a person having this magnetic quality. Conversely, one hears people say: "He seems to drain all the strength from me."

Reference to Section I tells of the means whereby this cosmic energy can be sought for a patient. Magnetic healers possess these energies in abundance and usually are in vibrant and radiant health. When a magnetic healer gives of his vitality to a number of patients, then he is liable to feel a sense of depletion and consciously needs to replenish his energies.

Most healers have the faculty of imparting this strength to a patient, as they blend in with him when they direct strength to flow from themselves into the patient. If a healer feels at all depleted after treating patients, it may well mean that he has given more than he should of his own strength. If depletion is felt, the healer should sit relaxed for a few moments, and by characterised breathing, open himself to receive a fresh supply of the cosmic energies he has expended.

Magnetic healing can be very helpful to a patient who is weak—but this is **not** spiritual healing. The energies do not come from a spirit source—they are of physical origin only. Magnetic healing and spiritual healing can merge, but it is not possible to draw any dividing line between them.

Associated with this subject is the "Psychic Gland" referred to later on.

Spontaneous Cures. When a sudden recovery of a patient cannot be explained by medical science, doctors often term such a recovery as a "spontaneous remission", and say "in some strange way Nature has asserted itself". Very little medical research seems to have been conducted so far into these spontaneous cures which can, of course, take place naturally; but more often than not, it is when spiritual healing has intervened that sudden changes for the better are seen, being brought about by the introduction of forces and energies which are beyond the knowledge of medical scientists.

Behind every state of change there must be a reasoned process, and this must apply to spontaneous cures also; thus in the majority of such cures spiritual healing may well be a large contributor to such a "reasoned process".

Medical Co-operation. Spiritual healing and medical practice are complementary to each other and healership continues to seek that closer liaison with medicine. Healers are not, therefore, opposed to doctors, nor do they advise patients to refrain from seeking medical help, for it would be unreasonable to deny a sufferer the benefits which medical treatment can bring.

Sometimes patients are afraid to go to their doctor, or they do not tell the doctor all of their troubles for fear they will be sent to hospital for surgery. Women suf-fering from breast conditions are an example of this. When a healer knows of such a situation, he should advise the patient to "obtain a medical opinion". This will safeguard the healer (and healership) from criti-cism, or more serious repercussions, should the patient pass over from a malignant or other disease without having been under medical care.

The general practice in such cases should be that spiri-tual healing and medical treatment should both be given. Healers should avoid the mistake of wishing to to take all the credit for a recovery, for the most important thing is that the patient should be helped to get well as quickly as possible. To whom the healing credit goes is not important.

A different situation arises when a patient is said to be suffering from an "incurable" disease, and the doctors declare they can do no more for him; then there is no purpose in recommending further medical treatment.

Treatment of Children. Where it is known that the parents are NOT receiving medical attention for their child, healers are most strongly advised to secure the signature of the parent to a statement in the form set out below BEFORE treating or continuing to treat the child:

"Mr. . . . . has warned me that I ought to call in the doctor to see my child."

Treatment of Animals. It is an offence for a person not qualified as a veterinary surgeon to practise as such, and this includes both diagnosis of ailments and advice as to medicine. In practice, however, healers treat animals in the same way as if they were human beings. After all, humans are animals too, subject to the same laws as the animal kingdom. The processes governing birth, bodily functions, organs, bone structures, circulation, breathing, and other systems—even the emotions of love, dislike, care for the young, are all very similar to those concerning the human. Diseases have the same causes, and need the same treatments. While in law healers are not allowed to prescribe medicines for animals, there is no regulation which states the healer cannot help an animal by prayer or the laying on of hands.

It is noteworthy that animals respond readily to spiritual healing, often when medical science can do no more. There is little doubt that animals, especially domestic ones, are conscious of receiving healing and even though a particular condition may be painful, an animal will not bite his healer whilst treatment is being given.

Treatment in Emergencies. The rendering of first aid in an emergency for the purpose of saving life or relieving pain is always permissible, as of course is prayer and the laying-on of hands. What constitutes an emergency must be a question for the judgment of the individual healer.

Legal Regulations. There are a number of legal requirements which spiritual healers must observe, and in view of the importance of this subject I have dealt with it at length under "Spiritual Healing and the Law"—see Section III, Chapter 14.

The Glands. The balanced operation of the whole of the glandular systems is a vital factor in maintaining good health. The study of the glands is an involved subject that cannot be catered for in a book such as this. The glands, including the ductless ones, are the governors of bodily growth, function and health. There is an intimate liaison between the glands, the mind and the bodily intelligence and they can also be influenced from Spirit.

The Psychic Gland. There is one vital ductless gland which has an important association with spiritual healing; this is what is termed the "Psychic Gland".

We each possess a psychic gland which has its receiving terminal directly behind the junction of the nasal bones with the frontal bone. It links up with the pineal and endocrine systems as well as with the brain. Its main "channel" proceeds down the spine and branches off contiguous with the nervous system, reaching all parts of the body. The psychic gland is a "condition" gland.

When we feel "on top of the world" and our whole being is filled with the joy of life, that is when the psychic gland is well charged with cosmic or spirit energies. If there is any truth in this, it explains why characterised breathing with intention is so strengthening, so beneficial. It may show the media through which stimulating healing energies can be passed throughout the body or to any given area.

It is a theory, and no more, that the pineal gland acts as the doorway between the Spirit and the physical; that healing influencing and energies from Spirit are received through the pineal gland and from thence are conveyed to the body.

Taking on Patients' Conditions. It has been sometimes said that a healer takes on, within himself, the patient's condition. This has arisen from the experience that the healer senses, or even appears to actually feel, the symptoms of discomfort the patient has. There is a logical explanation for this.

The patient's consciousness is actively recording all the pain and discomfort which he is experiencing with his complaint. By virtue of the healing gift, the healer's spirit-self attunes with that of the patient. Through his attunement, the healer's consciousness becomes aware of that which the patient is experiencing. When it is recalled that every sensation we have, of cold, hunger, pain, stomach ache, etc., is a mental experience, it can be understood that if the patient is recording, say, stomach ache, and this is received by the healer, the latter could have the impression that he is suffering likewise. It is, of course, not actual **but simply a mental appreciation.** As the healer realises this, so the experience is placed within its proper perspective and his reasoning mind will no longer accept the patient's distress. As the healing gift develops these sensations are no longer felt—although of course the healer can, in this way, receive knowledge of the patient's trouble and which is also observed by the healing guide.

There is one good point arising from this—it proves to the healer that he is able to establish attunement with the patient and with the healing guide as well.

The Washing of Hands. In the past it has been thought that it is absolutely necessary for a healer to wash his hands after treating every patient for fear that he may retain on his hands symptoms of the patient's disease and possibly pass these on to another patient.

Today, we know this idea is untenable. It is, of course, good to wash the hands for hygienic purposes, but it has no healing significance. If a patient is suffering from an infectious skin disease and is treated by the healer, then his hands MUST be washed in hot disinfected water.

Unnecessary Healing Passes. It has been observed that some healers have tended to make very vigorous healing passes over and around the patient. This is more often seen with healers who work under trance control, but may well arise from the healer's subconscious intervention, for no experienced guide has need to do this.

Such an unnecessary procedure is most likely to be

born of the healer's earnest intention and strength of desire to see the patient "cleansed" of his affliction, but as has already been pointed out, there is no justification for this technique.

Healing by "Blowing". Another undesirable practice needs to be mentioned, namely that of the act of blowing "healing power" into a patient by placing the mouth on the patient's body and blowing into it in a slow sustained breath. Sometimes a handkerchief is placed between the healer's mouth and the patient.

When this is done, the patient naturally feels the warmth of the breath and this can appear to have pentrating value, giving the sensation of receiving power; but the only virtue in this act is the healing intention.

This "warming effect" can be given by anybody and a moment's thought will show that this performance cannot be a healing act, for the breath does not penetrate, and the idea that healing energies are passed to the patient in this way is absurd. Psychologically, it may impress the mind of a credulous patient and whilst the healer may do this in all sincerity, it is only an expression of his good mental intention that the patient might be helped in such a way. This particular practice is undesirable and tends to expose healership to ridicule.

Healing Pads. The practice of giving "healing pads" to patients is based on the idea that if the healer holds a piece of flannel or other material within his hands, the material is impregnated with healing power. Then, when the patient places this on his body, the power passes into him and brings healing benefit.

In the past many patients have testified to the help they have received by this means, but here again, reflection will show that there can be no foundation for this practice in spirit science, for any benefit that arises can only be from the healing intention and not the pad.

Let us assume that the spirit healing energies flow into

the piece of flannel and that they have been transformed into their physical counterpart, what reason is there that they will reside dormant in the material and then flow into the patient's body at a later date, any more than the forces of magnetism or electricity can be so retained? The absurdity of this technique is further illustrated when the healer places the pad in an envelope to "keep-in the power". This is but another way of embellishing spiritual healing and trying to find some tangible means for impressing patients who know no better and are not sufficiently versed in psychic matters to question it.

Healing Passes and the Aura. In the past, some emphasis has been placed upon the healing of the aura. Surrounding the human body is a radiance, of varying width, usually about three inches as it fades away. The aura is seen clairvoyantly—it is not physically observable. It is composed of varying colour densities, which denote the condition of the person's bodily and mental states.

If a person is suffering from a complaint or is physically fatigued, depressed, or whose health tone is low, the colours shown in the aura are dull and heavy. Conversely, when the person is in full vigour of health the colours are brighter, scintillating and lighter.

The aura is no more than a reflection of the person's spiritual, bodily and mental health states.

In the past, the theory was commonly held that, if by healing passes the aura could be "cleansed", the cause of the ill-conditions would be taken away. This was the healing intention and as such was good, although it is now acknowledged that one cannot heal a reflection any more than one can heal a shadow, and, as through healing the physical or mental symptoms are overcome, so the change for the better is reflected in the aura.

Other Techniques. There are a number of other techniques that have been employed in the past in healing practice, such as using a "spirit embrocation" to rub into patients, giving patients "power water" to drink, and so on. They are supported by the testimony of patients who say they feel all the better for it and this is not doubted, for the healing can take place in spite of the healer's performances.

Happily these acts are now disappearing from healing practice. They are undignified and quite unnecessary. They arise from the healer's good motives and possibly from the desire to impress patients with his gift of healing and so adorn it further.

In these days, however, we should discard all rituals, and performances which decry the simplicity of the healing act which rather than edify it, tend to make it ridiculous in the minds of reasonable people.

SECTION III

HEALING PRACTICE

Chapter 1

INTRODUCTION TO HEALING
TREATMENTS

The understanding of spiritual healing advances with
the spiritual and mental evolution of both healers and
patients. It may well be that any form of treatment
including those suggested in the following pages is quite
unnecessary.

All spiritual healing is a result arising from thought
processes, i.e. the preliminary thought application for a
healing to take place, the ensuing diagnosis, and the
means by which the correct healing energies are created
and directed by the spirit guides (not the healer).

Absent Healing is as effective as Contact Healing when
there is no tangible contact between the healer and the
patient. It follows that if in Absent Healing both physical
and mental sicknesses can be overcome, then there is no
need for Contact Healing at all, or any need to adopt any
form of the use of the hands. It may be that, in the fullness
of time, spiritual healing will advance towards the employment of attuned thought alone; but in the meantime,
we have to recognise the limitations both within patients
and ourselves as healers.

If a patient went to a healer and did not receive

treatment through the laying-on of the healer's hands, the patient would be disappointed, his morale would suffer, and confidence in healing diminish. As a rule it is impracticable for healers to spend the time necessary to elevate the patient's mind to a high appreciation of the spiritual gift and how it can be used in its highest sense. This is an ideal to be achieved progressively as time goes on. It is also true to say that healers in general have not attained that high degree of spiritual evolution and knowledge which brings them into an attuned equality with Spirit.

The patient will go to a doctor to get treatment, but he goes to a healer to get well. Therefore, the psychology of the patient is an important factor, for he wants to feel that he is receiving healing.

At the same time, the healer needs to use his mind and personality to the fullest extent that they can be profitably employed, and therefore in the chapters that follow I am outlining the way in which treatments for various diseases can be given with the minimum of "technique", and which, if used at all, becomes simply an expression of the healing intention.

In the future, I have no doubt that even these healing methods may be further simplified, but they will serve for the present as a means of conducting healing treatment, simply and with dignity. They will avoid any extravagant passes, ritual or other ways of impeding the simplicity of the healing act.

Chapter 2

THE HEALING OF SPINAL CONDITIONS

Note: So often it is found that there is no rigid isolation between one disease and another, and it will be seen that treatment of the spine can apply not only to conditions directly affecting it such as slipped disc, curvature, spinal lesions, etc., but to a whole range of diseases such as arthritis, lumbago, sciatica, fibrositis, neuritis, paralysis, disseminated sclerosis, Parkinson's Disease, and so on. Even many respiratory conditions can be linked with spinal trouble.

With many complaints the spine plays a vital part. It houses the spinal cord conveying all the bodily nerves (except those of the head) concerned with internal functioning and movement.

The healer should study the structure of the spine to observe how it operates; how the individual vertebrae move with each other; the function of the cushioning and lubricating discs between each of the bones; and the function of the main nerves which branch out from between them.

The spinal cord is, in fact, part of the brain, being in direct communication with it. It has, on occasion, been found that where the cause of a **physical** trouble is situated in the brain, the healing directive applied through the spinal cord can reach the site of the trouble. In Contact Healing this method may be more direct than using the patient's head as the focal point for the reception of the healing influencing. It is stressed that this applies to physical afflictions only, such as forms of paralysis, effects arising from meningitis, etc.

Many of the causes of organic illnesses originate in mental stress. Nerve tension within the mind can cause spasmodic movements of the limbs, aggravate nerve weaknesses and induce lack of co-ordination as can be observed with disseminated sclerosis, Parkinson's Disease, and other troubles associated with paralysis. Thus the spinal cord is most intimately connected with many afflictions, and the healing directive applied to it is often found to produce a healing result.

With certain diseases the spine is seen to lose its flexibility; it becomes set and stiff and what is termed "poker-back" may set in. This is observed with slipped discs, arthritis of the spine and certain paralytic conditions. Such stiffness invariably indicates the presence of adhesions around the vertebrae, exerting pressure on the emerging nerves, making them numb, preventing co-ordination between the mind directive and the muscles controlling the limbs and at the same time creating very painful effects.

With lumbago and sciatica there will invariably be found this spinal stiffness. It can also arise when the patient, fearing pain, purposefully avoids bending the spine. Medical corsets are designed to prevent spinal movements and these, too, encourage poker-back conditions. Such corsets are palliative, just pain preventers (the exception being when support is necessary for acute spinal and muscular weaknesses). The purpose of healing is to cure, and this creates a difference of opinion between medical and spiritual healing practice. The medical intention is to render the spine immobile, for the reason that there is no medical alternative. The healing intention is to remove the causes of immobility, to enable the nerves to be freed from pressures, and so give them the opportunity of functioning properly once more.

So we come to the healing act itself. (See photograph opposite page 158.)

As the healer sits in front of his seated patient and lets his hand rest on the spine, he soon discovers there is little or no flexibility in the spine as he tries, with the patient's co-operation, to get any bending movement. The body can generally move from the hips, backwards and forwards, but the spine itself is stiff. (Hip movement may not be possible if the hips are locked with arthritis.)

The healing purpose is to restore mobility to the spine. The healer, now in attunement and blending in with the patient, places one hand closely on the waist (lumbar) region of the spine, and the other upon the patient's shoulder. All is then ready as the healer's thoughts turn to the guide to seek the dispersal of the adhesions and to restore mobility through the application of dispersing energies.

We know that the healing itself need only take a second or so, and after a short pause the healer then looks for the result.

The patient is told to relax and to go quite limp, and the healer should feel that this has been achieved before proceeding any further. The healer then asks the patient to let the back yield and bend slowly backwards over the hand, directed with gentle but firm pressure on the shoulder. **No force must be used.** It needs to be remembered that no physical pressure on the healer's part can bend a spastic spine—it must yield of itself.

The patient has become accustomed to a stiff spine and therefore any movement of it is a new experience; so the actual bending of the spine should be very gently encouraged to begin with upon this first movement, and only a little at a time.

As the patient is found to bend backwards a little, then the opposite movement is asked for, the healer telling the patient to "bend forward, letting the back bow over". As movement succeeds movement, so the mobility increases until the spine is reasonably free. The healer should, of course, seek this yielding along the whole length of the spine, moving his hand down towards the pelvis and upwards to the shoulders, and gently moving each of the neck bones.

When the forward and backward movements are reasonable, the hand should return to the waist region and the patient be directed to bend sideways in a gentle pendulum movement, keeping the waist quite still, for this should easily follow. As movements become easier, the patient should be encouraged to **do the swinging movement himself,** all the time seeking further looseness.

Finally, the healer should place his fingers on the spine between the individual joints and tell the patient not to move his legs or waist but simply to pivot and rotate the spine in a gentle horizontal movement, getting the individual vertebrae to rotate upon each other. All this should take place without any pain at all.

The neck should be similarly treated, again with that pause for the healing energies to dispose of stiffness, and then movement sought, with one hand being placed at the back of the neck with the fingers on the joints, and the other on the forehead to encourage movement as directed by the healer. These can commence with a general nodding of the head, and thence to each joint in turn, the healer working down from the top of the neck. As a rule, most stiffness is found in the 5th, 6th and 7th vertebrae and in the upper dorsal joints. The healer can then assess the degree of freedom obtained by asking the patient to let the head go backwards, looking up to the ceiling. The healer should always be satisfied with the extent of the betterment achieved at that time.

With all these spinal movements, it is helpful if the healer will speak to the patient, telling him what to do for every movement. This ensures the patient's co-operation with the healer's intention and helps the patient to avoid moving in a contrary way to that sought by the healer.

These spinal movements are not "manipulations" as is commonly understood by this word, but a gradual yielding of the patient's spine to the healer's directive. As a rule, a spine will yield readily, but if it does not, then the healer should be satisfied with the degree of movement that has been attained and await the next opportunity to treat the patient again. (With spondylitis, the spine can be very obstinate, perhaps yielding only very slightly at any one time. Several treatments may be needed for yielding to be achieved.)

It has been said that no pain should be felt by the patient during spinal treatment. If there is pain, the healing is not taking place and the discomfort is being caused by the excessive physical exertion. It is noteworthy in this respect that sometimes the patient will feel discomfort or pain in the muscles of the back or down the sides of the neck. This will probably be due to fibrous adhesions which have settled in the muscles, but a little massage (with healing intention) to soften up the muscles will often get rid of the distress.

It is good to advise the patient to seek to maintain each day the spinal movements and to have home massage—a simple "mother's rubbing", not a technical massage—using any oil, cream or talcum powder to act as lubrication for the hands. It should be known that no oil penetrates through the outer skin (epidermis). The value of massage is to stimulate the circulation to encourage the blood to carry away adhesions, etc. The use of a heat-producing ointment or embrocation conveys a sense of warmth through the epidermis, which is picked up by the minute nerve terminals of "touch", so creating a counter-effect of heat which at times helps to allay the nerve sensing of pain arising from, say, rheumatic tendencies, etc.

All through the treatment as described, the healer must retain his sense of attunement with his guides and the patient. So long as this exists, no pain should be felt. A patient who has had a stiff spine for years will find the new movements so strange that he may subconsciously resist them when the flexing is requested, but as the healer gently perseveres, the movements will come more freely. Patience is needed.

When flexibility has returned, the patient should be able to bend over backwards and forwards by his own efforts. When this is first attempted the healer can assist him, encouraging the new movements as far as they will go, and not forcing them. Remember, the spine cannot move until the healing energies have dispersed the cementing adhesions, or other causes of stiffness.

With the freeing of the back, the pressures on the emerging nerves are removed. Many body and limb pains are caused by these pressures. It will be observed that as the spine is freed, the pains vanish—for the cause of them has been overcome; and as the nerves are freed, they are able to function normally again, allowing the return of co-ordination though this may take a little time (see Chapter 4 on Paralysis). An exception may be found with spinal pain when this is caused by a chill on the spine, the nerves having become inflamed. Also with spinal stiffness, the nerves can be bruised or inflamed where there has been pressure upon them, but as a rule with healing these soon become normal.

If there is pain or stiffness with, or arising from, the spine in the pelvic region (the sacrum) the healer should place his hand firmly against the affected part, and the patient should be asked to keep the upper part of the spine stiff, and then lean backwards over the hand, and after, be gently encouraged to rotate that part of the spine without moving the pelvis. Although the sacral bones may be wedged into the pelvis, the healer will be aware of flexibility being restored to that part of the spine as movement is sought.

It is desirable for the healer to have an assistant when treating spines. A chair with a back is unsuitable, for it does not allow the backward movements to take place freely. A stool is much better. The assistant healer should stand behind the patient (acting as a chair-back) placing one hand on the shoulder other than that occupied by the healer, and his other hand over the healer's hand on the spine. The assistant should also seek a blending in with the patient, and at the same time, subconsciously allow himself to join in the movements as directed by the executive healer. He must remember that he is an assistant and should not seek to move the patient independently of the executive healer.

Spinal curvatures. Firstly, flexibility of the spine must be sought for as described. When this has been attained, the straightening of the spine is the next step. The healer, closely blended in with the patient, will place his hand on the outside of the lateral bend. He can get the patient to bend over in the opposite direction. Then— and this is important—will come the pause for the guide to render his correcting help, so the healer will then tell the patient to come up straight very slowly and, as he does so, the healer will slowly and gently move the body with the intention of correcting the curvature. **Again, no force must be used.** To apply force is useless, for the curvature has to yield to the correct alignment. The guide will do the work. The healer uses his hand to express the intention of straightening the spine.

If it is an outward curvature, as is seen with the familiar "hunchback" condition, the process is similar, except that the directional movement is inwards as the spine is straightened vertically.

Simple curvature may yield at the first treatment, but if pronounced and of long-standing then a number of treatments may be necessary to bring about the full degree of improvement that can be induced.

It is often seen in cases of curvature that the rib cage has become distorted, creating a bulge on one side of the upper body. As the spine is straightened, the ribs must yield with it, but this may still not be sufficient to take away the malformation. This we cannot expect to be magically removed, but it is found that as time goes on, with continuity of the healing purpose under Absent Healing, these malformations slowly yield or become noticeably less prominent.

With chronic curvatures, it needs to be remembered that the upper part of the body, the chest cage, as well as the pelvis, is joined to the spine. The chest houses the heart and lungs, which have become accommodated to the chest distortion, and therefore, obviously, the straightening up of the spine must be done stage by stage to allow the organs time to accommodate themselves to the readjustment.

When the curvature is in the lumbar region, very often the pelvis has become tilted, and it is a joy to healers to note that with the spinal correction, the pelvis becomes level and the patient is able to walk upright without limping.

Slipped discs and painful spines. With slipped discs the pain results from the inter-vertebral cartilage pressing on the emerging nerves, or it may arise from a misalignment of one of the vertebra with another. If it is the latter, the healer is often able to locate this as being the pain centre.

Treat the spine as described for flexibility, but in the earliest movements these should be minimal, and extremely gentle, slowly increasing as freer movement comes. There should not be any pain, and as mobility comes so the correction is made, with the cartilage receding and the misalignment adjusted. If this should not bring about the desired result, however, then the healer should rest his fingers lightly where the trouble is, and with gentle sideways or pivoting movements, have every confidence in the guide to bring about the correction.

With lumbago, sciatica, neuritis, leg pains, pins and needles, etc., first attain spinal mobility. When this is established, move the legs gently at the hips, first up and down and then rotating in the hip sockets. Finally, get the patient to swing the lower leg free, and as a rule it will be found that the discomfort has gone.

Similar painful conditions of the arms arise from the cervical spine, where there is pressure upon the emerging nerves. First, mobility of the neck bones should be gently encouraged, and then the arm being treated should be gently moved at the shoulder joint until it swings loosely, with the shoulder blade gradually becoming free.

A number of body pains, especially those described as girdle pains when there is a "belt of pain" encircling the body just under the chest, may also have their origin in spinal pressure in the area where the dorsal vertebrae link up with those in the lumbar region. These pains, too, are relieved by achieving full mobility of the spine in that area.

Spinal healings are now much more easily accomplished than a decade ago and healers should approach a spinal healing with full confidence, for if the above suggestions are carried out, simply and gently in attunement, then it will be the very exceptional case that does not yield, and for this there must be other reasons, for example where extensive surgery may have taken place, with bone grafts, or where the joints have permanently fused together, and so on.

Chapter 3

THE HEALING OF ARTHRITIS, RHEUMATISM AND KINDRED CONDITIONS

Arthritis, rheumatism, fibrositis, etc., are a family of complaints, grouped together. While each case needs individual treatment there are some main healing considerations that will apply to all of them.

As with most other human ills, if the trouble is taken in the early stages the healing is very rapid. If the disease has become chronic and deep-seated the period of time necessary to induce measurable relief or complete cure will take longer and will be found to be variable in each case.

Healers should be on the alert to notice the first symptoms of these troubles, and to deal with them. If a patient says: "I have a touch of rheumatism but there is no need to bother about that" the healer **should** bother. If only those people who are now crippled with arthritis, etc., had gone to a healer when the symptoms were first noticed we should not have the many thousands of sufferers, deemed to be in the "incurable" class.

Very often the seat of the trouble will be found in the lumbar region of the spine for hip and leg conditions, and in the neck for shoulders and arms. The actual cause of the trouble may not necessarily be situated there, but these are common centres, particularly with both osteo and rheumatoid arthritis.

Arthritis is a nutritional disease. The blood function

is weak and waste deposits from the cells are left in the joints and in the muscular tissues instead of being disposed of through the respiratory and excretionary systems. The primary cause may be psychosomatic, inducing a depreciated health tone, and so opening the way for the introduction of the physical ill-effects.

A common preliminary result arising from healing is the building up of the health tone of a patient, thus improving the blood state, and so assisting the healing through the bodily intelligence to disperse the adhesions.

When treating arthritis the healer should be on the alert to observe whether there is spinal stiffness and, if so, to treat the spine as described in the previous chapter.

In the treatment for this family of complaints it is of primary importance that the patient should be completely relaxed, allowing the healing to bring about looseness of the joints, etc., without any muscle tightness or resistance. The healer should assure the patient that if his body and limbs are completely relaxed, no pain will result from those movements for which the healer will be seeking.

The patient will probably have suffered pain with every movement of the body and joints for a considerable time past and it is natural that he will anticipate pain and will flinch or tense up the body in an act of resisting the movement that he fears. If the patient does this, thereby resisting the healing intention, pain may ensue. Therefore, the healer will use his persuasion and if necessary chat to the patient for a while to gain his confidence and so obtain complete relaxation before attempting any movement.

With the healer seated before his patient, he follows the same preliminaries as described in the previous chapter. The patient will tell the healer where his trouble lies to give the healer a full picture of the healing need.

After freeing the spine and neck from any stiffness, he will then seek healing for each affected joint in turn, a similar healing process being applicable to each. If, for example, the shoulder joint is stiff, locked or semi-locked, the healer will cup one hand over the joint and hold the patient's forearm with the other. Then, blending in with the patient, the healer will pause to allow for the healing energies to flow through and disperse the obstruction to movement. The shoulder joint is tested to observe the result. The healer (leaving his hand over the shoulder joint) will gently move the arm backwards and forwards from the shoulder. The healer may become conscious of the movement being a little stiff, but as he continues to move the arm, he will become aware of a much looser movement taking place. Gradually the arm can be moved back and forward a little more each time until it swings freely, as far back as can be reasonably expected, and forward until the arm stretches out straight in front.

The next step is to observe whether the joint can be moved in a circular manner, remembering that the shoulder joint is a ball and socket. With one hand remaining on the shoulder, the other will move the arm in the smallest circular movement possible, gradually widening the arc of movement until the upper arm can be raised horizontal to shoulder level. When the healer feels that full freedom has so far been gained, he can next attempt the upward movement of the arm.

In doing all these movements the healer is encouraging the patient to co-operate in a relaxed way by "talking" to the arm, such as: "let the arm swing freely"—"I shall not hurt you"—"now try and swing it yourself with my help"—"let the arm come up ... gently at first ... straighten the elbow ... now let the hand go right up".

With the healer's hands in the same position, the arm should be slowly extended upwards, the elbow should come in, until the arm is vertical. This needs to be done gradually, the healer sensing if any remaining tightness is still there. If it is, he will NOT use any force, for the movement needs to be a yielding one. Once the arm is up, the downward movement follows, and this is helped by the healer placing his hand at the patient's elbow, bending it, thus helping the arm to descend.

It needs to be borne in mind that before the healing this upward and downward movement would probably be very painful, and the patient may tend to hold the shoulder joint tightly. The healer's hand cupped over the joint will sense this, so he will again ask the patient to relax the shoulder so that it can move more freely.

The healer should repeat the upward and down movement several times, telling the patient to "let the arm fall freely from the shoulder". Then, when the arm can be extended upwards, tell the patient to bend the elbow and let his hand rest on his head. Very often, this will be an action the patient has not been able to do for a long time. It is stressed that these new movements need to be **very gradually** encouraged.

Next, the elbow joint should be circulated and the forearm bent upwards and extended as freely as possible. If there is a kinking of the elbow joint that prevents the arm extending quite straight, correction should be sought, after the necessary pause for the healing energies to free it. Only minimum of encouragement need be given to help the joint to yield and allow the arm to straighten; but if the kinking persists, then it should be left alone, until the next time of treatment.

Generally, the wrist will be found to be either locked or semi-locked. The healer then holds the forearm firmly just above the wrist and the fingers of the other hand placed under the patient's palm, with the thumb on top. This should be a firm hold also. Next comes the delicate movement of the wrist, and in this the healer must sense the degree of movement possible. Holding the forearm firmly to prevent it moving, the hand should be gently turned to see how far the wrist will yield. This movement may be very little at first, but will often be seen to increase as the yielding is sought. The healer should then try the sideways movement of the wrist and finally for the hand to fall and rise. If the healing is effective, the healer can ask the patient to "let the hand fall by itself".

Following the same process, direction is turned to the fingers and thumb. Each finger in turn should be circulated at the knuckles and the two finger joints encouraged to bend. Then the thumb, circulating this at the ball of the thumb, followed by the two upper joints.

In all this, the healer needs to feel within himself the extent of the movement that can be attained at the time. If there is tightness and further movement is difficult, no pressure or force must be used. The healer needs to be blended in with the patient and his attunement maintained. He should feel as if he is living in the healing purpose, and he should be oblivious to all that is taking place around him. **His brain and his sensing lies in his fingers as he seeks the yielding of the joints.**

If the patient's fingers are distorted and bent backwards, or the joints have become ossified together, destroying the mechanism within the joint, then it may be contrary to the healing laws to get the joint to yield. The healer should always feel within himself the supreme confidence that the healing will bring the **maximum relief possible at the time.**

If the healer's efforts should cause the patient any pain at all, then he should desist, for he is trying to do too much. Once again, let it be remembered that the healer does not heal, and it is useless for him to seek redress by his own efforts. As in all things it is experience that counts, and he will often find the joints becoming

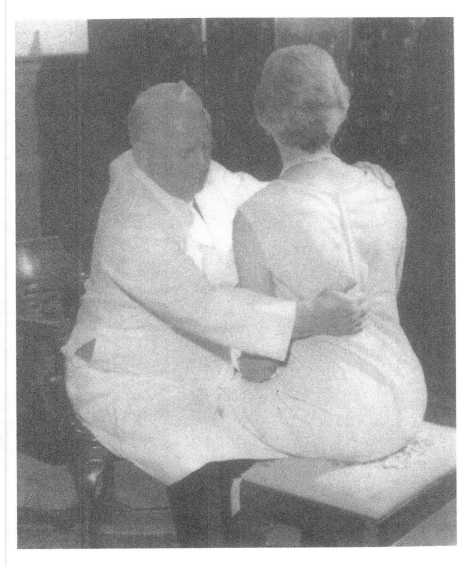

Harry Edwards restoring flexibility to the spine . . .

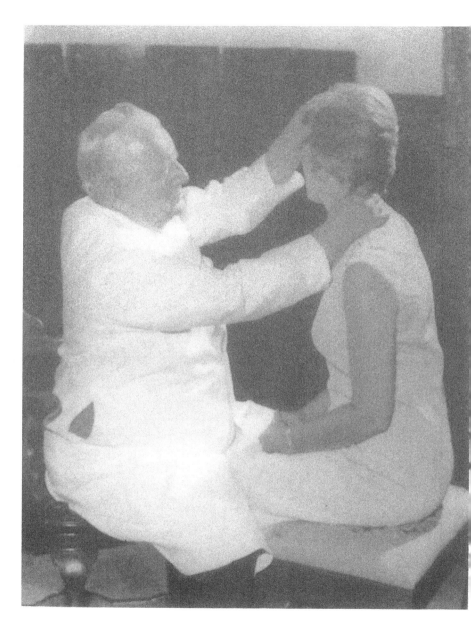

. . . and here seeks easement for the patient's neck.

free without the need for the preliminary pause for the healing act to take place as he progresses with the seeking of freedom from the condition. If any joint continues to be stiff, then the healing pause should be made to seek the guide's further help to free the joint to the fullest extent possible.

A similar process takes place for the legs. If the hip is locked, the knee should be gently raised, just a little, and freedom looked for within the orbit of that movement. The healer should then raise the knee a little more and so on. When the up and down movement has been attained to the fullest extent possible, the leg should then be circulated at the hip.

It is a common condition with arthritis for the tendons and ligaments to have become contracted and knotted with arthritic adhesions and the patient may feel a "pull" in the groin and in the buttocks as the leg is moved. This is only to be expected, but such pulling is not actually pain. The healing effort is to gradually restore flexibility and resilience to the tendons, etc.

For the loosening of the knee, it is helpful for the healer to lift the patient's leg on to his thigh, for remember the healer is seated before the patient. The healer should then ask for the knee to raise and descend. If this movement cannot be obtained, the knee-cap may be fast, but very gentle finger movements should succeed in getting the knee-cap to "float" and this will lead to progressive looseness within the knee joint. If the knee is very painful, there may be fluid and inflammation, in which case only the minimum movement should be sought. If necessary the healer should suspend treatment until the next time. When the leg is lowered, the patient can be asked to swing the leg from the knee loosely backwards and forwards. The ankle, foot and toes, should receive treatment as with the wrist and fingers.

Finally, the patient should be asked to stand up and

place his hands on the healer's shoulders, the healer then asking for the knee to be raised to ascertain the new movement in the hip which can invariably be done without any pain in either leg.

The patient must be encouraged to maintain all new movements day by day, and so build upon the improvements seen and to resist any further encroachment by the adhesions. The patient should also be asked to arrange for daily **home** massage as referred to on page 149, using any oil, cream or talcum powder to lubricate the hand massage. This will stimulate the circulation, energising the blood and so help to carry away the adhesions in a natural way.

It will be found at times that even after a patient has responded wonderfully to the healing, because his walking movements have for years been restricted by the arthritis, so he will continue to walk in a crippled way, because it has become habitual. In cases like this, the patient should be shown and encouraged to walk more normally, lifting the knees and using the foot movements. This can best be done by the healer walking with the patient, showing him the improved way of walking.

With severe cases, it may take a number of healings to obtain reasonable freedom with the joints, the healer learning to be content with the measure of relief that the healing gives on each occasion. With the chronic locking of a joint, when, for example, the fingers are clenched and incapable of movement, it may be some time before mobility can be restored. Thus, these pitiful conditions will need much patience on the part of both healer and patient, but once the easement begins, it should increase with each healing, and the healer will then feel that the time so spent has been more than well worth while.

When joints have been fixed by surgery, or have ossified into a solid state, it may be outside the healing laws to expect movement to be induced.

Chapter 4

THE HEALING OF PARALYSIS

There are a number of forms of paralysis, each having a different cause. Some have their origin seated in the brain as with strokes and Parkinson's Disease. Others arise from deterioration of nerve function, as follows from poliomyelitis. A further considerable percentage emanates from injury to, or stiffnesses within, the spine, creating pressure on the nerves where they emerge between the spinal vertebrae.

In all forms of paralysis there is a lack of co-ordination. The motor nerves receive their instructions from the brain, the messages travelling along the nerves to bring about muscular responses. For example, if one requests the movement of the little finger, the message travels down just those nerves connected with the little finger and no others, and the finger obeys the mental request.

Paralysis follows on from a lack of this ability, where the nerves have become numbed or have deteriorated, preventing the transmission of the messages; so the healing intention is to stimulate and re-awaken the function of the nerves to respond.

It may well be that the act of stimulating the health of the nerves themselves is the responsibility of the healing guide, but we can do much to aid the process and so help the patient to take advantage of the benefit the healing brings. In this we need to make an ally of the patient with the healing effort. Let us take an example.

A person has a paralysed leg and it is incapable of being lifted or only very slightly so. The patient has accepted the hopeless condition, and if the healer asks him to raise the knee, he will say he cannot, and to prove it he will tighten his abdominal muscles, make a spasmodic momentary effort to lift the knee and find that he cannot, and so he accepts this as final.

When patients are suffering from paralysis, and particularly in cases of disseminated sclerosis, there will often be found a poker-back condition of the spine. It may be that the paralysis has its origin there due to spinal pressure on the leg nerves. The healer will first seek to free the spine as previously described. He will then allow his hands to rest on the spine or the limb and pause for a while to allow the guide to improve and strengthen the nerve functions. The healer explains to the patient that the healing intention is to assist the message from the brain to travel down to contract the leg muscles more strongly in order that a degree of movement can be effected.

The healer then "talks" to the patient's legs, through his mind, saying that in a moment or two help is going to be given to carry the message along the nerves, down the spine to the leg nerves to get them to respond. He explains that as the nerves are numb and weak, it may take a little time for the message to reach the leg, and therefore the effort should be a gently sustained one.

The healer will have one hand underneath the leg, near the knee. He then speaks through the patient's mind to the leg, saying: "Lift the knee—NOW." A moment or two later the healer helps the knee to come up. possibly the healer has done most of the lifting. Still holding the knee up, the healer waits for a second or two, and speaks again, saying: "now let me feel you pushing the leg down slowly". It may well be, that the healer is conscious of co-operation from the patient doing this. The slower the movement, the more the nerve control is assisted.

The healer then asks the patient to try to be consciously aware in his mind of the sensation of movement, so that it can become a recorded experience that the mind will look for when the experiment is repeated; so the effort is made again, following the verbal request from the healer.

Often it will be found that there is a little more response the second time, for this results from the anticipation in the patient's mind of the reaction desired and there is a noticeable sign of improved co-ordination. To accomplish this will absorb considerable energy on the patient's part, which is very tiring, so the effort should not be undertaken more than two or three times.

Another way to help is for the healer to place his hand firmly around the thigh muscles and ask the patient to "clench his leg muscles". If the healer feels this to take place it is a good sign for the future. This is the principal way for seeking a more strengthened act of co-ordination with most forms of paralysis, in any limb or part of it.

If treatment is sought for the arm and hand, the healer takes the patient's hand in his. If the fingers are contracted, the healer helps to straighten them out by talking to the fingers to join in the healer's purpose. Then comes the spoken request for the fingers to tighten over the healer's fingers, helping them as may be necessary.

The healer then talks to the fingers, telling the thumb and first finger to tighten or straighten. Then the next finger and so on. In this way individual co-ordination is encouraged, finger by finger. Holding the patient's hand, the healer next directs the arm to move backwards, with the elbow close to the body, and then forwards. This should be repeated a few times slowly, asking the patient to be aware in his mind of the feeling of movement. The healer should be conscious of this as well.

A more difficult act is getting the patient to lift the

arm up with the healer's hand clasped in that of the patient. Before each movement the spoken request is given. At the outset, the healer may need to supply most of the effort as the patient raises his arm, but in the descending movement, the healer asks: "Now, pull my hand down slowly", and he should wait to experience the patient's effort as this is done. It is essential to induce the patient to co-operate with all movements and to get him to try to sense the action in his mind.

Having secured this, then will come the efforts to encourage the leg movements, first with the upper leg, then from the knee downwards and finally to seek a response in the foot movements. For this, it is good to lift the patient's leg on to the healer's thigh, and then to encourage movement of the foot up and down and round and round. Leg tension should be avoided, the only movement required being in the foot itself.

The healing of paralysis is usually progressive. Patience is needed. If the patient is accompanied by a friend, then the friend should be asked to help the patient in the same way, day by day. The patient should be asked to adopt the process of talking to his limbs continuously, anticipating every move with directional instruction. One cannot expect a patient who has lost the power of movement to persevere in this way for very long; that is why the sympathetic daily help given by a friend is so good. A general stimulating massage is useful, too, but this should not be stressful otherwise it is liable to tire the muscles.

Where there is paralysis of the bowels or bladder, this too, often has its origin in a spinal injury, or where surgery has taken place. The patient has no control of the natural functions. Normally such functions are controlled through the brain, and a message is required to give permission for action. This condition is often yieldable to the healing influences. In such functions there is a close liaison between the brain and the nerve control of the excretionary valves. There is no physical treatment for this, but the patient should be encouraged to look for co-ordination and control returning under the mind direction. This is usually a gradual process, but it can take place with patience and continuous effort.

Parkinson's Disease arises from nerve tensions and weakness of control. When a state of inertia is present, the healer should seek to attain freer movement of spine and neck as well as with the limbs, and the patient urged, with help from Spirit, to maintain the looser movements day by day.

Whilst the healing treatment is mainly the responsibility of the guides, who will tranquillise the nerve tensions and induce serenity to the outlook, much helpful treatment can be given through the healer, a primary task being to strengthen the patient's morale and inspire him to anticipate improvement day by day. The patient is asked not to try and physically stop tremors in the limbs, but to seek a relaxed condition for the limb and then very slowly to direct the movement needed. Fear is an obstacle to be overcome, and confidence restored.

One way in which this can be suggested, is for the patient to pick up small objects, watching the fingers do this in slow motion. Another idea is to suggest that the patient should pick up a light plastic empty cup and raise it slowly to the mouth. When the mind appreciates that this can be done smoothly with the nerves coming under better control, a little water can be placed in the cup for the patient to drink from it.

It should not be overlooked that the healing purpose continues with the patient all the time, and these positive little exercises help the sufferer to reap the advantage the healing brings in stabilising and strengthening nerve control.

It will often be found with the different forms of paralysis that the patient's breathing has become shallow, the chest having lost its ability to expand. When this is seen, the healer can give real directional help in restoring the ability to respirate properly by carrying out the treatment for this, as described in the next chapter.

Chapter 5

THE HEALING OF RESPIRATORY DISEASES

Under the heading of chest trouble comes a number of diseases amongst which asthma, bronchitis, emphysema, bronchiectasis, and tuberculosis are the most common. With the exception of the latter, there is a general ill-condition associated with them all and this is that the chest cage has become immobile with the ribs unable to expand, causing the breathing to become shallow. Because the rib cage will not expand the breathing has become diaphragmatic, that is, the lungs press downward onto the diaphragm, forcing the upper part of the abdomen outwards.

At the same time, it may be observed that the spine has stiffened into a slight curvature causing a hunching of the dorsal spine, and so constricting the lungs. Healers should be alert for spinal stiffness with chest troubles and should seek easement and flexibility of the spine as previously described. It will generally be found that any moderate curvature will respond, too, enabling the patient once again to sit up with a straight back.

With a fixed rib cage, the breathing will be found to be shallow, short and gaspy and any undue exertion on the patient's part, such as going up a flight of stairs, will bring on severe breathlessness and exhaustion. The healing purpose is to restore the function of the chest to permit full respiration and just as a stiffened spine can

167

yield readily to the healing effort, so the chest can like-wise respond.

With the patient sitting before him, the healer makes his first contact to put the patient at ease and help him to be relaxed. The healer will note the absence of chest movements with the breathing and if he places his hand on the upper abdomen, just below the bottom of the breastbone, he will be able to feel the swelling as the diaphragm presses downwards from the lung pressure.

When a healer has a positive healing act to carry out, such as to free a spine or to induce a return of flexibility to the ribs, it is helpful to tell the patient of the intention so that he will co-operate with the desired movements. In the case of the chest, the healer will tell the patient that his chest has become like a cage restricting any expansion of the chest as in normal breathing. He can point out where the breathing is felt, namely in the upper abdomen. He will also tell the patient that the healing intention is to free the chest, to enable it to expand and contract as the breathing takes place. The patient will then be on the look-out for this to happen and so co-operation is ensured.

The restoration of good breathing takes place in stages. The healer will place his hands firmly one on each side of the lower ribs and he will then ask the patient to breathe in through the nose very slowly, expanding the ribs where he feels the healer's hands are resting.

As soon as the healer feels a quantity of air has been taken in, he will tell the patient to stop, and slowly breathe out through the nose. As this is done, the healer will gently compress the ribs. **No great force will be used,** for it is neither necessary nor advisable. As this is repeated, the healer will feel the lower ribs expand and contract with the intake and exhalation of air.

Then raising the hands a little higher, the same process is repeated, bringing a greater area of the ribs into movement, until finally the hands are resting on the upper chest, when the healer should feel the full chest expansion with the patient's inhalation; and as he exerts a mild pressure on the chest walls, so he will feel the contraction of the chest as the air is exhaled. The patient's attention should be drawn to the ability of his chest to contract and expand. As the respirations become deeper the patient should be told to let his spine stretch, and the shoulders to go back, enabling the chest to expand fully. In all these movements it is important that the breathing both in and out should be as **slow** as is comfortably possible, thus helping to restore the sense of breathing control.

The next step in a successful healing of this sort is dependent upon the patient's co-operation. The old way of breathing has become habitual, and it is now necessary to change that habit for the new way of breathing. Thus the patient must be firmly impressed with the need to sustain the new style of breathing continuously until it, too, becomes habitual. It is suggested, therefore, that the healer tells his patient he must have the desire for full chest respirations with him constantly as if it were a "background" to all that he does. He can be told that on waking, his first thoughts should be of correct breathing, and to do this as he gets up and dresses; as he waits for his morning cup of tea; as he goes out and so on, the whole day through, until it is his final thought before sleep overtakes him on retiring. If this is conscientiously carried out for a few days, the habit of good breathing will soon be secured, and with this, there should be no more asthma, hay fever, or bronchial difficulties.

But this is only half the treatment, and it is necessary to divert for a while to consider the second part. It is obvious that with the improved respirations a greater amount of oxygen is being taken into the lungs to help the blood fulfil its work better. There is more to good breathing even than this. It is termed "characterised breathing".

We live in a sea of energies, of cosmic forces. Day by day, we subconsciously absorb these forces into our systems. It is the vital energy that the magnetic healer has in abundance and which gives him radiant health.

The simplest way to illustrate the presence of these forces is to study a tree. A tree does not thrive alone on the nourishment it takes from the earth through its roots. It absorbs from the sea of energies that eddy about it those other properties it needs for verdant foliage and vitality. The solar rays are but one example. The creation of chlorophyll is another. We all know of certain areas in pine belts where sanatoria are built to assist those suffering from breathing and lung weaknesses.

Some people are able to receive strength from trees and certain shrubs by consciously absorbing strength into themselves by breathing deeply with that intention. When we go to the sea-side we become aware of the healthful properties in the ozone and we take into our lungs long, deep breaths, knowing it is good for us. We do not have to be taught this, it comes naturally. We feel its health-giving properties and that it is going to make our holiday worth while, recuperative and health giving. It is the **sense of knowing** that is important. With ozone we can sense it, but we cannot sense this with cosmic forces, yet they are there just the same.

After having succeeded in getting the patient to breathe fully, the breathing should be repeated, but now with the **intention of consciously taking in the cosmic forces,** taking in new strength, more oxygen and healing power. The respirations should be slow and, after inhaling, the patient should then be told to exhale slowly to get rid of "waste" or trouble.

If the patient does this properly he will be conscious

of taking in strength and vitality and will feel the good clean "cool" effect as the air travels down the bronchial tubes into the lungs. The patient should be asked to do this characterised breathing a number of times a day in addition to the continual seeking of the habit of full chest breathing. During the time the patient is receiving this help with the healer attuned to him, the healing intention is to cleanse the lungs of congestion, or infection (if any), and to overcome any weakness. With asthma there is sometimes a mental link-up, referred to as "nervous asthma". In these cases it will be often found that the mind anticipates trouble as a matter of habit. For example, an asthmatical patient will say the attacks come on at three a.m. waking him up; or at a certain time each day. It can be helpful for the patient to be advised to have the mental directive of sleeping on right through the night until the morning, or to make an alteration in the daily routine and in this way assisting, with the right influencing from Spirit, to overcome habitual tendencies.

Characterised breathing with the healing intention mobilises all the bodily resources and intelligencies to overcome tensions, and symptoms of disease.

All healers will find this method of characterised breathing helpful not only to patients but for themselves, too. It is the natural way of absorbing new strength. It invigorates the psychic gland, and is the finest of all tonics. It makes one feel "on top of the world".

Chapter 6

THE HEALING OF MENTAL STRESS

It has long since been confirmed by medical authorities that the major percentage of all human diseases has its origin in mental tensions, frustrations and soul sicknesses. Such diseases come under the term "psychosomatic".

There is little doubt that the reason why so-called "incurable" conditions yield to spiritual healing is that the healing guides are able to direct good influencing to the patient's consciousness to soothe mental tensions, calm the fears, and bring balance and contentment to the outlook. This often means that the frustrations within the patient's spirit-self are tranquillised, and as these spirit and mind disharmonies are cleared, then the primary cause of the physical afflictions is removed, opening the way for the healing to master the physical symptoms.

During Contact Healing, healers through their attunement with the healing guide and the patient soon become aware of the presence of the mind and soul disharmonies within the patient. This has led to a number of ideas that are open to question.

For example, in the past, a diagnosis is given that the patient is suffering from a "split aura", or the patient's "etheric body is out of alignment", or the "aura is open and needs to be sealed off". It has even been said, that after a healing session the "healer needs to be closed up". Following this, we have seen how some healers will make sweeping passes down the patient's body with the idea of "cleansing the aura" and to "seal it off". A little consideration will show to any intelligent mind that such practices are useless.

The aura is a **reflection** of a person's spiritual and physical health. **It is a reflection only.** If a patient has a physical ill-condition, a psychic can sometimes observe this in the aura either as a dull or angry-looking colour. If mental disharmony is present then there is an adverse reflection generally. As the physical trouble is healed, then the aura automatically clears; and as the mental tensions are soothed, so the aura reflects the happier condition.

Thus it is not possible to heal an aura. One cannot heal a reflection. Neither is it possible for an aura to be "split", for no reflection can be split. Neither can it be sealed off. Any healer who is so ill-advised to attempt this "sealing" displays ignorance of healing's basic fundamentals, for any such technique is useless as a healing act, there being no reason for it. Its only virtue is that it is a mistaken way of expressing the healing intention.

Mental upset is the primary cause of almost all our physical diseases. This fact is now recognised by all medical authorities, and I would say that the principal causes are fears and frustrations. Consider "fears" first.

With some there is a basis for them: a lump is seen in the breast, and immediately comes the fear of cancer—it may be only a swelling from a chill, or a glandular upset that will soon yield to the natural curative properties of the body, yet the dread of cancer comes.

There is fear of insecurity, fears created by suspicions that are so often groundless; and it is true to say that in the great majority of cases there is no real foundation for the fears at all. Ask anyone, who has a fearful mind: "Where are the troubles you were afraid of last month? What were they?" It is doubtful if they can even be recalled, and yet they tortured the mind in the past days. How true it is that we are afraid of things that never happen.

Let me mention another cause of fear, it may be one of financial anxiety, or of some domestic situation that has arisen. Assuming that there are grounds for anxiousness, these concerns cannot be helped by continually worrying over them.

A more insistent form of mental stress is frustration. It is not always easy to realise what form this takes, for some of them dwell in the subconscious self. They comprise emotional and sex problems, failure to attain one's ideals, the desire of the inner-self for expression that the existing way of life does not permit.

It may be that the inner-self seeks expression in music, but the way of life does not allow this. There may be a yearning for travel and open spaces while the person is held down to a humdrum factory life. There are so many forms of frustration, often subtle, yet so harrying to good mental poise.

These, too, are productive of organic disease, and it is believed that some forms of cancer have their causation in frustrational conflict.

There are people who cause themselves mental suffering by being so sensitive they take other people's problems too much to heart, and sustain a deep concern about them.

Others suffer from a sense of responsibility, maybe at work, and instead of closing the office door on problems when they leave, they take them home with them, continuing to worry even in the hours when sleep should come. The fact that business executives are prone to gastric ulcers is evidence of this.

Consider first those mind upsets which can be described as "movable fears". Those small ones, that crop up from day to day, that we encourage and enlarge upon; exaggerating their importance until they assume unnecessarily high proportions. If they are dwelt upon they become very real, and only time will whittle them away, as their importance fades, and something else takes their place.

The general purpose of the healing is to soothe and calm fears and tensions, providing the opportunity for a true perspective to return. To give new and happier directives for the mind to engage upon. To provide that state of contentment from which refreshing sleep enables the exhausted energies of the body to be restored.

This soothing process can take place for this simple reason. Just as our physical minds are receptive to influencing through conversation, so our spirit or inner minds are receptive to spiritual influencing. Most mental disharmonies arise from frustrations that exist more in the inner mind or spirit-self of a person than in the physical consciousness. Because our inner spirit selves are on a similar mind plane to the spirit helpers and counsellors, so they are able to give to the troubled mind calming and adjusting thoughts to overcome the basic causes of stress.

This is not merely psychological healing, it is much more than this, although psychology is a science closely linked with these healings.

The next important thing to consider is, how a sufferer can co-operate with the healing effort. This is an aspect of healing in which the common-sense co-operation of the patient can greatly assist the response to the good guiding influences reaching him. The following advice should therefore be given to the patient:

(i) *Let the past belong to the past, there is no virtue in holding on to unhappy memories; this only perpetuates the trouble and there is no sense in it.*

(ii) The healing is a yielding process therefore do not fight in in the mind against anxieties.

(iii) Look for happinesses in the small things of life throughout the day. Consider the daily tasks that lie ahead with pleasurable anticipation of doing them easily and well. Look for happiness in the boiling of the kettle for the early-morning cup of tea; in washing up; and enjoy walking to the station or the shops.

Have a smile for all those you know, even the shop assistants or the ticket collector. More important have a smile for yourself. *Take care of your personal appearance, even if you are home all day; avoid dowdiness. If you are a lady, a little make-up and a bright dress. Put on the radio and join in with song and music. Have a song in your heart as you start work or dust around.*

This is the natural and happy way you want to be—it is what you are looking for. The healing is natural, too, so join in with it.

(iv) If you are in business, do not anticipate troubles in advance, deal with them as they come. Above all when you leave the business at night, leave it in the office, don't carry it home with you. Look forward to your evening hours and if there are dear ones to greet you, give them the warmth of your smile and take interest in the small home affairs. A few flowers or some sweets carry with them a lot of welcome. If you are a wife, try and make something special for your husband for his supper that you know he likes.

(v) Get out of the mental rut. Go out for walks or to the pictures, theatre, or anything else that gives a change. A Sunday picnic when the weather is good, and so on.

In this way you make a break with the past, and open life anew to happier days.

If it should be domestic disharmony the matter may be a little more complicated. The directive is to restore harmony and this will not come from long, sad faces. Pay those little attentions that are appreciated and appeal to the good conscience. Overlook any frustrating act by the other partner, do not add to it by quarrelling. The healing is trying to give good influencing and guidance and the way to assist this is by co-operation. As the happier temperament comes, so do headaches, neuralgias, tummy upsets, etc., go. If you like reading then get the type of book you like, and for a while each day, sit down, relax and enjoy it. If you like music, then put on your favourite records. Do the things that you like to do, and look forward beforehand to the enjoyment of doing them.

In this way, you assist the good healing influences to change your outlook, fears subside, anticipations of trouble lose their frequency, and the twin virtues of true perspective and contentment take their place.

So many times have we seen characters change, the hard and cold man becoming warm, loving and considerate and with a woman the same.

Innumerable people have been made well from mental stresses, at times chronic cases of obsessing ideas that created mental torture. Happiness has returned to many, and there is no reason why the great majority of sufferers should not respond also, for this is a field of healing where we are in our element.

If the patient's trouble lies in the physical mind, such as fears of insecurity, anxieties, fears of infidelity, responsibilities etc., the healer can play an effective part in soothing away such distress. One effective way takes place through the blending of the healer's spirit-self with that of the patient to enable good influencing and assurance from the healer to restore perspective and contentment.

The healer, seated in front of the patient and holding his hands, as a preliminary to closer attunement, and knowing of the disturbed state of the mind, should allow the patient to tell him freely of the nature of his trouble. The healer listens, showing his sympathy and understanding. Sometimes a great deal of patience is needed for this, but in this way the patient feels the healer is "with him"—he is sharing his anxieties with a compassionate friend, and therefore looks to the healer to free him from his mental stress.

The healer's attitude should be one of gentle yet dominant confidence when he speaks to the patient. The healer's common sense, plus the thoughts he receives intuitively through attunement, should govern his remarks to the patient and be positive and sympathetically helpful. There is no set way that can be laid down here as to how the healer can do this. He should follow his impressions to help clear away the patient's fears. The healer's confident, positive, sympathetic and understanding manner can do much to restore the patient's sense of perspective, help him regain his self-assurance and give him the full expectancy of becoming free from anxiety as each day comes.

Healers learn to be good psychologists but this is not psychology alone. It is much more than that. It is psychology **plus**, this being the help the patient receives through the blending of the healer's total self with that of the patient, plus the corrective influencing from the guide.

Sometimes the patient will want to return again and again to the mental trouble he has. With patients like this, it may be the best plan to tell them they must let the past belong to the past, and thereby discourage any continual repetition of the catalogue of troubles.

The healer should maintain an unostentatious confident control. When he talks to the patient, he should speak definitely and with confidence, and so convey a sense of assurance to the patient. If it is possible to let in a little humour, to get the patient to smile, it helps to "break-up" his tension. The purpose of such healings is that the patient will go away fortified, expectant of a happier outlook, and grateful for the help being given.

When, however, the cause of the unrest lies within the soul or inner-self of the patient, such as is seen with primary frustrations, emotional dissatisfactions, etc., which are coupled with ill-effects on the conscious mind, the only way these disharmonies can be overcome is on the same plane as they exist—namely, the spirit plane, thus becoming the responsibility of the guide. The guide will direct good influencing and right guidance to the patient's spirit mind. At the same time, the healer can play his part, as described, in a psychological way. The hands of the healer can play no part in this except, perhaps, to soothe and induce relaxation.

Returning to diseases which have a psychosomatic origin, it will invariably be found that as mental stresses are soothed, so the primary cause of the disease is gradually overcome and, with this, easement of the physical symptoms.

If the cause of frustration or mental upset is deeply seated, it may take a period of time for the good influencing and guidance from Spirit to produce perceptible results. Healers are aware how obstinately a patient can hold on to obsessing fears and remorse, and it may well be that those residing in the inner-self are just as obdurate. Thus if the consciousness and mind are so strongly possessed by these disharmonies, it can be that the healing influences are not being received, and so the trouble continues. This is one reason why, at times, we do not see all the success we wish for. It is when a patient's total mind condition becomes readily amenable to the corrective influencing we observe these spontaneous and rapid healings

The healer should, as far as possible, avoid giving advice to the patient on **personal** problems, except where it relates directly to the nervous condition. All help of that sort must **ultimately** be self-help, inspired by the healing. All mental illnesses are individual and very personal, so there can be no set rules that govern the healing or rate of recovery. The healing of mental stress is often indirect. It has already been shown that with the commencement of spiritual healing, whether by Contact or by Absent Healing, patients become aware of a feeling of inner upliftment.

The opening paragraph of this chapter states the truth that the majority of physical afflictions have a psychosomatic cause. Thus the healer has taken the first steps to induce a more serene state within the patient. The happy change just comes, and with the good calming influencing from Spirit, the mental stresses are soothed and the patient begins to take fresh interests and to enjoy life again.

When a patient is suffering from gastric troubles, the cause may well exist in mental tension, and here again one observes progressive betterment and as the nervous stress is calmed, so the symptoms of abdominal upset lighten and disappear.

Mental conditions that can be described as cases of obsession or possession are dealt with in Section V on pages 295 and 298 respectively. They are in a class by themselves and need particular understanding and treatment by one experienced in dealing with them.

The healing of mental stress is so often a part of general healing treatment. The guides are easily able to diagnose this and therefore treat it as part of the overall healing help the patient needs.

Chapter 7

THE HEALING OF INTERNAL DISORDERS, FUNCTIONAL TROUBLES, BLOOD AND CIRCULATORY CONDITIONS, GROWTHS, ETC.

It is not possible to give any direct advice on the way of healing the many diverse ill-conditions that come under the heading of this chapter. No healing can be effective until the cause which has created the trouble is overcome. The treatment of symptoms alone is helpful, but only palliative. Therefore, in dealing with this large range of complaints, little guidance can be given when the causes may be many and bearing in mind that every condition is individual. The primary causes of sicknesses in this category may well be psychosomatic or organic, or both.

If one considers sicknesses caused through functional disorders, like diabetes, epilepsy, etc., it is observed that the healing process is usually a gradual and progressive one as good changes are induced, and healers need to recognise this. One of the noticeable ways in which patients are helped is by the giving of new strength and vitality to the bodily health tone, and the happier outlook that comes with the feeling of inner upliftment.

In Contact Healing of this category of diseases, the healer's contribution is the attunement he establishes between the guide, the patient and himself, conveying to the guide the necessary knowledge of the physical symptoms, and then simply being the channel through whom the healing energies flow. The healer plays only a small part in the actual healing treatment.

In conditions such as anaemia, jaundice, leukaemia, thrombosis, and all other troubles that are connected with the blood, heart action and circulation, patients are often helped by the inducing of good respirations and characterised breathing. This materially assists in building up a healthy condition of the bloodstream and encouraging rhythm of the heart. If the patient can appreciate that as he breathes with intention to absorb healing and health-giving strength, then he consciously allies himself to the healing purpose.

In the healing of cancers, tumours, goitres, cysts, etc., the healer, in blended contact with the patient, should have the healing purpose firmly in his mind as his hands are placed in contact with the appropriate part of the patient's body, looking for the guide to disperse and take away the trouble.

Similarly, if the patient is known to have stones in the kidney or gall bladder, or indeed any other "unwanted" condition, the seeking of dispersal, or correction, should be "looked for". In all these healings the healer should follow his impressions. In his state of attunement, he should not question the impressions he receives, but feel that he is a conscious co-operator in the healing purpose.

With skin afflictions of all types, there will invariably be found a psychosomatic cause, in the form of anxieties, fears, past mental stresses, frustrations and so on. Skin troubles even of long duration are amenable to spiritual healing, and here again there is little for the healer to do in Contact Healing apart from his initial attunement. As in dealing with mental stresses, the healer's sympathetic yet confident attitude in helping to bring contentment to the patient's outlook, seeking tranquillity, and putting any mind troubles into their correct perspective, will materially help the healing purpose.

Some skin diseases are infectious, of course, and, when a healer comes into contact with such a patient he MUST take every precaution to prevent passing on any contamination to another person. Hands should be thoroughly washed in hot disinfected water. Chapter 9 deals with the healing of skin diseases in greater detail.

Healers are often asked whether or not a patient should undergo surgery. This is a very delicate question, involving a high degree of responsibility. Healers are advised to avoid giving any definite "Yes" or "No". Actually it is not within the healer's province to give such advice for one simple reason: the healer does not know what the surgeon intends to do, neither can he be responsible for the surgeon's skill or for any mistake the latter may make; or for any complications that may ensue. It is the purpose of healing to avoid surgery if possible, but healers need to recognise that for some conditions it can become necessary, such as in a case of acute appendicitis, or strangulated hernia, etc.

When a patient has been advised to have an operation and he comes to a healer hoping that through healing he can avoid it, the healer should be very circumspect in his words to the patient. **It is not within the province of any healer to make any promise or give any undertaking, in advance, of what the healing can or cannot do. This applies not only to severe conditions but mild ones as well.** Therefore the healer should counsel the patient to this effect and that while it is hoped the healing might avoid an operation, the final responsibility of undergoing surgery is one that the patient and his advisers must accept.

If it is found that following the healing, the symptoms of stress, swelling, size of a growth, pain, etc., have appreciably diminished, the patient should be told to see his doctor, and tell him of the improvement, asking whether the operation could be postponed for a week or two, to observe whether further improvements take place. It is often found that the doctor will agree with this and thus give further time for the healing to carry on its good work.

If an operation is inevitable, then the patient can ask his doctor for permission for the healer to visit him in hospital before surgery takes place, if there is time for such a visit.

The patient can also be asked to inform the healer of the day upon which the operation will take place and the healer should then seek through Absent Healing for strength and vitality to reach the patient to build up his resistance and to help him through the operation speedily and well, avoiding operational shock or complications.

If the healer is unable to receive a diagnosis of an internal disorder, etc., he should not worry about this, for it is the guide who is responsible for the diagnosis and treatment, and while he is blended in with the patient he should have supreme confidence in the healing guides to render all the aid possible at the time.

Sometimes, and especially in Absent Healing, the aid of spiritual healing is asked for when the patient's weakness has become critical with the disease having made such inroads into the body that it is not within the "scheme of things" for a recovery to take place. This again is not the healer's responsibility, but not questioning or limiting the power of Spirit to heal, he should continue to seek for all the help that is possible to be with the sick one. It will often be found that when a passing follows, the patient is given fortitude and inner peace, the pains are soothed and so much help is given during the critical hours that the passing into spirit life takes place peacefully and without any stress at all. When a passing takes place, or when there does not seem to be a reduction in the state of the patient's infirmity, that both patient and healer would wish to see, there is reason for this. As there is a reasoned process behind each successful healing treatment, so there is also a reasoned process to account for non-success. Firstly, it may be outside the scope of the physical and spirit laws; secondly, the cause being psychosomatic may be so firmly embedded in the patient's inner-self, mind or consciousness that the healing influences cannot penetrate; and thirdly, it may be that the patient is continuing to maintain the cause of the trouble.

For example, if a patient is suffering from acute arthritis and he continues to live in damp unhygienic conditions, the cause is maintained. A person who should diet and ignores this, or a person with diminishing sight through eye strain and who continues to over stress the eyes, will negative the healing by failing to co-operate with the healing purpose.

As has been mentioned earlier, when a healer does not see all the progress he would wish for, he should not blame the patient, the guide or himself and he should not think that his healing gift is "not strong enough". In this connection it should always be remembered that spiritual healing is the outcome of a spirit science that can only operate within the total laws that govern human existence in this life. Within the scope of those laws, we are happy to see inestimable benefits given to the human family through our kinship with Spirit.

Chapter 8

INSOMNIA

Insomnia is a common complaint, and is not generally treated with the seriousness it deserves. Mental activity can be more tiring than manual labour, and uses up just as much, if not more, bodily fuel than a hard day's physical work. Nothing reduces the health tone more quickly than sleeplessness, and anaemia results from this.

You have only to look at a person suffering from sleeplessness to see the result of utter weariness in the eyes and the drawn tiredness of the face. I remember a man coming for healing who suffered from chronic insomnia. He said he had "not known a night's sleep for twenty years" and dreaded going to bed to lie awake with a tortured mind, so he never went to bed at all, but sat up in his chair, and slept when he felt like it.

I sought help for him, and gave him the advice that follows later in this chapter. When I next saw him a transformation had taken place, his eyes were alert, a smile was on his face and he looked thoroughly fit.

Sleeplessness is due to over-activity of the mind; it will not rest, it continues to work and work. The old-fashioned suggestion that a sufferer should count sheep jumping over a stile is rarely successful for the simple reason that this is adding just one more activity to the mind and does not soothe the underlying anxieties and worries.

Doctors usually prescribe sleeping tablets in varying strengths; these are just palliatives and they do not cure. They blanket the consciousness without soothing the mental activity that continues underneath, and the patient wakes up more tired than ever. Spiritual healing has as its objective the removal of the cause. This cause has its origin in mental tension, frustrations, fears and anticipation of troubles. It lies deep within the subconscious mind. This part of the mind can be reached on the same plane that it exists, namely, the spirit-self, by the correcting and soothing influences from Spirit.

In this way, balance and perspective, with gentle discipline, are restored, and the natural function of refreshing sleep comes back. This is what happened in the case of the man I mentioned, for he reported how contented his outlook had become, and he could tackle his business problems easily and with confidence.

The soothing of nerve stresses, neuritis, and even unbalance in the mind, invariably follows the commencement of spiritual healing by the Absent Healing method. A sense of inner upliftment with freedom comes to the patient—the heaviness that weighs down so constantly is removed and when the patient retires to sleep it comes naturally and refreshingly and in the morning he greets the day and its tasks with confidence and pleasure.

The spiritual healing does its part but it is common sense to co-operate with it. This help a patient can give is partly psychological, for the first thing he should do is gently look forward to what he so dearly needs, and that is sleep.

If he should go to bed, thinking of all the other restless nights in the past and prepares himself for another, then it will negative the healing effort. The healer, therefore, should advise sufferers from insomnia to look forward to restful sleep some time before going to bed. It is good for the patient to take a warm, comforting beverage, such as Bourn-vita, Horlicks, or just cocoa.

If it's a cold night the bed should be warmed, thus preparing for the sleep to come. On retiring, the patient should first enjoy the luxuriousness of the physical comfort the bed can give, lie firmly on it, with the limbs relaxed in whatever position he likes the best. The patient has the thought in mind that the bed is the place to sleep and he looks ahead to sleeping right through the night until daylight comes, or the proper time to get up. This will avoid the troublesome waking in the small hours. As the patient makes an ally of himself to the healing effort so will sleep come.

If a person is accustomed to taking sleeping tablets, with chronic conditions he can still do so for the first nights and then gradually ease off taking them as the sleep improves, but I suggest with the average case of insomnia, this is not necessary. But there is no harm in having the tablets near by to take, just in case they are needed. They rarely are, and eventually find their way into a drawer to be forgotten.

If sleep is a little time in coming the patient should not let all the daily worries revolve round and round, like a mouse in a wheel; he should recall pleasant memories of the past, such as last year's holiday; or contemplate what he hopes to do in the coming holiday, or some other happy desire. He should build a "castle in the air" by wishful thinking. This leads the mind into smoother avenues of thought and the worries are bypassed. As a rule one will not get very far in happy contemplation, for sleep will overtake.

The same process should follow each night and it will not be long before the insomnia is a thing of the past.

I remember a case of a small child who, so the parents told me, never slept, except fitfully during the day, but never at night. I learnt that he was afraid of darkness, and could only be pacified when taken into the parents' bed. I told them to give him a night-light and a nice cuddly animal that he could hold close to him, and that we would seek calming influences to be with him.

They did so, and the very first night the boy slept right through and they had no trouble after that. In this way, his fears were soothed, he had the companionship of the cuddly toy that he held close to him. So was his little mind calmed and with the added help he got through the healing effort so natural sleep came.

At the end of a day the body cries out for relaxation so that the expended energies can be replaced. The active physical mind needs this, too. It is only unpleasant thoughts that keep it awake, no one suffers sleeplessness from continual contemplation of happy thoughts; they are always thoughts associated with responsibilities or fears. Therefore the patient should go to bed happily, looking for a rest from worries. Let a smile come into his thoughts, and tell him to look forward to the refreshing sleep that will then so surely come.

I have not known any cases of sleeplessness, even chronic ones, that have not responded to this treatment, especially when spirit help and protection have been asked for through Absent Healing.

Chapter 9

THE HEALING OF SKIN DISEASES

There are few diseases the doctors find more difficulty in curing than dermatitis, eczema, psoriasis, etc. They are particularly obstinate and special hospitals exist for the treatment of these maladies alone.

Yet with spiritual healing they are often the most easily healed. There is a reason for this, and I suggest it rests on the fact that medical attention is largely directed to the healing of the symptoms and not the cause of the disease. Thus medical treatment almost solely rests upon ointments and lotions and sometimes radiation treatments. These may be helpful in a few cases, but for the majority are of little help, for the simple reason *that the cause remains untouched.*

In my experience I have found, with the exception of some types of infectious skin disease, that the origin lies in some form of nervous or emotional stress, and therefore this unbalance must first be rectified before the skin will clear . . . and this is just what spiritual healing does.

Healers are often called upon to heal children, mostly boys, who are said to be "born with skin trouble". These unfortunate youngsters are invariably outside the scope of medical science to heal them, and they continue to suffer year after year, causing great sorrow and inconvenience to the parents. They rarely have a restful night, and I have known cases where the parents have never known a peaceful night because of the cries of their children.

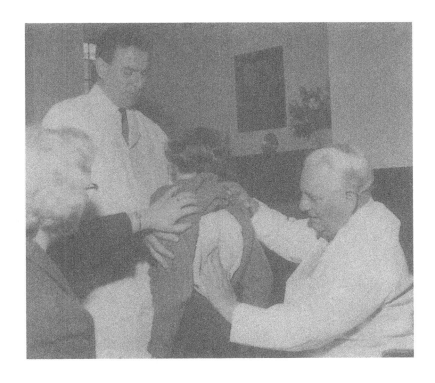

Harry Edwards, assisted by Ray Branch, checks a spinal condition prior to giving healing; and below, the partners at work in The Healing Sanctuary at Shere.

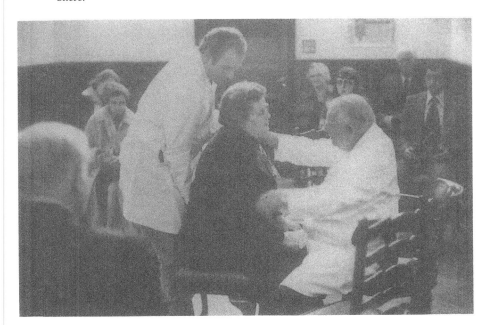

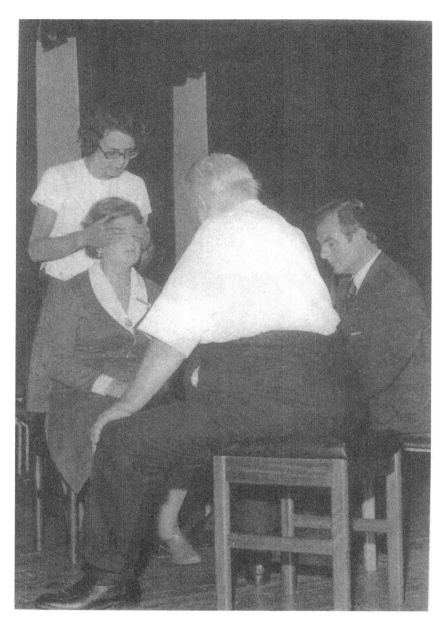

The healing of sight. Joan Branch seeks help for a patient at a public healing demonstration as Harry Edwards (foreground) and Ray Branch also attune to the healing purpose.

I have yet to learn of a case like this, when healing has been asked for, where speedy relief has not soon followed, and been maintained.

It is not proposed to detail here the means by which skin eruptions follow mental stress or sickness of the inner mind. Suffice it, that, because the cause lies within the spirit-self of the sufferer, this can only be calmed and soothed on the same level as it exists.

In the same way that we see the neurotic, the vicious-minded, the alcoholic, the drug addict changed—in which a happy and contented outlook replaces the former maladjusted one—so through spiritual healing are the emotional causes of unrest in the mind of a skin sufferer removed and the healing of the skin soon follows.

Doctors now recognise the truth healers have put forward for the last twenty years, that the causation of the major portion of our physical diseases lies in some form of nervous and emotional frustration and mental unrest. This applies to skin disease particularly. The doctors now know this, but what can they do? No medicines can cure mental stress.

This is the way of the healing of skin disease by spiritual means, and which is best effected by the Absent Healing process. Following the application for the healing and intercession, a feeling of mental ease, contentment or "inner upliftment" comes to the patient. The outlook becomes soothed. With this, the anger within the sore places on the skin fades away; the redness disappears. Next the areas affected begin to diminish and the new clean skin appears until the whole area is healed.

Care has to be exercised to avoid any further mental upset, disappointments, frustrations, etc., especially with children, in the weeks that follow the healing, until the good results are consolidated.

Any cooling or soothing lotion is helpful to keep the skin cool and moist while the healing goes on. This helps to allay the physical irritation. At the same time the first law of health in keeping the bowels free is essential, so to assist the bloodstream to carry away the waste products from the skin; and deep breathing should be encouraged. Apart from this I do not suggest any other treatment, except for the patient to keep the mind as contented as can be. The healing will do the rest.

An *infection* of the skin does not come within the above category and usually the natural corrective functions of the body will remove the invader. Though here, too, we generally see the healing process accelerated by healing.

A doctor once asked for my help to heal a man who had suffered for years from a vicious type of skin disease, which followed his incarceration in a prisoner-of-war camp. For three years the doctors "tried everything" but to no avail, the condition spread and became worse. But as soon as the Absent Healing commenced the skin cleared completely and within three weeks showed no scars or blemishes. No doubt the mental stress the man endured was the cause of his trouble, but with the soothing influences reaching his spirit-self, his mind was soothed and calmed and the symptoms were soon removed.

A young lady was about to be married and was very worried over skin trouble that she had suffered for years. She said in her letter: "When I take my clothes off the skin flakes fall off like confetti." Her marriage was to take place in three weeks, and before the happy day arrived she wrote to say that all her trouble had completely disappeared.

Can there be any other explanation for such healings to take place than that which I have given here?

Chapter 10

THE HEALING OF SIGHT

In view of the many different troubles that can affect the eyesight, it is rather difficult to give any precise indications of how eyes can be helped by spiritual healing; but in general, I can say that there has been much evidence of success with the healing of vision.

I often point out that no one case of healing can be taken as a precedent for another, and this is particularly true with eye diseases. For example, with one case of cataract we may see a rapid clearance of the obstructing film, yet with another, possibly less severe, the dispersal of the film takes a longer time and in some cases there is no apparent clearance.

In the Contact Healing sessions in the work here at Shere there is hardly an occasion when we do not have patients seeking help for eye conditions, mainly with people past middle age but often with a surprising number of young people, too.

There have been occasions when, from our visual examination of the eyes, there appears to be no hope at all; for the eyes have lost all appearance of organisation and look like a whitish blur. Yet, at times, the seemingly impossible happens and sight is restored— possibly just a little at first, increasing in strength as the Absent Healing continues.

I have found that the greater percentage of success is seen when the eyes have not been operated upon. The eye structure and function are so delicate that surgery while possibly doing good work for those people we do not see, invariably brings most difficult conditions to heal with those patients who apply to us for help.

I divide eye troubles into two main classifications: those whose causation lies in some form of mental and nervous tension, and those like cataracts, which appear to be of a more physical nature. With the former, an appreciable measure of success is obtained often leading to complete recovery. With the second category the healing result is more problematical.

There is a third section, mainly with people whose sight is failing as a result of old age or a senile condition. While spiritual healing is unable to put back the clock, it has been found that with these cases the sight is maintained in a stronger state than would otherwise be the case.

Conjunctivitis, which is an inflammation of the membranes, is one of those common troubles that respond easily to healing, and this is seen by the lessening of the redness and watering, until the eye is clear.

With cataracts the healing manifests in the gradual dispersal of the opacity that obscures the lens, and success is not infrequent. The delicacy of the structure of the eye indicates the wonderful way in which healing works to disperse just the unwanted matter and without injuring any other part of the eye.

Iritis, nervous twitchings of the eyes often promoting double vision, is also a malady that can be helped by healing, for with the soothing of the nerves the eyes respond. More difficult are detached retinas, with their painful effects. This is an affliction where the healing is not often seen after surgery has intervened, but if the trouble is not chronic then restoration comes; but when this does not seem to be possible, the pains and light flashes are soothed and lessened.

The ill-results following a haemorrhage also yield to

the healing effort, but with this a further period of healing is necessary to remove the ill-effects. Glaucoma is the only other disease I need mention specifically. This usually is seen with people who are past the prime of life, and if the trouble has not developed seriously it is often overcome. In all cases where spiritual healing is invoked for eye troubles, I strongly advise patients to avoid eye strain and strong light. Correct glasses are also essential and a constant check-up with the oculist is recommended. Sometimes patients come with weakening sight, images become blurred and there is pain and tenseness in the eyes. When I ask what their employment is, it is often found that this involves tedious and close work. So long as the cause is maintained then the eyes will continue to suffer, and I find that the majority of people in this class would rather continue their employment and ruin their sight than seek something new that would be less exacting to the sight. However, if close work cannot be avoided, I advise that as often as possible the focal length be altered by looking elsewhere for a short time. When people hurt their arms they rest them, but rarely do they rest their eyes when these are suffering from some ill-condition.

There is another difficulty we meet in healing: when a patient has been in regular attendance for his eyes and the doctor has formed an opinion that nothing more can be done, or he has advised the best glasses possible. Following this the patient receives Absent Healing and the stress is taken away; the sight is relieved; and the strengthening becomes obvious. The doctor recalling his prognosis is unwilling to recognise any change or to recommend different glasses.

If any patients are in this position, conscious of ease-ment from stress and clearer vision, even if a little, they should consult a new optician and ask for an examination. In these circumstances new glasses may be given to help the sight and relieve strain.

I recall one lady who, through a blow, became blind and was registered as such. With the healing her sight came back, but the hospital doctor would not consider this or give her glasses because she was "Registered Blind".

Another case concerned a man who had been completely blind for fifty years and who recovered his sight with spiritual healing. It returned as long sight and the specialist optician declared it was perfect and miraculous. He observed "Vision perfect, eye clear, bright, and in splendid condition, no fear of deleterious effects".

I submitted this case to the doctors concerned for their comments and recognition of spiritual healing as the healing agency. The excuse they offered to account for the recovery was "suggestion, the patient began to see, after being encouraged to look".

Believe it or not, the suggestion was seriously put forward that after being totally blind for 50 years, the eyes cataractous and the lens dislocated, all I had to do was to tell the patient to look and he could see! This is not a fairy story, it appeared with this doctor's excuse in the *British Medical Journal*, 4th December, 1954.

Strange, is it not, that there are some doctors who will not "see"!

Chapter 11

THE HEALING OF DEAFNESS
AND HEAD NOISES

The story I like best to relate of healed deafness took place some time ago, when a lady came one afternoon to my healing sanctuary to see if we could restore her hearing. We were told that when she was a baby her mother poured hot oil into her ears and from that day she could not hear any sound at all.

She did not appear to be a very suitable case for a healing for she had been deaf so long, and it seemed that the childhood experience had destroyed the faculty. For the reason that it is not within our province to limit in our minds the power of healing, we sought help from Spirit for her.

At ten o'clock the same night there came a knock at the door and there was the lady bursting with excitement and all she could say was "I can hear! I can hear!" The sequel to this story came a few days later when the lady again came to see me. She worked in a laundry, and her comment was: "I never thought girls could swear so much".

Like most other diseases, the response to healing depends upon the individual condition and cause. When an eardrum is badly perforated we are usually told that medically the trouble is incurable, and yet it is with this condition that we frequently observe a return of hearing. The implication is that the perforation has been healed over, and this is not so remarkable when we remember

197

how wounds and bones heal readily under directive treatment.

Another common cause is catarrhal deafness, and this often means that the hammer and anvil bones of the middle ear have become clogged and can no longer carry the sound vibrations to the inner ear. Arthritis in the ear can produce a similar locking-up of these essential small bones. Once again the healing is frequently able to disperse the clogging substance and the hearing strengthens. With perforations and clogging a little time is needed for the correction of the ill-condition and for the hearing to return.

A more general cause of deafness is due to the weakening of the hearing nerves in the inner ear. This may have been the result of severe nerve stress or disturbance such as an explosion. If the former, then by soothing and calming the general nerve state we do see the hearing nerves respond and function once more, but when the cause has been a violent explosive noise, success is not so often seen.

Weakness of the auditory senses often comes with the wear and tear of life, and when age takes its toll of the delicate hearing mechanism.

With age, the functioning tends to be less virile, and healing cannot put back the clock, but what we do find as a common experience in such cases is that with the placing of the healer's hands over the ears, with the healing intention to improve the quality of the hearing or to soothe away noises further deterioration is stayed, and the hearing is maintained—as well as the general condition permits.

There are other causes of deafness, some of which we do not know. For example, a person will come with one ear stone deaf, and yet with healing the faculty is restored. This is one of those mysteries that we cannot explain.

A clergyman of the Church of England once asked for help to prevent his hearing declining further; he was wearing a hearing aid for his right ear. His left ear had been stone deaf for thirty years and he had given up any thoughts of improvement with this. After Contact Healing, it was found that he could hear, even whispers, with his stone-deaf ear, and when he put his hearing aid back into his right ear the volume of sound was so great that it was "deafening". Thus it is, as with all other troubles, while no improvement can be seen in advance there is no limit to the good that can come through spiritual healing.

Associated with deafness there are the head noises, and these are most distressing. The continual hissing or booming, thumping and roaring tends to drive the patient frantic. The effectiveness of the healing is again dependent on the cause. Hissing may come from a perforated drum and this can be healed and the noises will cease. The most common cause is from nerve tensions, worries and anxieties, with accompanying headaches and neuralgia. These respond to healing but invariably take a longer time. Indeed, I rarely find a case of instantaneous healing of ear noises.

Generally speaking, as calming, healing influences soothe the mind and overcome the tensions, so the volume of the noises diminishes, and periods of total relief come to extend in time until the sounds are vanquished. With these patients care must always be exercised to prevent a recurrence by keeping the mind contented and not overstressed.

There are two main ways in which patients can help their healing. Watch any partially deaf person. When you speak to him his eyes are strained, watching your mouth, and they are tensed up to "hear". This creates a state of mental tenseness or agitation which upsets the nerve harmony, induces stress, and thus prevents the nerves of hearing carrying the message to the consciousness smoothly and easily. I therefore advise a passive mental state when listening to permit the ears to receive the sounds in a natural and easy way.

The ears do not hear—they receive the sound vibrations which are then conveyed by the many delicate auditory nerves to the consciousness, where the vibrations are translated into a mental experience. Thus any form of tense anticipation to hear can only impede the process of hearing.

The second way to help the healing is to encourage more selective hearing. It is said that with one ear that is weaker than the other the weak one gets lazy, and also that the consciousness becomes, as a matter of habit, content with what the aural nerves feed to it. Therefore the hearing requires stimulation to increase its selectivity.

I suggest that patients whose hearing has weakened should listen to orchestral music by means of a transistor radio placed firmly against the ear at just sufficient strength to enable the general sound effect to be heard easily. Then they should try to distinguish the various instruments in the orchestra, without strain. This will encourage the "ears" to "look into" sounds, thus building up receptivity. If one ear is weaker than the other, it is helpful to turn that ear towards the music and mentally seek hearing from that ear. In this way natural stimulation is obtained for the weaker ear.

In this way the weak (or lazy) ear can be encouraged in its functions. These exercises will also help those who find difficulty in distinguishing words in conversation. But it is important that there should be no mental stress in trying to guess or anticipate the character of sounds or speech.

Healers are often requested to give treatment for other conditions associated with the ears, such as Ménière's Disease, having the symptoms of giddiness, headaches, ringing in the ears, as well as other troubles associated with a section of the inner ear (the cochlea), and troubles connected with mastoid cells.

The anatomy of the ear is a delicate and complicated affair, and healers are, perhaps, best able to seek help to overcome such troubles by placing the hands gently over, or near, the ears with the purpose of providing a means for the soothing and restorative healing energies to reach the weakened areas.

It is inadvisable for healers to take any action to interfere with the ears—even the removal of wax from the outer ear should be done by a doctor or a nurse.

The healing plays its part in reviving the nerve faculties to hear, and to overcome any physical cause that impedes the hearing. Therefore the carrying out of these suggestions will effect co-operation with the healing to produce the greatest benefit in the shortest possible time.

Chapter 12

THE HEALING OF
CANCERS AND GROWTHS

Note:
1. *This chapter takes into account all such growths as tumours, cancers, goitres, fibroids, cysts, etc.*
2. *The reader should also refer to Section IV, Chapter 3, page 259, "Organic Diseases and the Bodily Intelligence".*

The law is definite that no person should advertise that he can cure cancer, but all the Acts on the Statute Book cannot prevent the seeking of healing of a cancer either by Absent or Contact Healing. Therefore, if, in conjunction with prayer or attunement with the spirit source of healing, a healer places his hands over a part of the body where a cancer growth is said to be, seeking in his inner-thoughts for the malignancy to be dispersed, there could be no successful prosecution.

Although this law was made many years ago, the author is not aware of any prosecution having resulted. Therefore, in effect, healers can continue to seek healing for cancer sufferers as they have previously done; but, should any person be so ill-advised as to advertise a "Cure for Cancer" and at the same time offer to supply a medicament for that purpose, then the law would have an easy victim.

In view of the legal position, the healer should protect himself by advising the patient to have a medical examination where a serious condition is suspected.

Healers are free from any legal proceedings, providing they adopt the way of spiritual healing by means of prayer, intercession or the laying-on of hands. In this way, uncounted numbers of cancer sufferers have been, and continue to be, treated by healers. The percentage of cures of malignancy may not be very high, but time and time again healings do take place, with tumours being dispersed, and the patients declared to be medically free from cancer. These are termed by the medical profession as "spontaneous recoveries" or, in the doctors' language, "in some very strange way nature has re-asserted itself contrary to all medical expectation", which in other words means a successful spirit healing.

When a healer learns that a patient with cancer symptoms has not consulted a doctor, the healer should advise the patient to do so. Some women with breast "lumps" refuse to see a doctor for they know the usual procedure is for him to send them to hospital where surgery or deep radiation, or both, follow on. It is therefore for the healer's protection that he advises any patient with suspected cancer to obtain a medical **opinion**. Whether the patient accepts the healer's advice is his (or her) responsibility, just as it is the patient's responsibility whether or not to heed his doctor's advice.

When the presence of a tumour can be felt with the healer's fingers, then, in attunement with Spirit, the healer should place his fingers over the growth and direct the intention from his mind for the ill-condition to be dispersed. It is a common experience for healers to feel the hard consistency of a tumour softening and lessening in size. With a small growth, its complete dispersal is often seen.

Unfortunately, it often happens that the aid of the healer is sought when the disease has become chronic, with the doctors having stated that the patient's passing will shortly take place, so the percentage of success in these cases is smaller; but what invariably happens is that the patient receives a sense of fortitude, an inner peace, restful sleep, and absence of acute stress, and so his passing into spirit life takes place gently and peacefully. The healing may be said to have failed but the help so given is worth more than any words can tell.

Through observations of many cases it is clear that there are different ways in which the healing guides are able to disperse growths.

In the case of a growth situated in the bowels, it has repeatedly been found that, after spirit healing has been invoked, there is a most unusual heavy rectal discharge, of such a character that it cannot be mistaken for an ordinary motion. Whenever this has occurred, an immediate betterment has followed, even with patients whom the doctors have given only a few days to live. The obvious inference is that by some unknown means the healing guides have been able to dissociate the growth and expel it from the body. Sometimes the growth can be felt by the healer's fingers during Contact Healing, and invariably it is found that it begins to lose its "moorings", becoming emulsified and soft around the edges.

After healing has begun for growths, the patient often experiences excessive perspiration which is a sign of dispersal taking place. This comes from under the arms, in the groin, and particularly from the hands and feet and sometimes this perspiration is so profuse that the part where it discharges becomes very sore. This excessive perspiration sometimes lasts for a number of days, but generally when it ceases the growth has disappeared.

There is an abundance of evidence, fully supported by psychic science, to show that the spirit operators are able to employ forces to change the state of matter. This is seen in the phenomenal act of apporting objects. When this takes place, the object is changed from its physical condition into another state that is superior to the physical laws. In the act of apporting, the object is brought in an instant from a far place; it is not affected by friction or the physical law of heat; it is passed through solid walls and re-formed in its original physical state in the seance room.

As this is performed with one form of matter, so it can be with another, such as living tissue, and it has even been established beyond any doubt that live birds and fishes have been so apported. Therefore, prima facie evidence exists that organic matter can be also changed in this way, and it is important to bear this in mind as we consider the dispersal of growths.

The healing of growths has been found to be equally successful with both Absent and Contact Healing. In Contact Healing, the healer will blend himself, as one, with the patient. He will place his hand over the area where the growth is and he will feel that his hand is "welded" to the patient, as if it is part of him. The directive in his mind will be for that of "dispersal", with his fingers moving gently and "erasingly" over the growth. This directive for dispersal should be gently maintained and there is no need for the healer to lose time or break off contact by "throwing-off" passes.

It may be that a number of healings will be required, but after each there should be seen some sign of the growth diminishing or getting softer. There may be fluctuations in the size of the growth during the period of healing, but this need not deter the healer, who should continue his help for the patient, having every confidence in the outcome.

Sometimes when a growth is situated in the chest, throat and abdomen, the patient has afterwards been known to vomit a mass of foreign matter, and when this occurs it is a good sign that dispersal is taking place.

Because internal growths are difficult to "feel", it is

not easy to ascertain, after a treatment, whether improvement has taken place or not. When, however, a patient loses the symptoms of discomfort, pain ceases, flatulence subsides and weight is increased, the signs are that a healing is taking place.

In cases where a discharge occurs as has been described, or there is a clearing away of stressful symptoms, no harm can arise if the healer recommends that the patient has a further medical examination, should there be any question of the patient being faced with an operation.

There are, perhaps, few other diseases where the doctors have had to change their diagnoses more often than with patients said to be suffering from cancer and who have benefited by spirit healing. The doctors have been unable to understand why the patient's condition has undergone such a major change for the better.

Unfortunately, the help of the healer is often called in too late for a healing to take place, especially in cases where the patient has been opened up and found to have an "inoperable cancer"; or when the disease is so far advanced that the medical opinion is that the patient has only a few days to live. Even with these extreme cases, restorations have been seen, but not so often as with growths in their earlier stages.

The healer will often meet this difficulty with advanced conditions for which he has been asked to intercede. The doctor has made up his mind that the patient must die, and has started the dosage of morphine or some other powerful drug. I have known a doctor to say under these circumstances: "The patient has got to die anyway, so why not from morphine poisoning as from cancer?" In a case like this, even if it would have been possible for spirit healing to effect a recovery, the continual dosage of poison would not only prevent the healing but triumph in the end. The drug is used to give easement from pain,

HEALING IN PUBLIC

The scene at The Royal Albert Hall in London in May 1973 when Harry Edwards, then at the age of 80, gave one of the greatest public healing demonstrations of his career before a capacity audience of 5,500 people.

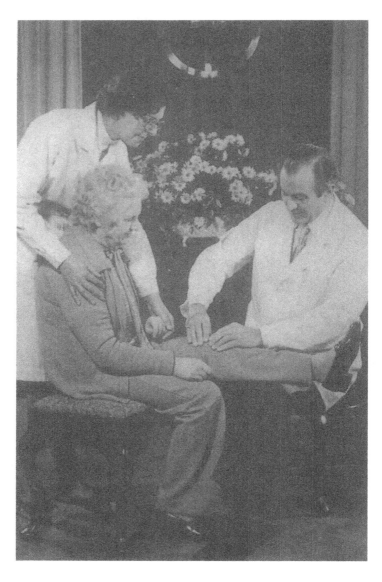

Ray and Joan Branch seek to restore
movement to a locked knee joint.

but when, following spirit healing treatment, it is seen that the patient no longer suffers from pain, then it can reasonably be suggested either by the patient or his relatives that the drug be discontinued and so give the healing its chance.

In my experience, cysts and fatty tumours are conditions that generally yield only gradually for there is not that more rapid dispersal as is seen with goitres and cancers. Therefore, patience is again needed, both by the patient as well as the healer.

The most common form of dispersal of a growth is through blood clearance and perspiration, as well as excretion. The patient should be impressed to follow all the elementary laws of health, bowel freedom, cleanliness, hot baths, and so forth, to aid the blood and excretory systems to discharge the extra duties they are called upon to bear.

Chapter 13

THE HANDS OF A HEALER

Remembering that the healer's hands possess no healing qualities of themselves, apart from soothing away a headache or a troubled area where there is pain, we use our hands as part of our minds to express the healing intention.

For example, if a patient has pain and we seek easement for this, then our hands will move in such a way as if to soothe it away, the hands thus expressing the healing intention. If we touch a lovely piece of wood carving or a piece of soft material, we use the sense of touch through our fingers to convey to the mind our appreciation of the beauty of the handicraft and the texture, etc. We love to feel the hands of our dear ones, or to touch the face as an act of endearment, showing that our hands possess a sensitivity that is very intimately associated with our emotional processes.

Thus, as the hands with all their sensitivity are aids to mental appreciation, so they are indeed servants of the mind, and in healing they become extensions of the mind—as if our brains are in our fingers. It is difficult to imagine any other activity where the intimacy between the hand and the mind is stronger than in healing.

In considering these things, it is fundamental to remember that it is not the mind or the hands that heal. Every healing is an individually planned act, needing the intelligent application of a particular corrective healing force to master a given ill-condition. The human mind does not possess, nor has it ever possessed, the knowledge to administer these forces; and as the hands are used as an expression of the mind intention, they cannot heal either. Yet the mind plays the vital part in the healing, in so far that it is through this and the spirit-self of the healer that the aid of the spirit doctors is summoned, and information given.

When a healer seeks healing for a patient, his hands naturally become a part of the healing intention to soothe away pain and to make contact with the patient, so that the healing forces may be directed to that part of the body where the affliction lies.

In the previous chapters it has been indicated how the hands are employed to assist the patient to appreciate the change for the better which the healing has been able to induce, such as showing the patient that his spine or neck is no longer set and stiff; or the joints having been given freedom of movement from arthritis; or the return of movement becoming possible through streng-thened co-ordination as with the healing of paralysis.

There is, however, the greater range of human mala-dies when such an aid to the patient is not possible, such as with the healing of the senses or of mind stresses like migraine or insomnia; and so in the treatment of the diseases which follow a different attitude on the healer's part becomes necessary.

Basically, all the healer has to seek—in a state of attunement—is for the affliction, whatever it may be, to be mastered and overcome. For example, with the heal-ing of a stiff spine, the healing itself takes place in a very short period of time and it is after that the healer seeks to ascertain the extent of progress made by checking the degree of freedom which has been achieved.

So, when we come to the healing of internal disorders,

functional troubles, growths, insomnia, and so on, the healer will expect the healing to be as effective as can be at the time. If the trouble should be a growth such as a goitre which can be felt by the fingers, the healer will place his fingers gently over it, and as he looks for the healing doctors to bring about its dispersal, so the fingers can gently move the mass of the growth with the intention of softening, and dispersing it.

The healer, in attunement, blends in with the patient and his thought directive is for the trouble to be taken away, and he anticipates that an improvement will take place.

If it should be that the patient cannot report any improvement, the healer has to accept that it is of no purpose for him to try further, for if the spirit doctors do not succeed in getting an improvement to satisfy the patient's and the healer's wishes, the healer will not be likely to succeed. In these circumstances, the healer should not blame himself, the patient, or the guide, but be content for the present and look for benefit on the next occasion or through the healer's Absent Healing intercession, which becomes more favourable because of the closer union established through Contact Healing. The healer should bear in mind that it may take some preparation and time for the cause of the patient's malady to be mastered before the symptoms can yield. Healing can only take place within the scope of the laws of creation which govern us from our birth to our passing.

Chapter 14

SPIRITUAL HEALING AND THE LAW

In the United Kingdom, spiritual healers have almost full freedom to practise spirit healing and it is quite lawful to do so. This privilege also extends throughout the Commonwealth, Canada and New Zealand having been given charters authorising spiritual healing. However, it is not permitted in most European and other countries or in certain states in America.

Any person is at liberty to call himself, or herself, a Spiritual Healer, a Divine Healer, a Psychic Healer, or any other similar title. The healer can set up his clinic in any house without the need for a licence but he may be subject to local bye-laws. Nearby residents have the right to complain about any noise, even including the singing of hymns. There may also be some reservation that no "business" may be conducted on the premises. If the healing is conducted privately and by invitation, then it may not be considered a "business", in which event there should be **no public advertising**.

General advertising is permitted, but to avoid the implication that it is a "business" no costs of treatment should be mentioned, indeed it is far the best thing to state: "No fees are charged".

Healing does not include professional massage treatment, as for this a local authority licence is required.

The following is an official notice issued by the National Federation of Spiritual Healers which recommends certain safeguards regarding the healing of children and animals, as well as conduct which would be an offence under the various Acts of Parliament.

All spiritual healers should know the dangers whereby they may infringe the law. Also patients should know these limitations so that they will not expect healers to do what they should not do.

The legal advisers to the National Federation of Spiritual Healers state that there are a number of dangers which can be divided into those matters which are regarded as being of major importance, and those matters which will have a somewhat limited application and which in practice may not present quite the same dangers.

It is desirable that as far as practically possible the healer should work in close conjunction with the medical profession. In the following two matters great care is needed.

The First Group

1. *Children.* A parent or guardian who fails to provide adequate medical aid for a child under 16 commits a criminal offence. Spiritual healing is not medical aid as known to the law and a healer who treats a child whose parent refuses the orthodox medical aid runs the risk of being considered an aider and abettor to that offence.

Where it is known that the parents are NOT receiving medical attention for their child, healers are most strongly advised to secure the signature of the parent to a statement in the form set out below BEFORE treating or continuing to treat the child:

"Mr. . . . . has warned me that I ought to call in the doctor to see my child."

2. *Animals.* The rendering in an emergency of first aid

for the purpose of saving life or relieving pain is always permissible as of course is prayer and the laying-on of hands.

What constitutes an emergency must be a question for the judgment of the individual healer.

Apart from that, however, it is an offence for a person not qualified as a veterinary surgeon to practise as such, and this includes both diagnosis of ailments and advice as to medicine.

The Second Group

If healers fail to comply with any of the matters set out hereunder, they may, and probably will, be guilty of a breach of law which could result in a prosecution. In case of doubt the healer should present the detailed facts to the Secretary of the National Federation of Spiritual Healers for consideration and advice.

1. Do not practise dentistry (treatment, advice and operation on teeth).
2. Do not treat venereal disease.
3. Do not attend women in actual childbirth or within 10 days thereafter unless in an emergency.
4. Do not sell herbal medicines without checking that it is legally permissible.
5. Do not treat animals by physical as opposed to spiritual remedies.
6. Do not publish any advertisement that specifies healing for any particular disease.

NOTE:

All the observations in this chapter constitute a general guide only to the law as it applies to spiritual healers.

All practising healers are advised to obtain

a copy of the National Federation of Spiritual Healers "Members' Code of Conduct" which sets out in detail under the section 'Healing and The Law' specific requirements to be observed by healers practising in the United Kingdom. The N.F.S.H. "Members' Code of Conduct" is basically the same as that issued by The Confederation of Healing Organisations.

SECTION IV

THE SCIENCE OF SPIRIT HEALING

Chapter 1

INTRODUCTION

This Section is intended for study and discussion. It does not claim to establish any new truth. It is hoped the chain of reasoning and logic will allow of conclusions which will bring our understanding of the science of spirit healing within the classification of "The Theory of Accepted Probabilities".

The purpose of this first chapter is to study the character and composition of the "healing energies"; how they are formed and manipulated; how they are transformed from one state to another; their direction by the healers in Spirit and use by our bodily intelligences; the hereditary factor and the maintenance of health and purpose in the life of the individual cells.

This section is not for the scientist who may not be willing to look in a different direction to that in which his microscope directs him, but it does take advantage of his discoveries and it is intended to assist the spiritual healer who wishes to become a more intelligent instrument of the Spirit, thus co-operating more consciously with the healing intention.

In the past, the conception of what spiritual healing

is has been nebulous. Healing has been credited to some abstract power wielded by God or the spirit healing guide. There has been talk of "split auras", "etheric bodies", "vibrations", of "rays"—sometimes blue, golden, grey or other colours—being directed on to the patient's body through the fingers of the healer to ease some specified malady.

Some of these explanations and instructions have come from revered healing guides, but we should realise how handicapped they have been through being unable to convey thought pictures to human minds incapable of comprehending a more technical explanation. Such a situation would arise with a scientist trying to explain to an aborigine how a television receiver works; he would have to be content with using his hands to convey the idea of "pictures coming over the air".

Different aspects of our study will need to be sectionalised and treated independently from each other though they are all part of the total healing picture, and at the end of this section I have endeavoured to bring them together to form a complete picture.

While it may be said that the conclusions cannot be proven as factual they come within the "Theory of Probabilities" resting on logical deductions arising from known facts, and should stand until disproved, or give way to an alternative reasoned thesis.

Reference will be made to certain scientifically established data, such as in the characterised construction of molecules, but it is NOT necessary for the healer to become conversant with such detail. The references are given to provide the healer with a glimpse of the character and nature of the energy formations which come into operation during the healing process.

In order to approach an appreciation of how spiritual healing manifests, and for the reason that we can only appreciate things in the physical realm in which we live, we need to work backwards. There is no disputing symptoms of many of our diseases, e.g. joint distortion through arthritis, pathological evidence of the presence of malignancy, the deficiency in the blood content of the leukaemia patient, cataract, and so on. There is positive proof of their existence, and with "incurable" conditions there is no known human treatment to overcome them. It is when spiritual healing comes into the picture that a change takes place: the swollen, distorted arthritic joint loses its ill-effects, and the joint is free to move; the blood content of a leukaemia patient becomes normal; the hard, malignant swelling becomes softer and gradually disperses and so on. It is unexpected changes of this nature which are summed up in the admission by the British Medical Association with the words "recoveries take place which cannot be accounted for by medical science".

So in this Section we shall ask by what means the changes take place. We know that nothing takes place by chance, and for every change there is a reasoned law-governed cause. We shall look to see how states of matter can be changed and from this build up a Theory of Probabilities.

Leaving infectious diseases on one side for the time being, it can be said that physical diseases have as a common denominator an injurious chemical state which interferes with healthy bodily functions. This can be easily seen with arthritis, diabetes, stones, liver and kidney upsets and indeed throughout the catalogue of diseases right down, say, to fungoid finger nails.

Let us recall the postulates which govern all spirit healing. These have been established in Sections I and II. These are:

"Consequent on the emission of a thought appeal by a human mind in attunement with a spirit intelligence, the spirit intelligence is able to receive the request, form a diagnosis, and administer the correct quality of characterised energy to bring about the law-governed changes necessary to overcome the particular disharmony in the mind or body of the patient."

Chapter 2

HEALING ENERGIES

The Atom

We start with "energy". Everything which exists is energy in a characterised form. Every material thing is composed of atoms—the chair you are sitting on, the paper on which these words are printed, and so on. Every atom is ordered energy. The whole of our universe is a state of energy: the sun and the light and heat it gives off is all energy; also the stars and the light from them—all is a form of ordered energy.

Energy is the basic material of all creation and for the reason that healings take place through spirit agencies it follows that energy is common to spirit life, too. It is said that energy (or ether) is the clay and stone of spirit life as it surely is of ours.

Energy enters into an ordered form with the atom. Every atom, which is far too small to be seen with our most powerful microscope, has precise order, function and purpose. The simplest atom is that of hydrogen; it has a central nucleus and a single electron which rotates around it at amazing speed. If a hydrogen atom could be enlarged to the size of St. Paul's Cathedral, the nucleus suspended in the centre of it would be no larger than a football; and the electron which races around it, no larger than a golf ball.

Every element has its determined number of electrons which rotate round the nucleus, varying in number from one to several hundreds. We can think of an atom as a tiny solar system with electrons (the planets) travelling around a nucleus (the sun) in determined orbits.

Formation of Molecules

When two or more elemental atoms are placed together they form a molecule. By associating atoms together so a compound material is formed. The simplest example is the amalgamation of two hydrogen atoms with one oxygen atom to form water, chemically expressed as H_2O. Science is based upon the association of atoms with other atoms forming composite molecules and studying their behaviour under varying conditions. It was from this study that the atom bomb was formed.

It is important for the healer to understand this, for it forms the foundation for spirit healing science as it does for human science. This will become much clearer as we go on.

Whenever we suffer from a physical affliction there is set up an injurious chemical condition; for example, the arthritic deposits which cement up a joint and cause so much pain. To overcome the trouble, a change must be induced within the injurious chemical state. The chemicals causing the trouble are, of course, molecules composed of energies which are out of harmony with the bodily functions. With every ill-condition there is a troubled state of chemical imbalance, for which there is a definite cause.

We cannot escape from responding to the law of "cause and effect". Wherever there is a cause then the effects or symptoms follow. If one goes out into the cold wind and rain without adequate protection then one can expect to contract a chill—the ill-effects following the cause. When a healing has been effected it means that the cause must first have been removed for mastery to be established over the symptoms. In most cases of physical disease this requires a chemical change to be induced at the site of the trouble, and most forms of medical treatment have this end in view.

Molecular Structures and Healing

Let us again hold in mind that every healing is a planned effort—it has direction and purpose; every state of change in the universe is law-governed; and that every achieved state of change results from intelligently applied law-governed forces and energies to the subject.

All spiritual healing must come within these precepts.

We know that by associating one form of energy with another, so a change in the energy state takes place, and it is this which forms the basis of all physical healing, medical and spirit.

Medical scientists, as a result of research and experimentation, are sometimes able to predetermine the course of a desired chemical change within a patient when a new drug is introduced. In recent times the growth of the use of antibiotics is eloquent of the advance in medical knowledge. However, it is lack of more detailed knowledge of the patient's molecular make-up which often results in adverse side-effects with one person as compared with another.

In spiritual healing, the spirit intelligence (or guide) is not only able to obtain an accurate diagnosis of the patient's illness but is able (a) to analyse the chemical substances causing the ill-condition, down to its molecular components and (b) to direct to it a spirit-generated molecular force designed to bring about the chemical change in that molecular structure for the patient's advantage.

If there is any logic or truth in this conclusion, we

arrive at a new principle in healing which transforms the old ideas of "blue" or "golden" healing rays into an acceptable and soundly reasoned aspect of spirit science.

Spirit Analysis

We may ask how it is that spirit people are able, with physical conditions, to make such a close analysis of injurious molecular structures. Reference has already been made to energy being composed of polarised forces, positive and negative, i.e., neutrons and electrons, being the "clay and stone" of the spirit people. It follows that when they are able to effect healings after medical science can do no more, their knowledge of the manipulation of energies must be profound.

After all, when dealing with matter, the number of elemental atoms is limited, so that which appears to us to be an intricate problem in assessing the composition of energies in any given molecular structure may be far more simple to those possessed of advanced wisdom in the science of energy. Let us remember that human scientists can set out on a blackboard all the atomic components of a very complex molecule. They can also set out the components of other structures in the same family of molecules, so that they know the manner in which different energy components can merge with, overcome, or disperse, components in a given molecule. This is what spiritual healing accomplishes.

In order that a wider view of structures can be visualised, we can go from the simplest molecule which produces water to more complicated ones, such as in the diagram of a simple sugar molecule, see Fig. A opposite page 223.

Figure B shows a diagram of an intricate structure of molecules which builds up the substance of a chromosome. It is thought that there are twin strands spirally

HARRY EDWARDS

A
A simple sugar molecule
made by a plant

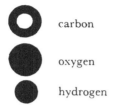

carbon

oxygen

hydrogen

B
Structure of the DNA molecule
Two strands made of
sugar and phosphate
groups wind around one
another. The strands are
joined horizontally by
groups called bases

twisted together and pinned horizontally by other groups which unwind and separate into two parts when a cell reproduces itself, thus maintaining its hereditary characteristics. This exceedingly complicated structure of energies is now termed nucleic acid, and one of the groups composing it is the "sugar deoxyribose", so this molecule is called DNA for deoxyribonucleic acid.

It will interest the student to know that it is these DNA molecules which make us the creatures we are through the control of the chromosomes and the genes. They guide cellular growth and character, cell by cell. If we proceed one stage further we find these DNA molecules serve as patterns for shaping molecules of another kind of nucleic acid called RNA and from this the RNA molecules serve as patterns for the making of protein which is the food of the cells. The picture after this becomes too complicated to elaborate further in a work of this kind, but shows us in clearer detail the wonder of our bodies and how they function.

The healer is NOT required to make a study of the science of these structures, for this is not necessary. This brief allusion to the DNA molecule gives just a glimpse into the complexities of atomic energies and molecular structures and groupings which have to be taken into account by our spirit doctors in treating disease.

If the author may be allowed a prophecy, it is that the story of the DNA molecule is only beginning and the components of the thousands of genes contained within the chromosomes have yet to be found, and when they are, it will be seen that spirit thought influences are contributory factors in the character composition of those genes that have to do with the emotional and spiritual qualities, contributing to the total make-up of an individual.

Changing the State of Matter

It is worth remembering in our study of energies how, through physical mediumship, the phenomenon of apporting takes place. Apporting means the bringing of a solid object from a distance to a given place without physical means. An example of this took place when I was attending a sitting with Jack Webber, an exceptionally gifted physical medium. In the dim red light of the seance room a trumpet was taken up near to the ceiling where it rotated at an exceedingly fast speed; gradually, my friends and I heard a knocking sound from within the trumpet and following this it tipped an object into my hands. This was an ancient Egyptian amulet, which expert investigation proved to be 3,500 years old. Where it had come from is not known, but as with other apports it can be safely assumed it came from a distant place. The act of apporting was photographed at another Webber seance*. The objects apported were brought at terrific speed from where they had been to the seance room and must have been rendered impervious to the friction of travelling through the atmosphere at that speed; and furthermore to have been in a state where they could pass through physical material, such as walls, etc. All the time the objects being conveyed had to retain their identity and shape. There does not seem any reasonable alternative to the theory that such objects were rendered into a higher vibration of energy which, while retaining their identity, became superior to the physical laws of friction and substance. On the occasion referred to above, the process of slowing down the energy vibrations of the amulet took place gradually until it resumed its original state.

This is further evidence of the power of Spirit to

* See *The Mediumship of Jack Webber* by Harry Edwards.

manipulate energies and provide an explanation for the instantaneous removal of a growth. The doctors call it "spontaneous healing", and such occurrences are recognised as medically factual. It follows that if the spirit people can so manipulate energies, then it is also within their ability to dissociate a growth from the body and, by accelerating the energy vibration of its molecular structure, thus remove it from the patient's body.

Healing Energy in Action

It is now the purpose to see what happens through healing when a chemical change is needed to overcome a disability. Perhaps the most simple example is the unlocking of a joint cemented up with arthritis. Let us first appreciate the situation and then apply the conclusions we have so far reached.

To keep the picture simple, we shall consider the stage when the bloodstream, having deposited waste from the cells around and within the joint, has caused the latter to become hard and fixed. In other words, the joint has more or less become cemented up so that it cannot move, or move only slightly. Medically, this creates a totally incurable condition.

When healing enters into the picture, movement is restored to the joint, either instantaneously or over a period of time. In public healing demonstrations instantaneous healing of chronic arthritic conditions has often been witnessed. For this to happen, it must mean that the cementing substances have been removed. When the healing is progressive then it indicates the substance is being changed gradually. What is certain is that a **chemical change** has been induced within the affected joint, removing the arthritic deposits.

What implications arise from this? First the joint has been freed from the adhesions. With a chronic condition of long standing, the arthritis has spread into the surrounding tissues, impoverishing and contracting the ligaments so much that, even if the joint were freed, the limb movements would be very restricted, because the ligaments have lost their elasticity and most likely have contracted into "knots". Therefore the arthritic adhesions have to be dispersed for the whole of the affected area. Another fact must be remembered, that the act of dispersal must take place in a fraction of time. Time taken, for instance, in getting an arm to move freely is not an act of healing, but simply the time needed to encourage the joint to move after having been immovable for so long. A parallel is that when a metal hinge has been rusted up and is treated with lubricating oil, it takes a little movement and time to get it working as freely as it should.

For such a mass of hardened matter to be so dispersed in a fraction of time, indicates that the chemical change in the substance must have been complete and instantaneous.

Arthritic adhesions are chemical in substance and to change the nature of this substance is the healing purpose. If changes must follow the application of law-governed forces, then the healing must provide those forces to induce the change. These forces are the spirit-created energies composing the molecular structures which, when they come within the association of the arthritic molecules, induce a change of state, which either disperses them or enables the bodily properties to assimilate or evacuate them.

The main arthritic substance is calcium carbonate. It is a simple molecule, $CaCO_3$, i.e. one atom of calcium, one of carbon and three of oxygen. The simplicity of these components renders it an easy subject for chemical change. When the force of heat is applied to it, it changes formation. In the next chapter dealing with the healing intelligences, reference is made to the quality of heat transferred from healer to patient, and it is suggested that this spirit heat (of which we are physically conscious) is a means of bringing about the chemical change to convert the calcium carbonate into another form.

There are other ways to change the chemical state of calcium carbonate, but the above illustration should suffice to explain how a chemical change in the state of matter can be induced.

Origin of Spirit Healing Energies

There are two questions which spring readily to mind and are worth analysing:—

(i) How do the spirit doctors produce the particular energies to create a dispersing force?

(ii) How does this reach the affected part of the patient?

We do not know the factual answers, but we can assume certain possibilities.

Man is now able to split the atom, as we know through the exploding of the atomic bomb. By subjecting an atom to very great heat, it causes it to break up, releasing the vast store of energy within it which, in its turn, creates a chain reaction with other atoms. This means that the energy agents, the nucleus and the electron, are returned to the primal source of all energy, or ether.

We know that when man splits the atom he requires an array of powerful apparatus to accomplish the act. If, therefore, he has to employ such crude means to do this, then surely we can give credit to the spirit intelligences to do the same, yet far more simply? Man directs the force energy of heat to overcome the force energy which holds an atom together; in spiritual healing, the spirit doctor, through his knowledge of spirit science, simply directs a counter energy to achieve the same result.

In our hospitals, doctors employ deep-ray therapies in treating carcinoma, the intention being to burn up the cancer cells, and they claim a measure of success with this. In spirit healing we have seen the entire mass of cancer cells, not only the primary mass, but infiltrations, too, disappear—sometimes instantaneously—which implies that the chemical composition of the cells has been so drastically altered that it is no longer physically traceable. We shall be dealing with this more extensively in the coming chapters.

Returning to the arthritic shoulder, the cementing adhesions are largely calcium carbonate, so as the spirit doctor directs to the molecular structure an energy or force which is able to break up the molecules, not only in the joint itself, but also in the tissues and ligaments, so the tissues become free and the ligaments are able to function again. While this may give a general picture of the healing process, it is by no means as simple as this.

Firstly, if the dispersing force dealt only with the calcium carbonate then it would still leave any other harmful components to cause trouble later. This implies that a spirit doctor is able to appreciate the nature of the **total** molecular structures, in order that the dispersing energies he directs will be able to disperse or change all the other harmful chemical structures at the same time. Secondly, the dispersing energies must be applied with great care and discrimination, for otherwise the dispersing energy for calcium carbonate would not only break up the molecules in the arthritic calcium carbonate but in the natural healthy calcium carbonate content in the bones as well.

Whilst medical science achieves its results through the use of massive technical apparatus, spirit science operates in a far easier way by the application of what we call "Thought Energy".

Thought Energy

As all things within creation are forms of energy, then thought is an energy, too. Through thought we have the ability of making assessments and arriving at conclusions based on known facts. We can find answers to problems which were not hitherto known.

Just as every variation of sound and every form and facet of light in all its colours possesses a particular form of energy, i.e. recorded music and colour television, so a particular thought does so as well. If a dozen people of different nationalities and language were to think of a cedar-wood black lead pencil, the thought picture registered on the consciousness would be the same. The word to name the pencil would be a different one, but the thought energy would be of the same construction and vibration.

Similarly, when a healer conveys to a spirit doctor the complaint of, shall we say, arthritis, there is a positive form of thought energy which is received and interpreted by the healers in Spirit as "arthritis".

We referred earlier to energy (or ether) being the "clay and stone" of the spirit people. It is suggested they employ their thought forces to manipulate and use structural energies for their purposes in spirit life.

We have to obtain all the materials that we need from the earth. We have to dig for the clay and quarry for the stone. No one would suggest the spirit people need to do the same . . . it is surely more probable to conceive them directing through their knowledge creative thought energies to manipulate the primal etheric energies into particularised substances they require for their needs.

If this reasoning is tenable, then if follows that the spirit doctors, having observed the nature and composition of the ill-condition within the patient are able, through their wisdom, to form a correct amalgamation of spirit elemental energies to effect the necessary chemical change in the patient's ill-condition.

Like will yield to like; and the chemical formula is so delicate and balanced, that if it be its purpose, for instance, to disperse calcium carbonate molecules in an arthritic deposit, it will do that **and nothing more**. No harm will come to any other character of molecules in the healthy bone.

Thought transference is now generally accepted as factual, and for thoughts to be conveyed they must have some established form. **All spiritual healing is a thought process,** and this specially applies to Absent Healing in which the healer conveys a thought request to heal a disharmony, this request being received by the spirit guide. The guide contacting the patient is able to study his healing needs, diagnose the trouble, and then determine the character of the healing treatment. All this is done by a thought process which must be based upon some kind of appreciation or measurement which is the purposeful direction of characterised spirit energies.

It is suggested that wherever "things" or "matter" is concerned, then most often they can be "pictured" like our earlier example of the black lead pencil. However, if we think of a silver propelling pencil, instead of the wooden one, then at once the brain computer will give to our conscious mind a picture of this new image — a picture which would be instantly recognised by an attuned spirit mind; and as we have already seen that thought itself is a form of energy, then it follows that the picture is transferred from one visual image to another by a characterised form of frequency, vibration or energy.

By way of further comparison, let us consider television. A picture of the subject in the television studio is transformed into a series of precise energies, which travel, maintaining their formation, to satellites in space, to be reflected and received back in another country on the other side of the world in perfect and precise detail and colour to be seen on television screens, where it can be studied, valued, criticised and appreciated.

With healing the process is far more simple. We have the healer's mind transmitting the thought request to be instantly received by an attuned spirit mind, which then, in various ways, is able to assess the situation, establish where the cause of the upset lies, and analyse the symptoms; and from this to direct to the patient the remedial energies to overcome the cause and master the symptoms.

It is accepted that the primary causation of the greater percentage of physical diseases lies in some form of mental disharmony, frustration, or soul (spirit) sickness. No healing can be effective unless the cause of the sickness has been removed. Thus, when the spirit doctor enters into affinity with the patient, he is able through the patient's spirit-self to observe the emanation of discordant energies which reveal the nature of the symptoms and the cause of the sickness. In order to soothe and pacify any disharmony within the patient's mind, corrective thought energies are directed to the patient, and providing that these can gain access to the patient's conscious mind then a more contented outlook comes to him—the cause of the illness is overcome, and the removal of the symptoms then becomes an easy task.

It is understood that if the patient's mind is so obsessed with the nature of his trouble, real or fancied, and that this totally dominates his mind and being, then it may not be possible at that stage for the correcting influences to be received by the consciousness, and the healing purpose has to continue until an opportunity occurs to permit an entry. Even then it may be ignored, but more often than not, it is accepted and acted upon.

Nutrient Energies

Chapter 4 devoted to "The Cell" should be read in conjunction with this section.

The use of healing energies is to effect a state of change to the patient's advantage, but there are different ways of doing this. So far we have been studying those which promote the dispersal of an ill-condition through a chemical change, but we now turn our attention to another wide avenue of healing in which supporting, sustaining and re-building energies are given.

As we used the subject of arthritis to explain the healing processes in the first part, so we shall use "pernicious anaemia" and "malnutrition" in this next section. Pernicious anaemia is mainly caused by lack of proper nutrients in diet or the inability of the digestive system to take advantage of them. The red blood cells are ill-affected and they become unable to transport oxygen to the other cells of the body, resulting in physical debility, lack of strength and vitality, fatigue and instability of function. Sometimes the nutrients are not produced.

The red cells of the blood are mainly composed of a protein called globin and an iron-containing pigment called haemin, and in anaemia, as well as in a number of other deficiency sicknesses, there is a marked deficiency of haemoglobin in the blood.

Cells are nourished by protein, and this is a very involved process but it is helpful to have a general picture in order to appreciate how the healing deals with the situation.

It is believed that DNA molecules provide patterns for shaping molecules of another kind of nucleic acid called RNA molecules, which in turn provide patterns for the making of protein.

Each kind of protein molecule must be built according to a plan, for it is a very complicated chain of energies having hundreds or even thousands of amino acid groups linked in a precise order. This is to provide the right nutrient for the individual cell according to its nature and purpose.

So it follows that if the body metabolism is unable to supply the full and complete requirements the body needs for the nourishment of its cells, then anaemia follows.

The amino acids are, of course, formulated energies in molecule groups. So when cells are suffering from malnutrition or starvation, because they are not being fed with their particular nutrient, the spirit intelligences observe the deficiency and supply to the cells just the protein molecules the cells need.

When healers recall the many cases of recovery from functional disease which take place daily through spirit healing, the restoration of strength and vitality, the building up of tissue, and the return of proper function, as well as the overcoming of blood diseases and weaknesses (often said to be medically incurable), then there must be a process by which these recoveries take place. One needs to get to the origin of the trouble, but if it cannot be dealt with by overcoming the primary cause, then the second task of healing is to master the ill-effects.

We can again remind ourselves that if our scientists are able to differentiate between the structures of the many amino acid molecules, then surely the spirit guides with their greater knowledge can do so, too.

In healing there are no set rules. The guides are able

to use whatever method is best, and this will be illustrated by the study of the causes of anaemia, where the process of metabolism has become erratic, causing a lack of balance within the body chemistry leading to cellular starvation. By correcting this imbalance and so restoring normal metabolism again, so spiritual healing overcomes the effects of cellular starvation, or anaemia.

Let us briefly look at the digestive process so that we have a clear picture of it. After food enters the stomach it is churned, and at the same time receives a chemical action of enzymes and acids, breaking it down into nutrient molecules. In this way, the food is transformed into a thick fluid called chyme. Entering into the intestine, the chyme comes into contact with its walls which are lined with millions of small projections called villi which telescope in and out and so push the nutrients into the circulatory system. It is here that the nutrients and complex carbohydrates are changed into simple sugar molecules, protein molecules, and then broken into their constituent amino acid components. In these digested forms the nutrients are small enough to pass through the villi cell walls.

Although this is only the beginning of the story, it will suffice for our purpose. It is when there is obstruction or non-fulfilment of these digestive processes that trouble commences.

If the breaking down of the nutrients into the amino acids is impaired by a lack of converting fluids, then this deficiency is made up by the guides who, through their intimate knowledge of chemistry of the human body, are able to direct the desired characterised energies where they are needed, and so restore chemical balance. Again, if the villi are not functioning through some lack of energy then "stimulating energies" are given.

In this way we can begin to understand the means by which healing is often able to restore proper digestive

functioning and overcome long-standing painful conditions.
In cases where there is wasted muscle and tissue, often
connected with paralysis, it is observable how such
waste is repaired. The cells have not been reproducing;
they have become weak and are in a state of inertia. By
the introduction of stimulating energies and an effort to
re-awaken the cell's intelligence (see Chapter 4 on "The
Cell)," by supplying them with additional nutrients—
such as are found in invalid foods—so the cells receive
not only nourishment but a strengthening of their
directive intelligence for the body's welfare. Again, the
means by which this is done is by spirit-directed characterised energies in the form of molecular structures to
supply just that which is needed.

Direction of Healing Energies

A question remains: how do the healing energies
reach the patient and the special area where they are
needed?
Everything which originates in Spirit is Spirit—it is
not physical. Hence the healing energies created by the
spirit intelligences are, in the beginning, non-physical.
Yet there must come a time when they are converted
from their spirit formation into their physical counterpart.
It seems obvious this must happen in a condition
where there is a merging of Spirit with non-Spirit, and
this can be through the healer's spirit mind and body
attuned to Spirit. Thus in Contact Healing the healer
can be used as a transformer of those spirit energies
which are in molecular form and also in harmonious
association with the healer's spirit-self, and thus change
them into their physical counterparts; and it is through
the blending of the healer with the patient that these
energies are passed into the patient. Healers often have

the common experience of sensing this flow of spirit energy in Contact Healing.

Another explanation is that the act of conversion takes place within the spirit-self of the patient. This is the process with Absent Healing. For the patient to be able to receive from Spirit, it means that he is in a state of attunement with Spirit and so the conversion of spirit energies is a natural one.

It is appreciated that the spirit guide has diagnosed the precise area of disease, and has created the corrective energies and directs them to that particular area where they are needed, no matter how small it may be.

Molecules are too small to be seen through the microscope, yet we know much about their form and the atomic components of which they are built. It is surely tenable to think of a superior spirit intelligence being capable of manipulating etheric energies into a precise construction for associating certain molecules with other molecules for the purpose of dispersal or to change their nature; or in another instance, to give to a cell the nutrient it needs; or to the villi, the energised fluid they require to change carbohydrates into amino acids.

Stimulating Energies

There are cosmic forces which abound for our use. These pertain to the physical realm, though it is thought they are the "half-way link" between physical and spirit life.

Cosmic forces or energies are all around us. Every day, we subconsciously absorb these forces into our systems, according to our needs. It is the vital energy that a magnetic healer has in abundance and which gives him radiant health and strength (see Section II, Chapter 13).

To illustrate the presence of these forces let us study a tree. A tree does not live alone from the nourishment it takes from the earth through its roots. It absorbs from the sea of forces that eddy about it those other properties it needs for verdant foliage and vitality. Furthermore, we have certain areas where there are pine trees, for instance, that are beneficial to those suffering from tuberculosis or other respiratory diseases. Some people are able to absorb energy from trees and certain shrubs by consciously drawing this strength into themselves by breathing deeply with this intention.

After a healing session, or treating an individual patient, healers should devote a few moments to intentional characterised breathing, explained in Section III, Chapter 5, for it will overcome any sense of depletion, and will replenish the reservoirs of vital energy. It is a direct way of building up the health tone and it is good to encourage ALL patients to do this, whatever their trouble may be.

It is the **sense of knowing** that is important. With ozone we can physically sense it, but it is not possible so to sense other cosmic energies, although they are present just the same.

The Psychic Gland

Let us break off, and think of something else. Each of us possesses a ductless gland that I will call the "psychic gland".

It has its receiving terminal at the back of the nose and its main "trunk" proceeds down the spine, where it divides off into the whole of the body, in a similar way to our nerves and circulatory system. Another branch of this gland goes to the head and brain, and links up with the pineal gland and the endocrine glandular system.

It is this psychic gland which acts as the receiver and conduit for the cosmic energy. Thus we add to our knowledge of ourselves, for in addition to the nervous

and circulatory systems with their main arteries and
nerve branches with their intricate arrangement of
capillaries and nerve fibres, so this third system of the
psychic gland inter-penetrates the tissue in a similar way.
Another name for this gland could well be the "condition" gland.

Healers know how to take in their fill of cosmic
energy by characterised breathing through slow, gentle
and full inhalations, being conscious as they do this of
drawing into themselves cosmic energy and strength,
thus giving a sense of exhilaration, vitality and power,
in the same way as being conscious of absorbing vitality
when breathing in the ozone at the seaside. Upon
exhaling, so one is conscious of discharging waste and
weakness.

Healers can freely give to a sick person healthful
power from their own reservoir of cosmic energy thus
"recharging" a patient who is weak and lacking in
stamina. When healers do this, they should purposefully
replenish their natural energies through the way of
breathing referred to.

There is a reason for every state of change. Is it not a
common experience for patients, after being treated
through spiritual healing, to feel uplifted and conscious
of more strength? This is particularly so with Absent
Healing, for then we see not only physical buoyancy but
inner-upliftment as well—the two so often go together.
What happens when a person finds himself "full of life"
and brimming over with vitality? The answer is that his
reservoir of cosmic energy is full.

The spirit healing guides use these energies. They are
not built up of molecules (as far as we are aware). They
are "forces"—but forces are energies, too. The spirit
guides are able to stimulate minds, and obviously our
bodily functions, too. They can accelerate the flow of
blood to areas where there is a need for it, such as for

the dispersal of infections, or fibrositic or other deposits. We have mentioned the need for stimulation of the villi, to put more life into them to carry out their duties more efficiently. We observe stimulation given to weakened and lethargic nerves.

In the next chapter, dealing with the healing intelligences, it will be shown how healing influences can activate the bodily intelligence, so as to employ in a directive manner both cosmic and physical stimulating forces.

In considering these things we must try to avoid limiting our appreciation or comprehension of spirit healing to the operation of our physical laws alone. As this Section proceeds we shall try to enter a little way into an appreciation of the spirit laws which are intimately associated with our known laws, and upon our acceptance of this association, then a new vista of potentials comes into vision, and we can begin to see the mechanism whereby healings take place with other diseases.

The keystone on which the whole concept of spiritual healing rests is that the spirit doctors are able to make a true diagnosis of our diseases in such depth that they can accurately assess molecular structures of a harmful nature and create, through spirit science, corrective energies to induce a beneficial state of change. Every patient is individual, every disease has its individual characteristics, too, and this implies that the character and strength of the health-giving energies are individually prescribed.

How often do spiritual healers hear statements like: "the doctors have changed their diagnosis"; or "there has been a mistaken diagnosis", because the doctors have been unable to account for an unexpected recovery? Is it not now more usual to hear doctors use the term "spontaneous recovery"? This especially applies to patients diagnosed as having a malignant cancer—often pathologically proved—who, on being opened up, are declared to be cancer free and are described as another case of "spontaneous healing". This term relates, medically, to recoveries which cannot be explained by medical science.

Behind every case of spontaneous healing there must be a reasoned process to account for it. Nothing takes place by chance. There must be a law-governed process behind every state of change. Until it is disproved, we affirm that the majority of spontaneous healings result from spiritual healing.

Every healing is a planned act intelligently carried out by a non-human intelligence, so when the healing of a medically incurable disease takes place involving an organic change in the body, this can only be done by the application of correcting energies to bring about the required change; and furthermore this must be accomplished through structures of molecular energy acting upon, and changing the state of, other such structures. Thus we believe that spiritual healing is indeed a spirit science of the most advanced kind our minds can conceive.

In this book I am expressing my belief that the application of a spirit energy force can change the chemical nature of diseased organic matter, and the reaction of one form of energy with another creates a state of change. It is only a theory, but a highly probable one, for the reason that man is doing the same thing every day, as we see in our hospitals when radium or cobalt rays, laser beams etc., are directed to diseased human tissue, whereby chemical changes in the molecular structure take place, destroying the diseased cells.

Chapter 3

THE HEALING INTELLIGENCES

It is a fact that nothing takes place by chance; there is a reasoned process behind every state of change in the universe. It is the same with our bodies; there is a reason for every change, even to the winking of an eyelid. What induces a wink? It can be the subconscious action to clear the fluid lubrication; it can be the spontaneous action to protect the eyes from a strong light; it can come from instinctive fear when we are threatened, or from the noise of an explosion; it can be a purposeful wink announcing a sense of humour; it is used to convey a flirtatious invitation, "the glad eye", or it can help to provide a sense of benevolent satisfaction; demure people will lower their heads and eyelids, while those who are arrogant will keep their eyelids open in a menacing glare. Behind all these various forms of the wink is an intelligent purpose, even an instinctive one at times of fear or mishap.

In the human nervous system there are nerves which function subconsciously like those which control digestion, register touch, and so on; they do not need direct instruction to fulfil their purpose, and are not governed by the computer brain. Apart from those nerves which function automatically, there are those nerves which do not work until they receive an instruction from the brain to carry out a given task.

The purpose of this chapter is to try to establish that there are other forms of intelligence apart from the brain, and that these other intelligences have a direct bearing on healing and can be used by Spirit as well as by the conscious mind, when it knows how to do so.

Every cell in our bodies has its own separate life; it possesses a purpose and has its own intelligence which is influenced by the pituitary glandular system. The heart has its own nervous system and is responsive to mental frustrations. The principal intelligence apart from the conscious mind and brain is the "bodily intelligence".

The Healing of a Wound

The healing of a wound will illustrate how the bodily intelligence works. As soon as the wound is inflicted, an instruction goes to the heart to lower the blood pressure to minimise the bleeding. The ability of the blood to clot is accelerated. Orders proceed to the spleen to empty its reservoirs of blood into the circulation and for the speeding up of the leucocytes. At the site of the wound, the tissues are damaged, the cells, nerves and capillaries are torn apart. The wound is open to invasion by a host of disease germs. The intelligence is aware of the danger and a constant supply of leucocytes, phagocytes and macrophages is directed to the wound to devour the bacteria, to consume the dead cells and dispose of other debris. Lymph and plasma are released to keep the wound moist. Thus we see the first phase of cleansing the wound and protecting the body from infection.

Normally the blood resists clotting, but within the wound it is given the ability to clot very quickly. Another constituent of the blood is the platelets, which bridge over the surface of the wound and are directed in a continuous supply until the need is satisfied. As the platelets settle, so they create a substance called thrombin and from this comes a cottony substance called fibrin which seals off the capillaries and plugs the open ends of the lymphatic ducts and capillaries to prevent the incursion into the body of harmful bacteria.

From the capillaries, the leucocytes pour out to cleanse the wound of germs, waste and contaminants. These leucocytes are assembled in their millions, and if the wound is very severe, orders proceed to the bone marrow to speed up their production to supply a constant flow of reinforcements. There are other intricate changes which take place in the preliminary actions before the actual healing process begins.

The healing of a wound is like a campaign, requiring a commanding intelligence to organise and administer it. There is no direct contact between the wound itself and the bone marrow or with the supply of platelets. Regulation and control is essential and this is a function of the bodily intelligence. The mechanism of the brain does not possess the initiative to give the specific orders relative to the detailed needs of the wound, neither does the mind. The directing intelligences, therefore, must be a faculty apart from the brain and the mind.

All the preliminary processes to cleanse the wound and protect the body from infection proceed in an orderly manner. When the need for an excessive supply of leucocytes is over then the production of them eases, otherwise the blood content would become out of balance.

To continue the story. A new component is created from the blood on the wound site, called fibroblast. This acts as a kind of scaffolding and reinforcement. Fibroblast is a living substance, which fills in over the surface of the wound creating a patch. Very soon the patch strengthens and the fibrin trellis is no longer needed, and because there is no blood circulation in the wound, it is converted into nourishment to feed the cells.

A constant supply of material is required to carry on the healing process. These materials are obtained from other parts of the body where they can be best spared and the demand becomes a matter of priorities. Tissues are broken down and changed into amino acids and these materials are transported to the wound site, being taken from places where they can best be spared.

From whence comes this direction? Obviously not from the sufferer's mind. It must come from an inherent faculty that is knowledgeable of the body potentials in order to select those places from where muscle tissue can best be taken without weakening the resources of the body. To say that this operation is just "nature" or "instinct" is an evasion. There **must** be a knowledgeable faculty to make a correct assessment, to determine the quality and quantity of materials needed and to arrange for their transport to the wound site. Therefore, there must exist a bodily intelligence to function in this way. Finally, there is the creation of granular tissue, with the marshalling of capillaries and nerve terminals, until they are directed to meet the other terminals and join up. Muscle fibres grow, meet and are spliced together. New skin has to be formed under the scab by the skin cell elongating and stretching out until a fine covering is formed, followed by the final reinforcement of the outer skin cells until a strong enough covering is formed. So the campaign proceeds in a most orderly and intelligent way until the wound is fully healed.

All this surely represents a picture of constructive and engineering skill that dwarfs by comparison the planning and skill necessary to build a suspension bridge or a twenty-storeyed block of apartments. Such achievements need a superior mind to design and a "clerk of works" to interpret and carry out the plan. With the human body, it can surely be only the "bodily intelligence".

This proposal that we possess a bodily intelligence

apart from the brain and glandular control is significant, for it will have an important bearing on the manner in which healers will be able to co-operate with the healing intention in the future.

The Healing of Infectious Diseases

Here is another illustration. When we contract influenza or any other sickness arising from infection we discover another instance of a highly organised campaign to defeat the invading bacteria, which can be likened to the preparations necessary for the winning of a major battle in war, but with a difference. Conflict on the battlefield is one of skill and attrition and it usually ends there; but with conflict within the human body, a "peace" is ensured by establishing safeguards for the future by the building up of antibodies to act as a line of future defence against any similar incursion of the invading bacteria.

The hazards threatening our well-being are continuous. With every breath we take into our lungs, countless numbers of germs seek to establish and propagate themselves in our bodies, and if left unimpeded would bring about illness and even death. So it is with food and drink; they are subject to infection, too. As soon as an animal is killed so putrefaction commences. One of the causes of tuberculosis in humans was found to be due to infected milk, but this danger has been largely overcome through pasteurisation.

Such bacterial invasions are with us all the time and yet the vast majority of us do not succumb to disease as might be expected. It is worth some thought to appreciate why this is.

To combat the invasion of harmful bacteria there are lines of defence in depth. Behind each line is intelligent control. The leucocytes are our defenders, they attack the invaders and consume them. They are then, in turn, carried away by the phagocytes and further by the macrophages, which keep the battlefield clean and tidy. As one wave of leucocytes is fully employed, so another wave comes into the affray. Messengers have gone to the bone marrow factories to turn out more and more leucocytes to build up the reserve army of defenders and progressively they go forward into battle. The full battle scene is surveyed by the "intelligence in chief", and this directs where reserves are needed most and resolves the battle plan. It is when the defending leucocytes can be mustered in depth that a strong attack can be made to isolate groups of the enemy bacteria. Then, once this has been achieved, and the bacteria is surrounded and attacked on all sides, the end of the infection comes within sight.

By this time the leucocytes have become expert in the art of attacking that particular bacteria and this experience is not lost, for there is kept in store a supply of "specialist fighters" for attacking the same species of bacteria, should they come again, and that is why with so many an infectious disease, once it has been conquered, it never re-establishes itself again. A common example is the purpose behind vaccination against smallpox.

While the brain is the centre of a fantastic communication system and is able to give directives, it can be reasonably assumed that it is not aware when an infectious invasion takes place until the latter has established itself and commenced to create the symptoms of sickness. The defence system comes into operation immediately the invader arrives and during our lifetime this occurs scores and scores of times without our being aware of any symptoms because the leucocytes have done their good work **before** the brain has known anything of peril.

So, if the existence of a bodily intelligence is accepted, then we can go on further to see how it can be purposefully used in healing; but first let us look at the way the brain serves us.

Co-operation Between the Mind and the Bodily Intelligence

The conscious mind can be likened to a mirror on which thought pictures are received. With a wound, the injured state is reported to the brain, pain is felt, and this sensation of pain becomes a recorded experience on the conscious mind. When a musical sound reaches the ear its tonal qualities are transmitted along the auditory nerves to the brain from whence it is interpreted into a conscious mind experience. So it is that all physical experiences associated with the senses, memory, recorded information, knowledge, and motivation are acknowledged as presentations on the "mirror" and from these the mind can establish conclusions, appreciations, and subsequently motivate action.

When a wound is received, the general reactions sensed at the wound site are appreciated as an experience by the conscious mind and this will be far more vivid if the eye is able to see the wound, thus completing the mind picture. From the mind will go the instruction to the bodily intelligence to get busy. The mind will then be informed of the changes taking place, when the bleeding stops, and so on—**but these will be observable changes only.** The mind will not be conscious of the actual **process** of the leucocytes fighting and scavenging against infection. It will not determine the flow of reinforcing leucocytes summoned to the wound; neither will it control the act of bridging the wound with platelets and all the other precise organised states of change taking place in the healing.

The mind and the bodily intelligence are in

close co-operation with each other—there is the most wonderful team-work. If the mind has knowledge of the means whereby the bodily intelligence can be directed to take specific action, then it will do so. This is one of the ways in which spiritual healing intelligences can pass instructions through the patient's mind to the bodily intelligence telling it how to act.

The Organisation Behind the Healing Intelligence

The brain is a wonderful computer. Information is fed into it from countless numbers of nerves. They record every touch, every sound, and if there comes any experience which interferes with the smooth operation of our internal economy then the brain is informed of this and counter-action is commenced. The brain receives items of our knowledge and experience and is able to relate one item of information with another.

Even when everything is normal and all the body processes are carrying out their functions smoothly, the brain computer is kept informed of this. Through our senses the brain is bombarded with impressions from everything we see, touch, hear, taste or smell. Through our eyes an ever changing vista is being recorded, every moment. At the same time, if one is listening to music, scores of thousands of nerves are activated within the inner ear, receiving clearly every tone of the orchestration and conveying them to the brain, and thence to the mind, as "experiences". At the same time, the sense of touch is active; a ceaseless flow of physical impressions is transmitted to the brain; the tightness of the shoes; the touch of clothing to the skin; the pressure of those parts of the body pressing on the chair and so on. So sensitive is the touch that a tiny insect crawling along a single hair is instantly noted on the conscious mind.

Co-existent with the above, an incalculable number of messages is being continually fed into the brain, reporting the condition of each of the bodily systems and every part of the body. If there is any upset within, say, the digestion or circulation, this is reported. The brain is conscious of all bodily movements, of the heart beat, the breathing and so on, and maintains a strict supervision over them. It deals with the disposal of waste and the intake of health-giving energies. It supervises the working of the kidneys and every other organ, functional process, and the maintenance of the correct body temperatures. All this gives some idea of the fantastic communication system we possess of which the brain is the computer.

The brain is the servant of the mind, and apart from the subconscious control over the internal functioning, the brain possesses no executive ability.

All the experiences the brain records are available to the mind and the bodily intelligence which, when necessary, takes independent action. For example: if the fat deposits stored in various parts of the body are needed to supplement the fuel the body needs to consume, it is the bodily intelligence **and not the brain** which makes the decision where the fat is to be taken from and to arrange for its transportation to the digestive system. Such positive action requires direction and decision which neither the brain nor mind possesses. If we take in too much of any vitamin or if our sugar level is too high, intelligent supervision is needed to determine the amount of excess.

Bodily Intelligence Headquarters

Where there is a directing intelligence there needs to be a centre from which it operates. In considering the siting of the headquarters for the bodily intelligence there is no proven evidence where it exists, but there are conclusions worthy of consideration.

It is apparent that there is a close linking between the bodily intelligence with the physical mind, spirit mind and the brain. If this were not so, then spiritual healing could not take place. There must be a centre where thought direction is received from Spirit in order that it can be transformed into a physical experience. This centre is thought to be the pineal gland.

Not very much has been scientifically determined about its purpose or function. It is a small reddish structure situated on the upper part of the mid-brain and has been said to be the seat of the "third eye". In the past this gland has been associated with occult powers. It exerts an influence upon the spleen which is reactive to emotional stresses. It has an intimate contact with the endocrine system, the brain and the bodily intelligence and, perhaps most important, with the spirit mind, too.

The suggestion is put forward that this gland acts as the receiving centre for communication from Spirit (as with clairvoyance) and it is the centre for receiving and passing on spirit impressions and directives to the consciousness and the bodily intelligence on how to co-operate with the healing treatment.

We know that most physical diseases have their causation in psychosomatic disorders and it follows that if the pineal gland is closely associated with the spirit self, then such disharmonies are its concern and these may be the way in which mental and bodily health can be upset. Conversely, the pineal gland can provide an entry for spiritual healing to overcome sickness, restoring physical health and mind balance.

Employing the Bodily Intelligence

On the understanding that the bodily intelligence exists, we will now see how we can put the theory into practice and the suggestions which follow show some of the ways in which this can be done. At this stage of human wisdom, this approach will have to be superficial rather than detailed, for our minds do not yet possess the knowledge how, or when, to instruct the bodily intelligence to act in specialised ways; but we can apply our theory in a general way.

It follows that if we wish to "talk" to the bodily intelligence, we need to get into a state of attunement with it. We cannot expect this to be achieved in a casual manner. We shall need a little time to establish within ourselves a state of attunement with the healing purpose. We must picture in our mind what we want the bodily intelligence to do. Our conscious mind must possess specific intention to transfer our thoughts through the brain to the bodily intelligence.

Let us suppose that you, the reader, have a pain. Try to evaluate it (to attune to it) by mentally analysing it, gauging its intensity, the area affected by it and so on. In this way, the mind receives a true appreciation of it and is able to relegate its effect in relation to the total bodily condition. One of the results of this is that the pain will lose much of its intensity and importance. It becomes knowledgeably accepted.

Now seek to determine the cause of the pain. If it comes from a septic or inflamed condition, you can inwardly ask for the bodily intelligence to get busy—to energise the leucocytes to cleanse the condition and ease the pain as quickly as it can.

If there is a painful muscular sensation as with fibrositis, rheumatism, etc., follow out the same process, but with the thought directive to the bodily intelligence to overcome the cause of the pain by speeding up the circulation in the affected area with the objective of carrying away the particles which have become deposited in the tissues; and if there is allied to this effort gentle massage or the application of warmth, so with the combined effort, a speedy reduction of the stress can usually be effected.

During the healing of a patient, the healer is attuned to both the spirit doctor and the spirit-self of the patient; furthermore, the healer's spirit mind is linked with the patient's spirit mind and as the latter is intimately associated with the patient's bodily intelligence, then it is easy to understand how, through the blending of Spirit-with Spirit, the healing directive can influence the bodily intelligence of the patient.

In this way, the healer's body, mind and Spirit unite with the healing purpose, creating a state of affinity between them, through the directive of the conscious mind. This brings the patient's mental or physical disharmony into focus with the healing intention and enables the patient's bodily intelligence to be used to the fullest advantage to receive, and to put into action, any purposeful instruction from the spirit doctors and so accelerate the patient's recovery.

The healer's mind does not possess the wisdom to do this, but he can help to make conditions easier by which spirit instruction can be given and so instead of remaining a purely passive instrument of the spirit doctors, he tends to become a more co-operative attuned instrument, to be better used by Spirit.

To give a clear example of the way in which a healing intention can be employed to utilise the bodily intelligence, the following story will be of interest.

One evening, as my colleagues and I were discussing patients treated during the afternoon, we referred to a lady whose left eye-lid could not be raised, nor could the eye see, except mistily. In our conversation, it was mentioned that, 'they were the kind of eyes one could talk to'. This incident happened some years ago, but it was from this that came the beginning of an idea about the functioning of the bodily intelligence.

In the case of the lady's eye that could not open or see very well, by talking to the eye, through the patient's mind, the nerves and muscles controlling the lid received instructions and were induced into action. This was successful and the lid responded and the vision improved towards normal.

When I asked just what my colleague meant by 'the kind of eyes one could talk to' she said, "I think they had the kind of trouble that could be overcome by speaking to the eyes, through the mind, to give them encouragement and instructions on how to respond to the healing." We then realised we had been doing just that in our healing work, without realising the truth or its implications.

The story of the eye-lid can be carried further in the healing of paralysis. An appreciable measure of success is now commonly observed in treating most kinds of paralysis, such as that resulting from polio, disseminated sclerosis, strokes, etc. If it is a stroke, the directive is to restore the functional balance of the brain; with sclerosis, the origin of the trouble is often seated in the pressures on the nerves where they emanate from the spinal column. Usually the spine is very stiff or locked, it is immovable and has thickened with deposits, and fibro-sitis has entered into the adjacent tissues. The restoration of spinal mobility is usually brought about in a short time and quite painlessly (See chapter on Spinal Healing in Section III.) By removing the pressure on the nerves they have the opportunity to function again. In paralysis, the function of the nerves has become inert and so they need to be re-stimulated and encouraged to carry the messages from the brain to induce muscular movement.

The stimulation of the nerves is the responsibility of the healing guide, but the building up of the return of co-ordination can be so much helped by talking to the limbs, or in other words, the intelligence which controls movements. For example: if the leg is heavy, inert, incapable of being lifted or has but a limited response, we "talk" to the leg so that, through the mind, the message is carried down through the nerves to tell it what movement it is asked to make. A little time may be needed to allow the message, faint as it may at first be, to travel down and to sustain the intention for the movement to come. The patient is gently encouraged to move the limb as directed, assisted with the minimum of help.

In this way, perceptible progress often leads to a reasonable degree of restoration, sometimes completely. The healer needs to change the patient's outlook from one of hopelessness, of "cannot do this or that" into one of expectancy for as long as a hopeless attitude is held nothing much can be done. We need to make the patient's mental and bodily intelligence an ally of the healing intention.

Very often, with long-standing conditions the mind and body have accepted the situation that the limbs cannot function and therefore no effort is made to seek it. The bodily intelligence has also come to accept the situation, the brain being no longer instructed to seek movement, and so a state of inertia has come about. If, through spiritual healing, a happier condition can be restored, then the first effort must surely be to arouse the bodily intelligence to start working again, and the mind to send messages down the nerves to restore movement.

Harry Edwards in thoughtful mood at the end of a day's healing.

Vincent and Jean Hill carrying on the healing work at The Sanctuary.

This is what we term "talking to the patient's limbs" but actually it is the mind and the bodily intelligence to which we appeal.

There are other factors as well to be included in the healing, but the above will suffice to indicate the liaison between, on the one hand, the healer's attuned self, and on the other, the patient's physical and spirit minds, his brain, nerves, and muscles, and the bodily intelligence which is so intimately associated with the whole process.

Will-power and Faith

It is not uncommon to hear of a recovery from an "incurable" or serious condition being due to the patient's faith or self-determination and will-power. It is very true that when a sick person has indomitable faith and a strong, positive outlook, not "giving-in" and striving against weaknesses, we do see recoveries take place which cannot be accounted for medically.

That such healings do take place is beyond question, and as we know that no change ever takes place by chance and without a reason for it, there must be a planned process behind the recovery. In the past, these healings have been attributed to "will-power" and left at that. It is reasonable to ask, how will-power can be responsible for healing the causes and symptoms of disease, when medical science can do no more. It is begging the question to suggest that it is "instinct" or "just nature", or that the computer brain has planned it.

In the recovery of a condition of a purely physical nature we have seen how some form of chemical adjustment has been induced to bring about the change and furthermore that this must have been accomplished through intelligent direction and control. Neither the patient's mind nor brain has known how to achieve such a result but it is logical to assume that through the mental attitude of "no surrender" a strong stimulus has been given to the bodily intelligence to act.

Let us recall that in the healing of a wound there is direction for an increase in output of both red and white blood cells, that there is stimulation given to the blood to make certain chemical changes in the structures within the wound, and so on. Therefore it follows, that with a persistent request from the conscious mind to the brain, and from the brain to the bodily and glandular intelligences, so constant direction is given to the bodily intelligence to maintain a continuous healing endeavour in the ways that are needed. Other implications arise from this supposition.

Influencing the Patient's Bodily Intelligence

It must be admitted that the bodily intelligence has a high degree of knowledge which it can call upon in times of need, such as combating an infection. It is this knowledge which can be effectively utilised through a sustained demand from the patient's mind to organise, for example, the stimulation of the heart action, improve the circulation, regulate the temperature, increase the activity of the blood in certain areas to aid nerve centres to increase function, and so on.

However, there is ample evidence that there exists a superior intelligence behind any act of healing which is far more advanced than even the capacity of the bodily intelligence. When this superior intelligence is tuned into the patient's conscious mind it follows that it can communicate instructions to the bodily intelligence direct.

This can be understood by healers more simply when we recall that with clairvoyance, pictured impressions are transmitted from Spirit to the medium's conscious mind. In the same way, intuitive thoughts are likewise given, so it is reasonable to assume that a flow of thought from Spirit can reach the bodily intelligence of the patient through his conscious mind.

Another way in which instruction can reach the patient is via the healer, who is attuned to both the patient and the spirit doctor. By means of this attunement the healer's spirit-self and mind are very close to those of the patient and therefore the patient's conscious mind can be contacted by the healer's mind. This has two important implications.

The first is that the spirit doctor can give instruction to the patient's bodily intelligence how to proceed and deal with a disease problem, using the healer as the means of communication

The second implication is important in relation to the healing of mental conditions, for with these the patient's conscious mind is given corrective thought influences via the healer's spirit mind which is closely attuned to the spirit mind of the patient. Thus we have a situation in which the healer's own repository of knowledge and experience can be drawn upon to become an influencing agency to soothe and calm frustrations, give guidance to induce a better sense of perspective, and so help the patient regain a more contented outlook upon life.

The Heart and the Bodily Intelligence in Healing

This chapter would not be complete without some reference to the heart. The heart has a very intricately adjusted nervous system and an intelligence of its own, which is intimately associated with all other intelligences. It is responsive to emotional states and can be soothed by thought-given influences. The beating of the heart accelerates with fear and apprehension, and as fears and tensions are subdued, the heart action returns to normal.

The overcoming of these conditions can often be attained as the healer talks to the patient in a sympathetic and assured manner. The soothing of the mind and Spirit from frustrations is the primary way to overcome nervous tensions which induce palpitations. Just as the healer's comforting words will tranquillise the mind and subdue the rapid heart beating, so by talking to the mind by thought from a spirit level, it is brought into a more happy and more serene state.

The heart is very obedient to direction, as witness the betterment coming through the soothing of nervous tension. Through the affinity that is established between the healer's self and that of the patient, the remedial directive reaches the bodily intelligence to regulate the muscular action controlling the function of the heart. No word need be said—a few moments of purposeful direction is all that is needed to bring about a change in the rhythmical working of the heart valves and invariably there is a perceptible change for the better.

Other ways of improving the rhythm of the heart through characterised breathing has been dealt with in Section III. Here again, thought is the agent to encourage the body to take in refills of cosmic energy, for the patient's inner strength and well-being. It follows that where thought is received, there must be a form of intelligence to act upon it.

When a healer attunes to the patient, he may place his hand over the heart region and through his mind ask the spirit doctor to correct the irregularities and establish normal function. The act of placing the hands over the heart area is not, of itself, the means of bringing about the beneficial change of function. The hands are used to express the intention of the healing within the healer's mind; this can better be explained by the healer "feeling that his mind is in his hands and fingers".

Similar conclusions can be reached with other heart troubles and particularly with thromboses where the clotting breaks down and disperses and at the same time there is improvement in the consistency of the blood itself. The effects of phlebitis also readily yield in the same way.

Organic Diseases and the Bodily Intelligence with Observations on Cancer and Leukaemia

So far, this chapter has endeavoured to establish that we possess a number of intelligence systems each capable of independent action but at the same time combining together as a whole. (This will be more clearly shown in the next chapter dealing with The Cell.) In addition to these, there is that superior spirit intelligence which can influence and instruct the mind and body intelligences; can direct dispersive, constructive, strengthening and nutritive energies for our well-being; and finally can induce good influencing and guidance.

The healing of organic diseases takes place with the full co-operation of the bodily intelligence. The exception may be when the healing energies are able to bring about very rapid dispersal, such as with a growth or other unwanted matter; but in general, there is co-operation, and if we accept this as a fact, then it follows that the bodily intelligence is working in harmony with the healing process and can be given direction to further co-operate and implement its own inherent healing potentials.

Healers who possess knowledge of the bodily intelligence become conscious collaborators with the healing purposes. At the present time, the majority of healers tend to be passive instruments through whom the healing energies flow, but as the gift of healership improves, through more perfect attunement and that conscious reception of intuitive thought directives, so they will fulfil a more co-operative purpose in the healing act. To healers who have been able to gain considerable experience in the field of healing, the art of attunement comes easily as "second nature". With this, the ability to receive and impart intuitive thought direction from Spirit brings them into the way of becoming more conscious collaborators and thus able to influence the patient's bodily intelligence to play a more active role in the healing directive than it might otherwise do.

To explain this process let us take, as an example, a patient who has a serious growth, which may be a form of cancer. Although the healer knows that medically there is little or no hope for sufferers of these diseases, he seeks healing to reach the sick one in every way which can be. At no time does he give up hope, but whilst recognising that a healing may not be possible within the scheme of things, he maintains confidence in the power of Spirit to heal to the fullest extent. This applies to both Contact as well as Absent Healing.

In Contact Healing, the healer will place his hand over the area where the growth is located and his mental directive will be attuned to the act of dispersal. The healer is conscious of this; the patient is aware of the healing objective and thereby becomes receptive. There is unity of purpose, and if the dispersal is taking place through the gradual process of changing the atomic energies in the structure of the growth, then through the patient's conscious mind the bodily intelligence will co-operate by directing additional scavenging leucocytes and phagocytes to the area to carry away the injurious matter, which has now been changed into a new form.

We know that under the direction of the bodily intelligence, chemical changes can be induced in the body systems, so it cannot be ruled out that under the direction of the spirit intelligence, the bodily intelligence is shown the way to assist in changing the nature of the substance of the growth in order that it can be assimilated and subsequently excreted.

It is because of the untiring devotion of spiritual healers that there have been recorded many cases of cancer cures, which the doctors call "spontaneous healings". That cancers can be cured in this way is an accepted medical fact, although the doctors do not know why or how the recoveries occur.

There are now established patterns seen in the healing of both cancer and leukaemia. For example, with leukaemia, it can now be expected with the commencement of spiritual healing that a marked improvement is observed in the blood count. These improvements have been dated from the actual day when the healing intercession has commenced.

These better periods are called remissions but which the doctors invariably expect to give way to regressions within two years. **It is very important that the healing be maintained continuously to prevent regression so that if it should occur, it can be speedily overcome.**

Cases are on record of children suffering from leukaemia and doomed to die within a few weeks, but did not do so, some having lived for years. In many cases, with the continued good health of the child, the parents have ceased to bring the child to the healer, or maintain reports for the continuity of the Absent Healing. We have later heard that a child who has been doing very well, has succumbed to a fresh onset of the disease which might have been avoided had the parents maintained contact with the healer.

In treating leukaemia, medical practice and spirit healing are complementary to each other. The healer cannot give blood transfusions as the doctors can, or other treatments designed to be helpful; and the doctors cannot give that special strengthening help, the stimulating energies or instruction to the bodily intelligences, directing them how to increase the production of haemoglobin, to deliver healthy leucocytes, and maintain the vitality of the patient.

Healers will find it helpful to encourage purposeful characterised breathing for cancer and leukaemia patients in particular, as well as, of course, for sufferers from bronchial complaints, anaemia, and indeed for all other ill-conditions; but especially for cases of carcinoma in all its forms. The patient should be shown how to breathe in slowly through the nostrils, expanding the chest, and at the same time be strongly impressed by the healer **to be conscious of breathing and taking in with the air, extra oxygen, cosmic force, new strength and healing energy; and when expelling the air, to be equally conscious of breathing out waste and disease.** (See Section I, page 31.)

The advantages are obvious; it sustains the patient's morale so that he is consciously helping the healing process, becoming a co-operative ally with the healing intention. It gives purpose and stimulation to all the bodily intelligences to become active in giving the patient new strength, and to cleanse the body of unwanted matter; also to build up the health state and the body's resistance. The patient's relatives can be asked to join in with this special breathing to keep him company and so help to maintain the benefit which results.

Co-operation Between Heat Force and the Bodily Intelligence

It is an almost universal experience with healers when treating organic conditions to be aware of a sensing of a strong heat emanating from the healer's hand, with the patient also being aware of such deep heat penetrating his body. Should a thermometer be placed between the healer's hand and the patient's body, no rise in the temperature will be seen, though both the healer and the patient are aware of the exceptional heat. Although this heat cannot be registered on a clinical thermometer, it is nevertheless factual. The heat obviously represents a force. The healer cannot create it at will, and in fact, if he moves his hand away from the affected area then the sensation of heat vanishes, only to return when the hand again comes back to the affected part.

This is significant, for it implies that the super-normal force being directed through the healer only operates when there is a reason for it to do so. No one is able to create an increase in temperature in one small part of the body, i.e., the hand, by will-power and in a matter of seconds; or induce fluctuation of it, as described. It is something additional, experienced only through healership.

This heat force is characterised to carry out a planned intention. It is purposeful and in a case of, say, arthritis has the directive of stimulating the blood action, inducing a chemical change in the affected part and dispersing adhesions within the tissues or bringing about some other desired change.

That the patient physically feels this heat is noteworthy, for this indicates that the healing energy has been transformed into a physical expression. The invariable result is the removal or considerable lessening of the painful symptoms. Thus, once more, comes the indication of co-operation between the healing and the bodily intelligence.

At the risk of being repetitive, it is worth recalling that the main arthritic deposit is calcium carbonate. It is a simple molecule, one atom of calcium, one of carbon and three of oxygen. When the force of heat is applied to it, it undergoes a state of change. The heat energy experienced through a healer is a super-normal heat, it cannot be physically recorded, and it may well be that this **spirit quality** of heat is able to transform the calcium carbonate deposits from one state into another, which accounts for the remarkable change sometimes observed in the instantaneous removal of "cementing" within a locked arthritic joint.

If this point is established we should not mentally limit the extent to which the bodily intelligence can be made a partner in healing practice; nor should we limit the methods by which it can be used and how it can profit from any new instruction which can be given to it. With the future evolution of the physical human body, we should expect to see its bodily intelligence progressively evolve, too. In the next chapter on the influencing of a cell's intelligence we shall examine another aspect of bodily and mind intelligences.

Conclusion

The healer is justified in asking how this knowledge is going to assist him in his usage by the healing guides; for, remember, a healer is an instrument of healing. He is used by the guide to convey healing energies to overcome affliction. In carpentry, for example, the sharper the chisel used by the carpenter, the finer and more intricate the work he can produce. So it is with the healing instrument being used by the healing guide. It is important to remember that the healer's primary function is to be in an attuned condition with the guide and the patient. **If he is not, he is not serving any purpose.** With the healer attuned to the patient, the guide is able to use him in quite a number of ways: conversion of spirit energies into their physical counterpart; the conveying of stimulation; being able to blend more closely with a patient and so assess his outlook; to use the occasion for conveying direction, instruction and purposes to the various intelligences of the patient, and so on. It cannot be denied that, via the Spirit, direction can be given to the heart and bloodstream; and, is it not common within healing experience for a thrombosis gravely affecting the patient's life, to be dispersed rapidly, sometimes, overnight? Is it stretching credulity too far to believe that the blood cells, by reason of their individual intelligence, as we shall examine in a further chapter, can actively co-operate with the healing directive when the opportunity and right conditions have been established through attunement?

Thus in all healing we learn to avoid mechanical processes or techniques and instead to harness the total intelligences to the healing intention. As this more advanced form of co-operation with the healing guides is employed and the patient's intellectual faculties used, so more easily will disharmonies and disease be overcome.

Chapter 4

THE CELL: ITS INDIVIDUAL LIFE AND INTELLIGENCE

It may be thought by some that a study of the life and intelligence of a cell is outside the scope of a healer's need to understand more of the healing processes. Indeed it may be so, but this depends upon the limit the healer wishes to impose on himself, for his healing gift will still continue to be as effective as it always has been whether or not he embarks upon further study. On the other hand, the study of the cell is one of the most interesting of all aspects of the human system and leads to some very important conclusions concerning the functions of spiritual healing, especially in relation to the healing of psychosomatic disorders and the prevention of disease; and even to the very happiness of a person.

Every one of the fifty thousand billion cells in the human body is a complete, individual, living organism. The cell has similarities with the human body and mind. It has skin; it breathes; it takes in protein food; it possesses a digestive system; it excretes waste. The nutrients the cell absorbs are used as fuel to maintain abundant energy. It possesses a "brain", which is the nucleus; it has individual purpose to fulfil and therefore a consciousness, an intelligence.

The cell can be contented or frustrated. The intelligence which it possesses maintains control over its purpose and when it loses this control, it can become insane.

Every cell is subject to the law of disciplinary control. Every second, millions of new cells are born in the ceaseless programme of self-renewal. They are responsible for maintaining our hereditary characteristics and are responsible for the evolutionary changes in life. They possess the very "Spirit of life".

The cells are units from which all living matter is made. They are able to perform chemical transformations and although they exist in billions, they work in harmony and play a part in contributing to the health of each other.

Within the human cell are some forty-six chromosomes, each of which houses a large number of genes. It is the purpose and function of the genes with which this chapter is mainly concerned, for it is the genes which are the cell's central intelligence. Each cell also contains a bodily intelligence to record experience, harmony and disharmony in its mental and physical health.

The Genes

Genes are passed directly from the parents to their children and have been so passed since the commencement of the human story. Thus the cell's characteristics possess influences from earliest human life and occasionally we unfortunately see "throwbacks" resulting in mongolism simply through the presence of one additional chromosome.

The genes are influenced by the person's outlook and way of life, and it is through this influencing that the evolution of human and animal life has taken place. In the order of vegetation similar evolutionary processes occur.

It is recorded that there are thousands of genes contained within the human system. Every cell has its own personality, its own motive for existing. Its period of life is variable according to its function. Take, for example, skin cells: these are reproduced every few days while nerve cells do not reproduce at all. If we study a section of human skin we see how the lowermost layers of cells, nourished by the blood vessels, constantly produce new cells and how the newcomers push the older cells towards the surface of the skin. These older cells, cut off from nourishment, gradually starve, their nuclei disappearing, and the protoplasm becoming dry and flaky. Whenever we wash, some of the top layer of skin is sloughed off, but replacements keep coming up. So our skin is always fresh and new.

The blood cells live only about three to four months, the liver cells not so long, and the brain and bone cells persist for an indeterminate length of time. We can assume that about a billion cell divisions are always in process and that about twenty billion divisions are completed each day.

Like ourselves, the health of a cell is maintained in two ways, through its bodily functions and its mental harmony. The latter is dependent upon it being able to carry out its life's purpose. The cell has a consciousness which is a facet of intelligence. So long as a cell is able to fulfil its function it is contented; and when it reproduces itself, this state of contentment can be passed on to the new cells. Conversely, a cell in a state of discontent reproduces cells of a similar nature.

Different characters of cells need different forms of nourishment. When certain groups of cells serving a particular bodily need suffer from a lack of proper nutrients the health tone is affected, resulting in a disruption of the functioning of an organ or part of the body, with the result that sickness follows.

When a disharmony is communicated to the brain and thence to the bodily intelligence, the brain does not report the general condition but the physical detail of the symptoms. For example, it is not enough to report that the kidney is not functioning properly, the information needs to be far more exact, i.e., which kidney? . . . what area? . . . which cells? . . . where is pain or inflammation? . . . is there blockage? . . . malnutrition? etc.

It is then that the bodily intelligence acts, and directs through the digestive processes the production of the chemical need to be conveyed through the blood and lymphatic systems to the cells to bring them back into good health, or take other action necessary. As we have already discussed, the right kind of amino acid molecule has to be given. If this cannot be produced through the action of the normal body chemistry, then through spiritual healing and the healer's attunement, the healing guides are able to "manufacture" and direct the missing molecular energies to where they are needed.

The Frustration Factor

Just as we suffer from both physical and mental sicknesses, so the cells can suffer likewise. If they are prevented from fulfilling their purpose they will become frustrated, inert or even rebellious. Let us take as an example the cells of the glands in the female breast which have as their sole purpose the creation of milk for a baby. These cells are individual, too, and exist for this special purpose.

The consciousness of the cells lies in the genes and there exists a subtle connection between these cells and the mind. We see this in cases where a woman may have some inflammation of the breast glands and which becomes steadily aggravated by the patient allowing her mind to dwell on it fearfully. The cause of the inflammation may be traced to a disturbance of the normal functioning of the mammary cells from the ovaries and the pituitary gland. It is the pituitary gland which plays a predominant part in maintaining the good behaviour of the cells under normal conditions and especially when the breast comes into its function with the feeding of a baby.

If a woman greatly desires to have children and for some reason cannot or is denied the privilege, a state of frustration exists between the mind and the spirit-self, and this is passed on to the genes within the chromosomes of the mammary glands. Again, if a woman conceives a child and does not want it, a condition of mind stress is built up within her inner-self and this frustration is conveyed to the cells.

Another form of frustration lies in the strong maternal domination over a daughter, preventing her from exercising her natural desire to associate with male companionship.

It is noteworthy that wherever investigations have been made to discover the psychosomatic cause of breast cancers, it was discovered in every case that the woman suffered from deep frustration due to one or another of the three causes cited above. The cells within the breast became frustrated, they were prevented from fulfilling their destiny, they became rebellious, cast off all discipline, ran amok; and so changed a normal disciplined cell into a renegade, insane one.

It is easily proved that our mind frustrations are conveyed to the genes within the cells when we recall that the evolution of mankind has followed the change reflected in the seeds of inheritance, which, of course, are the genes. The genes are subject to being influenced by the state of the mind and character. Strong tendencies in life, such as love of the arts and the sciences, the virtues of kindliness, mother-love, etc., and the opposites, such as sadistic tendencies, hates, jealousies, etc., are reflected in the nature of the genes and these qualities, good or bad, are conveyed to the offspring through the genes contained within the sperm or ovum.

It is for this reason a child will often have hereditary tendencies similar to those of the parents and it accounts for genius, because the genes are so influenced by parental behaviour and outlook. It follows that the genetic directive can be adversely influenced by parental frustrations, imposing a lack of opportunity for the cells to fulfil the purpose for which they exist.

It is apparent to healers that the inner or spirit mind is very closely associated with the genetic directive. Primarily, most of our frustrations, idealism, ambitions, emotions, loves and hatreds are residual within the spirit mind and so the healing process needs to commence in the spirit mind to overcome the causes of frustration, whatever they are. When the primary cause of an incurable disease lies within a spirit mind disharmony and through the healing influences the tensions are soothed away, then the physical effects are open to response to the healing purposes—and this may explain how a so-called "incurable" is made well through spiritual healing.

Control and Communication

It has been established that every cell is governed throughout its life by pituitary control. How wonderful this control is can be gathered from the manner in which discipline is maintained over the many thousands of billions of cells each of us possess. This function acts like the governor bearing in an engine, ensuring that the body mechanism and cellular reproduction do not proceed too fast.

It is the natural incentive for all living things to reproduce themselves freely and as frequently as they can under the laws of life. The ultimate purpose of all the cells (except, as has been stated, the nerve cells which do not reproduce) is to divide and create another cell to carry on the life cycle.

The pituitary control keeps our bodies in balance by ensuring an almost uniform physical development of limbs, features, bones and organs. When this glandular control weakens, then discipline becomes slack and a condition known as acromegaly develops, where the cells multiply without restraint, as is seen with patients with excessively large limbs, especially the hands and feet. **Normally not one cell is allowed to reproduce itself until its appointed time,** which indicates a system of communication and control so marvellous that it is almost inconceivable.

Where there is communication and control, there needs to be a form of intelligence to maintain it and use it to exert disciplinary influence over its subjects. As we have seen, every cell has an intelligence able to receive instruction, and furthermore this communication and control denotes a state of intellectual liaison between each cell and the pituitary mind.

The Intelligence of the Cell

A very similar parallel can be drawn between the cellular intelligence with the mind and Spirit. The cell is conscious of the desire to fulfil its purpose in life, of its well-being, and of its needs when there is a physical weakness. It has liaison with the emotions and outlook of the human personality and has the intelligence to accept that there exists a control over its life.

With the aid of the electronic microscope, a cell can be enlarged many millions of times, so much so, that a single cell can occupy the full area of a cinema screen. In this way we are able to observe the steady, orderly process of life's function within it.

Some categories of cells appear to have a more active intelligence than others. For example, the cells comprising muscle have a more humdrum existence than the cells concerned with reproduction. Muscle cells are able to fulfil their purpose more easily because there is less opportunity for them to become frustrated. From this we see how disease is more closely associated with cells which have a high intelligence rating.

The intelligence of a cell can be compared with that of the mind itself. When a person's mind has become obsessed with fear, grief, shock, great disappointment in love, and so on—all of which come under the classification of "frustration"—then the ordinary mental processes suffer, breaking down the health tone, inducing bodily wastage and creating the opportunity for the acceptance and development of disease. If frustration persists in force, it will distort the mental perspective and if maintained will lead towards **insanity and suicidal tendencies. It is just the same with a cell.**

When the Cell Loses its Reason

Let us once again consider the element of frustration and take as an example the mammary glands in the female breast, which under certain sensual experiences, become activated. This stimulation demonstrates beyond all doubt that there exists a direct liaison between the intelligence of the mind and the intelligence of the cells. One intelligence reacts upon and affects the other. If, however, continual frustration of sexual desire and its fulfilment upsets the mammary glands, the cells within them become frustrated with despair. **The genes become rebellious, frantic and intensely unhappy,**

and this leads towards the cells themselves be-coming insane, throwing off the yoke of control and rejecting the discipline of the pituitary influence.

If we were to examine through the electronic micro-scope the behaviour of one of these insane cells, we should see it reproducing itself without restraint at a furious rate, quite uncontrolled, and with every function within it grossly speeded up. The cell has become preda-tory, depriving the normal cells of their nutrient. It has in fact, run amok. **It is in this that we observe the primary causation of cancer.**

A further example of similarity between the mind and the cell can be seen when we consider that insanity can be hereditary. It is the same with the insane cancer cell, for when it reproduces itself, it brings into being another insane cell. This is a common denominator with malignancy, and leads to a conclusion which it is most essential for all healers to recognise. **It is that the cause of cancer is psychosomatic.** It is not the product of a virus infection, nor does it arise from irritants. **The important fact is that the intelligence of the cancer cell has become impaired to the point of insanity.** When our bodies are hurt in any way, such as through bruising, cutting, septic conditions, etc., the cells suffer, and with burning they can be completely destroyed; **but they do not become insane.** If irritants can cause cancer (as we are told by medical authorities) then surely a sustained form of injury such as burning or radiation should drive a cell insane and so create cancer; but it does not.

The conclusion arising from this is that cancer has a psychosomatic origin; there is frustration which upsets the orderly conduct of the physical and spirit minds, con-sciously or subconsciously, and when this obstructs the fulfilment of life's purpose as expressed in the genetic potentials, the genes are likewise frustrated, causing them to go berserk.

The manner in which a cancerous growth can be dealt with has already been discussed in the chapter on "Healing Energies" but what is more important, especially to healers, is the **prevention** of cancer. We recall it was Sir Heneage Ogilvie, the cancer specialist, who said: "A happy man never gets cancer." Further study will be necessary into the causes of frustration, to recognise their forms and to evaluate them according to the personality of the individual. Some forms of frustration causing breast cancers have already been mentioned.

When these characteristics are recognised, then healership must come into the picture, to seek through the healing guides the direction of those correcting influences to bring about a happier state of mind within the patient. We have stated earlier that the only way by which spirit mind frustrations can be subdued is on the same level as they exist, namely Spirit.

It follows that those who are receiving spiritual healing today, particularly those suffering from mental "dis-ease", are being protected from the onset of cancer. Whilst it cannot as yet be proved, it is logical to state that through spiritual healing there are many people who would have most likely contracted cancer, but have been saved from doing so through healership. The implications which follow this are very far reaching and which need to be dealt with in the following Section concerned with "Psychosomatic Healing".

SECTION V.

PSYCHOSOMATIC CONDITIONS AND MENTAL HEALING

INTRODUCTION

So far we have studied the healing energies, the healing intelligences, and the structure and life of the cell, giving a general idea how they are concerned with spiritual healing. They have not been studied in depth, but sufficiently for the healer to bring them into the healing picture. Before a fuller appreciation can be formed, however, one needs to be able to comprehend the whole picture, and it is the study of psychosomatic conditions and mental healing that contributes the vital link. The studies we have so far been engaged upon deal with the mechanics of healing and not so much with the causes of disease or the manner in which the healing processes are put into operation from the spirit side. As this chapter is so largely concerned with the functions and employment of the mind, we should first establish what the functions of the mind are.

The Physical Mind

Everything is a mental experience. The conscious mind has already been likened to a mirror which receives

277

thought pictures and impressions. When we hurt ourselves, are fatigued, have enjoyed a good dinner, are warm and comfortable, hear a piece of music, or see an ugly or unpleasant sight—these are all mental experiences received on the mirror of the mind.

We store up knowledge and details of experiences within the computer memory of the brain. When we purposefully recall them they are projected back to the mirror as a picture or a conclusion. For example, ask the brain the sum of two and two at once the answer of four is given. Ask for the name of the hotel you visited sometime in the past, and the computer will give to the mirror all the recorded detail it holds, the name, the appearance of the building, the gardens, etc.

The physical mind has to cope with physical matters only. It is concerned with our bodily comforts and our physical needs. It also acts in a computer sense by retaining items of knowledge and recording experiences. It can provide items of information for the conscious mind to consider and arrive at a conclusion.

The Spirit Mind

The spirit mind (or known otherwise as the "subliminal mind", "the psyche", "the inner-self", "the etheric mind", etc.) has just as free an access to the mirror of the mind as has the physical mind. It deals with the emotions and ambitions, of love and hate, of goodness and evil, of security and fears, kindness and cruelty, generosity and meanness, and, through natural selection, the choice of a mate. It provides the incentive for ambition and idealism. It provides the abilities of appreciation and cultivation of the arts and sciences. It gives the urge to fight against evil and work for good causes. It is the source of that love and compassion which motivates every healer.

Because the spirit mind is so intensely personal, so delicately adjusted, so sensitive, it is within the spirit mind that resides the motives for unrest, frustrations and psychosomatic disharmonies, all of which can become experiences on the mirror of the mind.

People possess a sense of conscience. When they find a neighbour in trouble, they go to his assistance. To come across a crying child, one seeks to find out the way to help the little one; to pass the child by would be repugnant to most people. To free a captive animal or protest against cruelty is a natural act of compassion. **These are qualities of the conscience.**

Other characteristics are observed in different ways; a person may have an opportunity to steal something with little risk of being found out, but he does not, for the reason that he knows it is wrong. We all have that inherent sense of what is right and what is wrong. Where does this sense of conscience spring from?

The conscience is a state of awareness, it is not a quality of the brain, though we can educate the brain to differentiate between a good and a bad act, such as stealing. **There seems little doubt that one's conscience is a spiritual faculty, which we shall see is the director of the spirit mind.**

Cruel, evil people, also possess a conscience—a bad one —but which nevertheless gives them satisfaction. We know that in all spheres of life there is good and bad and it is in this that we see the eternal conflict between good and evil. Spiritual healing is directly concerned with this conflict.

The good conscience, being a spiritual quality and the inspiration behind healing, is an inborn quality of a divine character. It is the link between us in physical life and spirit life.

It is now accepted as a truth (a truth being a demonstrable fact) that the major percentage of disease has its primary causation within mind disharmonies and, deeper still, sickness of the soul as expressed in frustrations, fears, and inhibitions as well as sins against good conscience. These are not only the origins of mental disorders but also of almost every disease of the body.

Thus we are able to see that the study of our minds becomes very necessary to any approach in understanding the processes involved in spiritual healing. This must be the concern of every healer who wishes to become a more attuned instrument of the healing guides. It possesses a tremendous significance for the future for the obvious reason that **if we arrive at a closer appreciation of the nature and cause of disease, then healership will play an eminent part in preventing the onset of disease.**

There are two main divisions of mind unrest: firstly, there are those associated with physical life, insecurities, anxieties and responsibilities, financial worries, overconcern for others, fear of cancer and other health problems, and so on. Secondly, there are those associated with frustrations, the inability of people to carry out a way of life for which they have an inner yearning; the desire to have children when they do not come; unrequited love and lack of opportunity to fulfil the natural functions of life. All of these ill-affect the health condition by upsetting, or even destroying, that perfect balance between outlook, desire and fulfilment.

Perhaps the main reason why those persons who are troubled with frustrations and inner-mind disharmonies are so rarely touched by preaching, drugs or psychiatry, is that the spirit mind cannot be reached by these methods. Because the origin of such disharmonies lies within the spirit mind, or soul, of the sufferer, it can only be reached on the same plane as it exists, namely the spirit plane, and thereby it comes within the influence of the spirit realm and the spirit doctors.

It is worth noting that the orthodox Church sometimes comments that healers are only concerned with the healing of bodies, whereas the Church heals the "whole man", body and soul. When it is remembered that the cause of disease is primarily due to "soul sickness" then the measure of success which healership is responsible for in the healing of disease must imply the healing of the soul sickness, and thereby the "whole man".

The study of how the good health tone of an individual is maintained by the perfect balance between the soul or inner-self, the mind and the body, involves many considerations, but the principles are easily understood. If there exists inner unrest, this is conveyed to the mirror of the mind. With unrest in the consciousness there comes concern, depression and heaviness in the outlook, lowering the health tone. So long as this unrest is maintained, aggravation follows, and there is no respite; so the body's resistance weakens and becomes prone to the oncoming of disease, of which perhaps, the most common symptoms are migraine with women, and stomach ulcers with men.

The government of our bodies, their growth and functions are largely controlled by the endocrine glandular system, and it is true to say that all our glandular systems are very intimately associated with the mental state. Mind urges induce the glandular systems to take action as, for example, we see in the case of fear which will energise the adrenalin glands. We have already seen in the previous chapter the control of the growth of every one of the uncountable number of cells in our bodies and their good function is the responsibility of the pituitary endocrine system, with all the associated dependent processes, to maintain the good health of each cell. Thus it can be seen that when a persistent mental hurt or frustration is maintained, upsetting the total harmony, the ill-effects are felt within the glands as well. Furthermore, when the nature of the frustration has a direct connection with a particular organic system, the glandular control of that system becomes disrupted.

This has been known by spiritual healers for a long time, but it is only more recently that medical opinion is arriving at the same conclusion.

It must, of course, be appreciated that not all human illnesses have a psychosomatic origin. Some arise from a purely biological fault, such as with haemophilia, or a heart defect of which "blue babies" are an example. Even certain mental states are in a category of their own and do not necessarily affect the good functioning of the glandular, or other, systems of the body. Cases of obsession, kleptomania, claustrophobia and so on can be taken as examples.

Our purpose now is to consider those ways by which we can direct spiritual healing—either by Contact or Absent Healing—in seeking to overcome various categories of mind conditions, or physical disorders created by them, bearing in mind the interplay that exists between the mind and the various bodily systems, and especially with mental disorder it must be dealt with on the same plane as it exists, namely the spirit plane.

The Healing of Allergies—Hay Fever

The cause of an allergy can be obscure; it can be psychosomatic, creating an erratic mental habit, whilst another may have a physical origin. With the latter, we have allergies created by pollen, dust, contact with certain plants, dyes, odours, etc. Perhaps the most common allergy of all is that of hay fever, which invariably yields easily to spiritual healing. The cause arises from the inhalation of offending airborne pollen at a certain time of the year and healing experience has shown that when healing aid has been sought prior to the hay fever season, the symptoms do not arise. There are a number of reasons which may account for this. It may be that the bodily intelligence is alerted to take steps to countermand the physical effects of the irritant dust; it may be that, psychologically, the mind and body are prepared not to accept the usual symptoms. It may be that following the healer's advice to the patient to practise characterised breathing (see Section III Chapter 5), the respiratory processes are strengthened and a resistance is built up to counter the irritants; or the healing may help the patient to develop a resistance to the habit of surrendering meekly to the allergy.

Thus we see how the healer can make a positive contribution to the avoidance of hay fever by preventing the onset. The healer will intercede for the guide to prepare the bodily defences against the disease, and as the patient is advised to adopt characterised breathing, he is told that the purpose of this is to enable the blood to absorb a higher oxygen content and so fortify the body against becoming a victim of the hay fever; and by replacing the patient's expectancy of the feverish symptoms by a more positive outlook of resistance, so the symptoms do not manifest.

The Healing of Asthma

We can use this example to show how nervous asthma can likewise be overcome. Asthma is often associated with hay fever. It is a common experience with those who suffer from nervous asthma to have attacks at regular times of the day and the night, say at five in the afternoon or at three o'clock in the morning. Attacks tend to become habitual; they are expected, and they come. When the healer knows such details then the treatment is more simple and he advises the patient to change the daily routine around the five p.m. time, so that instead of the patient standing by waiting for the kettle to boil for tea (the time the attacks usually come) she puts off teatime for an hour, and occupies herself with some other activity. It is then usually found that the asthma attack does not come. When attacks come at, say, three o'clock in the morning, the patient is asked to give herself the mental directive to sleep right through until daylight, anticipating sound and refreshing sleep, with the healing purpose being to link up with the patient to help the directive to be carried out. In the majority of cases the healing is effective and asthma is overcome.

With all asthmatical, bronchial and respiratory diseases, including emphysema, it is wise to get the patient to become an ally of the healing intention by so practising that slow, gentle, deep characterised breathing, taking in more oxygen and cosmic strength, overcoming the habit of shallow, gaspy breathing.

The Healing of Gastric Ulcers and Digestive Troubles

It is well known that the cause of gastric ulcers is invariably mental tension, worry, anxiety, and so on. The greater responsibility a man has the more chance he has of developing a gastric ulcer. So it is with other forms of digestive upset, dyspepsia, nausea, flatulence, painful areas, and so on. There can be other causes, such as constipation, bile trouble or metabolic disorder, but the general cause is often found to be mental frustration of one kind or another.

While, of course, healing applied to the abdomen to soothe and disperse the trouble will bring easement, the main directive is to promote the soothing and calming of the mental outlook. At such times, it is good to recall that the healer is closely attuned to the patient, his spirit mind is able to reach the spirit mind of the patient, where the origin of frustration usually lies. If the healer is able to ascertain the trend or cause of the upset, then no doubt he will be inspired to convey to the patient the remedial thought influences which will bring about a more contented outlook with the patient; and as the patient responds to this beneficial influencing, so it is likely that a permanent cure will follow.

Causes of mental stress are not always easy to find. The healer may have a patient who is in good physical health and who will say he has no worries, all is well and happy at home, he has no financial responsibilities, and all is generally quite well with him, so there is no cause for nervous tension. However, the unknown reason may well be that the patient is unduly concerned about a sick friend and is harassed to think what will happen to the home and family if his friend should pass on. This kind of anxiety can indeed be more serious than wondering how to meet next month's hire purchase instalments. The patient is so open-hearted that he takes other people's problems very much to heart and sustains a state of anxiety in his own mind.

Mental Unrest and Skin Diseases

Healers pointed out, long before the medical profession realised it, that a psychosomatic cause lay behind almost every kind of skin affliction. It will be found that there is hypertension, worry or some form of frustration behind psoriasis, acne, shingles, dermatitis, and most other skin irritations and disorders (see Section III, Chapter 9). This also applies in the tragic cases of little children, who are tortured by eruptions and hard skin irritations which do not yield to any kind of lotion or ointment. We hear of little ones who are born with such skin trouble.

Generally, these skin conditions will yield to Absent

Healing, for as has already been pointed out, as the healing influences soothe away the cause of the upsets, so the clearance of the skin soon follows.

Sometimes with children, especially with boys, **fears cause skin trouble,** and if the healer is able to get the child's confidence, the child will tell the healer what is troubling him and it may even be associated with some form of home life, which the parents may not realise; or if they did, would not consider it serious enough. A common symptom is fear of the dark, and when this is known, the parents should be asked to let a little light be seen by the child to avoid the fear in his mind. It is wrong to make a child fight his fear. This is where a healer needs to be an understanding psychologist, not only to deal with the cause of the child's fears but how to advise the parents, too.

Bed Wetting

Connected with childish fears is the difficult problem of helping children over the weakness of bed wetting. Here again, we have a nervous, often an anxiety, complex. The causes can be one of several, but perhaps the main one is a greater need for nerve co-ordination and control over the bladder function. The healing of this trouble is often complicated by unwise parental treatment, for often the child is strongly lectured, bullied or threatened about the weakness and sometimes beaten every time the bed is wet. Unfortunately, a strong element of fear is developed, whereas the healing purpose must be to tranquillise the child's conscious mind and at the same time to encourage directively a stronger nerve control over the muscular action of the bladder.

Often the parents need more healing than the child, so the healer should, through Absent Healing, seek to direct a sense of understanding and tolerance to be with them. Naturally the parents are advised to see that the child empties his bladder last thing at night, and a little love and cuddle helps to put the little mind at ease and to be happily contented; and when, in the morning, it is found that the bed is dry, the child should be praised and rewarded in some way.

Diagnosis

It is worth repeating that the responsibility of diagnosis is not that of the healer: it is that of the spirit doctor. This is so, simply because the healer's mind does not possess the knowledge to heal. He certainly does not know the composition of the offending molecules, or how to apply such corrective energies to bring about a chemical change to destroy a disease condition. He has not the additional knowledge to give precise instructions to the bodily intelligence how to act; nor, for instance, does he know how to re-vitalise impoverished amino acid cells, nor how to adjust the metabolism or how to disperse a growth or a cataract. The healer, therefore, has to be content with establishing a condition of attunement with the patient and the healing guide, passing on known information of the symptoms and simply allowing himself to be used with understanding.

In all our instances of healing practice so far, it will be observed that the healing purpose has been by way of direction given through the mirror of the mind. The healer will also have noted that Contact Healing and Absent Healing are not two separate therapies, but are complementary to each other, and that after having given Contact treatment how it is necessary to direct further help by the Absent Healing method, too, and this particularly applies where there is a close mental or nervous link with the symptoms.

Thought Forces

The more one studies the science of spiritual healing, the clearer does one conclusion emerge, and it is that the "modus operandi" is that of **thought.** The spirit doctors cannot use a stethoscope or a thermometer in order to make a diagnosis. They diagnose through a thought procedure.

The healing commences with a thought request and thought communication is established and maintained by attunement through intercession; and during the time of contact treatment.

It naturally follows that the healing of the causes and symptoms of psychosomatic conditions must also be through thought influencing, just as the correction of unbalanced minds and the re-establishing of control and co-ordination in cases of paralysis must also be dependent upon thought direction.

In the chapter on "Healing Energies" it is stated that the creation of the correct molecular structures needed to induce a chemical change in an afflicted part of the body are gathered through the employment of characterised energy—in other words, through that of thought. At the risk of repetition, it will be helpful to dwell a little longer on the study of thought energies to give us a closer understanding of the psychosomatic cause of so much illness.

Telepathy between individuals is now accepted by most authorities as factual. How often do we hear of identical twins, sometimes miles from each other, each having the same thought at the same time, causing them to follow some specific line of action? Where there is an exceptional affinity or closeness between a husband and wife, telepathy between them is very common. In the animal kingdom, too, there are numerous examples of behaviour patterns in the various species which can only be accounted for by means of an exceptional form of mental communication. **For thought to travel from one mind to another indicates that this needs to be in an ordered form to account for its existence and a medium through which it can travel.**

Thoughts are positive things. Our brain retains and stores them and can present them to the conscious mind when called for. As everything pertaining to the universe is a form of energy, then thought must come within this definition, too.

Thoughts are not words. Words are used simply to clothe thoughts. When we think about things, we do so as pictures on the mirror of the mind, or they come to-the conscious mind as items of information or ideas. A descriptive word will bring a thought picture to the mind, for example; when the thought of a crucifix is given to a number of people of different nationalities, the thought picture will be similar but each person will receive its word representation in his respective language.

When a clairvoyant is in communication with the spirit realm, his conscious mind (the mirror) receives the vision in picture form, which he describes in words. When he receives intuitive thoughts these are registered as thought impressions, which he translates into words.

Every variation of light and sound possesses its individual frequency of radiation. It is a form of characterised energy, of definite construction, as is everything else in the universe. Similarly, each positive thought will possess its own definite energy formation. The energy frequency of a given object is the same, whether it is pictured in the mind of a Londoner or a Parisian. It is the same in spirit recognition or physical appreciation. **It is a positive thing with a definite structure.**

Sound frequencies travel at a much slower speed than that of light, which is 186,000 miles per second, taking five seconds to travel a mile. The frequency speeds up from the lowest sound to the highest. Within the range of normal hearing each minute variation of frequency has a different characterisation. If the frequency is speeded up beyond the capacity of the human ear to hear, there is a continuation of sound, but which only animals are able to appreciate. By continuing to speed up the frequency, it will eventually be registered as a light experience, commencing with the infra-red; and as the frequencies continue to increase, so it will reach the ultra-violet and beyond. Continue this speeding up of the frequency very much higher and it will begin to enter into the range of thought, which again is recordable by the conscious mind.

Therefore, just as every variation of sound and every refraction of light has its definite form, so has every thought its set form, capable of being recorded. If thoughts were intransient, possessing no ordered form, they could not be filed away in the memory and revived when needed. The brain cannot record nothing.

The number of recorded thoughts the brain computer stores is incalculable. It is said that no thought is ever lost and under psychiatric relaxation the brain can be induced to bring forth memories of the past, which could not be consciously aroused.

Therefore, if thought experiences are positive, characterised forms of energy, we can seek the way to relate them to the healing intelligence and observe what has hitherto not been recognised as a possible way of **scientifically changing** a mental state, by imposing on that state another form of thought energy which will merge with the original state and so bring about a change of outlook.

Just as with the chemical change, where one form of molecular energy can change the state of

another form of molecular energy, so we have a similar procedure high up in the scales of energy thought formation with the merging of one ordered thought energy with another, to bring about a change of mind picture.

As an example, let us take the thought formation of a wooden crucifix and then introduce the thought of a silver crucifix, so that the introduction of the thought energy representing "silver" would induce a change in the thought image of the crucifix from wood to silver.

This, so far as the author is aware, is a new conception. There is no evidence, as yet, to support it but it is an assumption based upon probability. If we dare to think ahead further we can visualise thought structures as being composed of "thought molecules" using non-physical (spirit) atoms. Furthermore, this can give a structure as to the means by which a thought flow can influence another thought flow, and so overcome frustrations.

If we are prepared to accept that in the spirit realm there are "things", then they must be made of something, and in view of the intimacy between Spirit and earth life, it may well be that substances in the spirit world are composed of energies, similar to those we have here, but of another frequency.

Thought Emotions

In studying psychosomatic causes of disharmony and disease, it is necessary to consider the emotional states which can have both stimulating and depressive effects on our well-being. If our supposition is true that positive thoughts take the form of determined energy formations, then we need to separate those from the "sensing" of feelings. Happiness, joy, misery and fear are not "thoughts" but "states of being"—a sensing. True

thoughts can promote and erase emotional states, which
are but effects.

When one has a fear, this tones the mirror of the mind
with a condition of fearfulness, which imposes its
influence on all our thoughts and consciousness and
troubles become magnified. Conversely, if one has the
sensing of confidence and happiness, then the consciousness is bright and one feels "on top of the world".

The emotional senses are built up by thought appreciations. For example, in daily life if our circumstances
or our sense of security is threatened, or we are given a
grave medical verdict concerning our health state, then
the sense of fear is aroused and dominates our well-being.
The same can happen in reverse: when success is in our
hands, or love is within our hearts then life is "rose-
coloured"; and when we are in radiant health, there is
the sensation of well-being and we can meet all life's
problems with courage and fearlessness.

So when we speak of frustrations, fears and anxieties
being the psychosomatic cause of ill-health, we can now
recognise them as "sensings" arising from thought
energies and situations.

The Healing of Fears

It is obvious that to master a fear or other adverse
emotional sensing, an opposite emotional state must be
encouraged. For example, if a person is fearful of
making a journey, a friend will seek to give reassurance
in all the ways he can; he may even arrange for a com-
panion to accompany the friend and he takes every step
he can to master his friend's fears by encouraging
thoughts and actions. We do this every day of our lives
when we say to someone "buck-up", or when we shake
hands with a feeling of affection and assurance.

So it is with the overcoming of unhappiness built up

in the spirit or inner-self mind. Because both the physical and spirit minds have access to the mirror of the mind, **so they can influence each other,** and thereby, in healing, the words and influence of the healer can make an impact on the patient's outlook and not only comfort the physical mind but can get through to the spirit mind, where most emotional states have their origin. It is often the case when the healer is in close attunement with the healing guide, that he is thereby able to receive intuitively thought directions from the guide, and so is able to speak the right words which will be most effective to soothe and calm the patient's mental unrest. It has already been stated that in healing it is necessary to deal with conditions on the same level as they exist. When there is a deep emotional upset within the spirit mind then it is best dealt with on the same plane, that is, the spirit plane.

Just as we can give expression to our desires physically, so it follows that the spirit mind can make itself clear to the spirit guide in the same way. The guide is then able to direct the patient's thoughts into other channels and so soften down and overcome the frustration.

Minds are like tortuous mazes. No clear path is easily seen and so many considerations impinge themselves, sidetracking the mind from reaching a solution, and when the mental state is disturbed, the situation becomes more involved and tangled up with fixations. The mirror of the mind is no longer clear but is full of unformed, unfinished, conflicting ideas and impressions which prevent any clear thinking.

To heal a mind disharmony, a clear directive line of thought must be imposed on the mirror of the mind for the conscious mind to accept it. This thought directive mainly comes from Spirit but it can also come from the healer's advice, too. Once the corrective thought has been noted and received then an entry has been made and the way to the healing is open. Much may depend on the follow-up flow of thought purpose to strengthen that good influencing designed to restore to the patient a fresh outlook and a better sense of perspective.

When a harassed mind is deeply obsessed with a sense of grievance, loss, or other cause, so that the mirror of the mind is dominated by it, then it may not be possible for the spirit directive to obtain an entry to the conscious mind. It is a fact, however, that a mind under constant stress ultimately rebels against the source of the aggravation and it demands a change, and it is at such a juncture that the healing directive, with its good influencing, is then able to reach the conscious mind.

When a healer feels specially drawn to a patient suffering from a condition having an apparent psychosomatic cause, and feels that he is sufficiently attuned to make a correct diagnosis with the resultant "blending" between the healer's and the patient's spirit-selves, the healer can then direct a positive flow of guiding thought to the patient.

Here, the spoken word will help to impress upon the patient's conscious mind those thought directives the healer is intuitively receiving from the guide. It may be, for example, that the healer is being impressed by the spirit helpers that "music" is going to benefit the patient, possibly suggesting to him that for a short period each day the patient listens to music of an inspirational nature, "looking into" the music, sensing its feeling and theme, so that his mind becomes uplifted by it, and so on. Again it may be that the healer is impressed to point out to the patient the advantages of some special creative activity which will enhance the primary purpose of the healing.

The Healing of Obsessions

The foregoing paragraphs have a direct bearing on the healing of those suffering from obsessions. "Obsession" and "possession" are often associated together and sometimes the symptoms are similar. However, they are quite different and have very different causes, and it takes an experienced healer to distinguish between them.

"Obsession" indicates a mind which is over-concentrated on a particular line of mental activity. Often it is only a matter of degree. Every reasonable person maintains a satisfactory degree of hygiene and cleanliness; but when a person becomes "obsessed" with the need to keep on washing, feeling that everything he touches, even door handles, is contaminated, then the condition becomes morbid and we can say he is "obsessed". Other common forms of obsession include persecution, the need to check something over and over again, deep remorse over a past misdeed, unbalance following a betrayal of friendship, and so on. Unfortunately the obsession can become so strong that it completely dominates the mind and is ever present, preventing the healing influencing having an entry to the conscious mind and so creating an obstinate condition to heal.

While every case of obsession is personal, needing an individual assessment, there are some general rules pertaining to the healer's treatment.

Primarily, the strongest way to obtain a healing for these unfortunate people is through Absent Healing, as usually there is not much help which can be given physically. It is mainly a disease of the spirit mind, therefore the logical way of treatment is by thought and influencing from the spirit guides. If Contact Healing should be given, then the healing directive should be maintained by Absent Healing.

Dealing Directly with the Patient

With Contact Healing there are some general directions which healers may find helpful. As a rule the healer will very quickly know that the patient is mentally troubled as he is often impatient to unbottle his emotions and relate his symptoms or the story of his mental unrest.

The healer's attitude to the patient is important. He needs to be patient, sympathetic and a good listener, but at the same time should maintain a dominant attitude of being in control of the situation. When he speaks to the patient, he should be kind yet firm. If the healer is to be effective, then through him must come the stronger influence that will impress the mind of the patient, and this may not be so easy, especially if there is a strong fixation maintaining the state of unbalance in the patient's mind.

After sympathetically greeting him, the healer should begin by asking the patient to tell him his trouble. Generally, the story is a long one, with a wealth of detail. The healer listens, showing the patient that he understands the situation and the trials the patient has undergone. During the narrative, the healer assesses within his own mind the basic or central theme of the patient's trouble, whether it is remorse, persecution, a complex, etc. He then determines the line of thought he wishes to superimpose on the patient's conscious mind to induce a change of outlook.

Firmness Essential

It is at this time that the healer needs to be kind, but firm. So often the patient will want to break in, interrupting what the healer is saying and wanting to repeat his narrative or some part of it. Indeed, often when the healer has done all that he can to persuasively steer the patient's mind into more orderly channels with a better sense of perspective and thinking "all is going to be well", only to find the patient ready to tell his sad story all over again! It is this that the healer must be on his guard against and try to prevent it, thus helping to break the fixation.

The healer speaks with confidence in a straightforward manner. He tells the patient he well understands the nature of his distress and he is going to help him. It should be remembered the patient has come to the healer to be healed of his trouble, to free his mind from upsetting thoughts. This is in the healer's favour and he should use this purpose in his plan of help. The healer will then speak to the patient in the way he is impressed to do so, with regard to the nature of the obsession. An obvious line being that the past, with all its troubles, now belongs to the past, and that every new day starts with a new strength of mind and purpose, with all the force of Spirit behind it.

If the patient then tries to relate again the details of the obsession—for this is a characteristic symptom of this trouble—the healer must insist that there is no need for this, because it now belongs to the past. This aspect of verbal influencing should not continue for too long, just sufficient to impress upon the patient's mind the new thought directive. The healer must do his best to speak positively and with assurance to impress the patient with the need to follow out the advice he has given.

The healer may, if he considers that the situation warrants it, give Contact Healing treatment, again with the positive purpose of removing tension from the patient's nerves and outlook. This may be only psychological, but it can impress the mind of the patient as a means of erasing the causes of mental fears and stresses. The healer should, however, be more conscious through his attunement with the patient of impressing the latter's spirit mind from the healer's spirit-self, and so helping to clear the mirror of the mind thus restoring a better sense of perspective.

The Healing of Possession

The healing of those who are said to be "possessed" by an undesirable entity is a more difficult procedure than in the treatment of an obsessed mind.

Possession and schizophrenia are akin to each other, but can have different symptoms. With the latter, the sufferer often believes he is a different personality, often a revered or important person, such as Jesus. Possession is an imposition of another mind onto that of the patient, which is invariably accompanied by what appears to be an audible voice telling the patient to do this or that, expressing opinions, and giving orders. Such voices are similar to those heard in "clairaudience" when this faculty is being used under proper control. With cases of possession these voices are crude, blasphemous, inclined to foul language and can be very stressful to the sufferer. They tell the patient what he is to do and at times they are very wrongful things. This is one of the most pernicious complaints anyone can suffer from—far worse than a physical affliction.

Here again priority must be given to Absent Healing, in which the spirit guides are asked to free the patient from the invading personality. This is not an easy task, for once an undesirable entity has taken hold of his victim, he (or she) sticks to him like a limpet.

One way in which success has been seen on a number of occasions is for the patient to be taken to a specialist "rescue circle" where an experienced medium can seek to isolate the invading entity from the victim. **This is highly specialised treatment to be conducted** *only* **by mediums who have developed this particular form of psychic gift.**

Contact Treatment

Healers are, however, able to assist especially when the sufferer is brought to the healer. Here again, the attitude of the healer must be understanding and dominant. He needs to impress the patient with his ability to be able to evict the intruder with the patient's co-operation, and to project on to the mirror of the patient's mind his strength through the power of good being stronger than the power of evil, and to create a state of expectancy and willingness on the patient's part to co-operate in defeating the invader.

The patient is told that from the moment of being treated, he will **totally ignore** any words, thoughts or impressions which enter his mind which he knows are not "good". If the voices call him or say something to him, he must completely ignore them. So that if, for example, the voices tell him to go into the garden, he will not, but proceed to do something else, even if only to make a cup of tea. In this simple way, he restores mastery over his own mind. The patient must be most strongly impressed to have with him, at all times, the over-riding determination that he will not take the slightest notice of the voices; to let the possessing entity know that it is wasting its time. When necessary, the patient should try to keep his attention occupied by, for example, reading, doing a meticulous pattern, going out for a brisk walk, singing hymns, ballads, even pop songs, and so on. The important thing is to mentally smother the voices.

When this has been carried out, experience has shown that before long the possessing entity gets tired and leaves the patient in peace. As far as the healer is concerned, it is best not to argue with the patient, or argue against what the voice has said to the patient. This only sets up opposition and strengthens the hold of the entity by having something to answer back to—remember, it is the entity that has the last word, for after the argument is over, it has plenty of time to assert itself, in a definite manner, most likely with vituperation and abuse. There is just one thing, though: if the healer is able to induce the patient to laugh at the voices, this is excellent, for the invading entities, as a rule, cannot bear to be laughed at.

It is good advice for the relatives of the patient to be urged to try and take him away from his customary surroundings and make a break from the daily routine. A new place, new scenery, new people, all serve to occupy the mind, and so awaken normal perceptions, giving the mind the opportunity to replenish itself with fresh experiences and so aid the healing purpose, especially the Absent Healing directive, by loosening the hold the entity has on the patient's mind. Sometimes, purely open-air manual work is ideal.

The Healing of Spastic Children and Those with "Lame" Minds

This is a tremendous subject, but one in which spiritual healing can make an effective contribution in adding to the sum of human happiness. It is most rewarding, especially to the healer. While each case is individual, there are common denominators which link them together.

The healing is divided into two functions. Firstly, through the help that is administered by the healer himself, and the other through ways in which the parents can co-operate with the healing purpose.

With these children, the healing brings into action much of which this book has already dealt with, i.e., the chemical changes necessary to induce freer movements, release from spasticity and activation of the bodily intelligences to arouse latent mental faculties. Generally, the healing directive is to induce a greater degree of co-ordination from the mind, through the brain, employing the bodily intelligence to get the nerves to activate the muscles, etc.; to soothe nervous tensions and fears; to stimulate nerve reactions; encourage the conscience to determine the difference between right and wrong and to allay mental apprehensions. Furthermore, the healing directs new strength and vitality to build up the health tone of the child, thus more easily enabling the disabilities to be overcome.

For the healing of these children a period of time is needed to allow the beneficial changes to be induced. The spirit side of the healing is the responsibility of the healing guides who carry out the healing purposes through the gift of healership. That which now follows is for the healer's guidance to try and show how the parents can co-operate with the healing purpose.

Children as a rule follow the line of least resistance, and if a limb does not function as it should, they accept this as a habitual state and make no positive effort of their own to overcome the weakness.

In cases of spasticity, the mental outlook may be bright and co-ordination may be good, the trouble with the limbs being limited to the physical inability to use them. The healing directive is to see that the vertebrae are mobile, and to free the joints and loosen up the muscles and tendons; but if no effort is made to help the child to take advantage of any improvements the healing brings, the little one will be content to continue just as before. The parents should therefore be urged to **gently** seek looseness within the joint, moving it as freely as it will, seeking just that little more and **gently** stretching the limb to straighten it as much as it will yield. In this, the child should be encouraged to join in with the purpose of co-operating with the healing intention. At the same time that this is done, the limb should be massaged to stimulate the circulation, encourage the muscles, and soften up the tendons.

Note: A technical massage is not necessary, just a gentle "mother's rubbing", using any oil or cream, or even talcum powder, to lubricate the hands in their movements. The value is in the massaging and not in the oil or powder.

When the limbs are lethargic with symptoms of paralysis, this is due to a lack of co-ordination from the brain, the nerves not possessing the vitality to carry the message conveying the intention, through the nerve cells, to operate the muscles. The child may have the mental desire to move the limb but cannot do so. Once again it will be observed that a child who has grown accustomed to the weakness is content to let things remain as they are and so makes no effort to seek improvement. Unfortunately some parents, too, accept the condition as inevitable, especially when the doctors say they "can do no more".

Showing the Parents How to Co-operate

In the healing of these conditions the nerves need to be stimulated to carry the message for a given movement from the brain, down along the nerves to the affected limb, and the only way to do this is to work through the mind and the bodily intelligence with spoken instructions, so that a muscular response is induced. For example, if the child has difficulty in raising the knee, the healer should show the parent how to take the leg in both hands and then tell the child "help me to lift the knee up," pause, "Now!" Then as the child makes the effort, the parent should give just that sufficient movement to help the knee to raise slowly. Then, supporting the leg, the parent should continue with, "Now, slowly, very slowly, press the knee down."

All this is directed at getting the nerves to work the muscles and to give intelligence to them. The healer will do this himself with the child and so show the parent what to do. The healer and parent should try to sense the child's response, and as this is felt, praise should be given and the child given further encouragement just to seek a little more movement.

This method should be carried out wherever there is muscular weakness and it applies equally well where the arms also are weak. Taking hold of both arms the healer should seek the child's co-operation through the spoken word, for them to be drawn back, then forward and upward, just as if the limbs are being "talked to". Similarly, for the fingers to bend and grip the healer's or parent's fingers as tightly as they can.

It should be kept in mind that these efforts are strenuous, using up a good deal of the child's energy, so not too much should be done at one time. **The essential thing is that the child's mind should co-operate with the intention.**

Even if little or no response is apparent, the treatment should be continued two or three times each day, to show the mind and bodily intelligence what is expected of the nerves. It will be observed that with repeated encouragement, the nerves begin to respond with progressive signs of movement and strength.

When a child or baby appears to have no comprehension and the mind does not function, the healing purpose is to try and arouse co-ordination through awareness. In these more difficult cases, still more patience is needed. The healer should try and show the parents that if the legs are inert, the feet should be held with the knees bent upwards and the one word "push" is used and repeated as the leg is straightened. By this means, the sound of the word "push" is received by the child and the mind will begin to associate the word with the leg movement, arousing the faculty of comprehension and so instructing the nerves to act. In the same way, associate the sound of a single word with a common action, repetitively, such as "milk . . . milk . . . milk", when giving a drink or "shoes . . . shoes . . . shoes", when putting shoes on. The child is receiving spiritual healing all the time, which seeks to arouse the conscious mind, so this kind of procedure can play an effective part in the effort to awaken and activate the mind and brain.

Most children whose mentality is not functioning possess two qualities. The first is that they are exceedingly affectionate and love to be made a fuss of. Even when showing affection to a child, a method can be adopted to help establish expectancy with awareness. In the fondling of a child, after the first expressions of affection, the parent should gently stroke one arm and then the other, leading down to the movement of the fingers, helping the fingers to curl round and hold one of the parent's fingers. Next the legs should be gently stroked one at a time, and the feet moved up and down. This, or any other procedure the parent adopts, should become a set form of procedure, and the child's mind will begin to look for it, thus commencing the mental awareness and awakening.

Secondly, these children are invariably fond of music, especially that with a good rhythm. When a child is fractious, music will often help to soothe him. Such music should be specially played, and the parent should try to enter into the child's way of responding to it so that if the arms are moved, to encourage this action in time with the rhythm. Finish with playing a lullaby to soothe the child's mind and help it to become more tranquil. This plan is often found helpful when the child is slow to go to sleep, as the soothing flow of the lullaby music assists sleep to come. If the child is afraid of the dark, a night light or other soft light should be left burning.

Another suggestion is to have a few widely differing sounds, a bell, a tuning fork, rattling a spoon in a cup, etc., and associating each of these sounds with a set function, such as time for drinking, bath-time, etc. All these things are designed to encourage co-ordination.

If healers can get parental co-operation in these ways and maintain both Absent and Contact Healing, they will find that handicapped children are greatly helped to better co-ordination and mental appreciation. The important thing to be kept in mind is that in "talking" to a limb, for example, the child should be encouraged to consciously co-operate and to try and "feel" what is taking place, so that the experience is registered on the child's conscious mind and can thereby be recalled when seeking the same movements later.

Paralysis in Children

In Section III, the treatment for paralysis is dealt with in some detail, and in which it will be noted that the principles for encouraging control and co-ordination are the same as for the treatment of spastic and retarded children.

Treatment of the Mongol Child

Healers are familiar with those sad and pathetic children who have been born as "mongols" with their typical mongoloid features and accompanying mental retardation. Mongolism is not a disease, it is a "throwback" to the earlier stages in human evolution. It is thought that it is unyieldable to spiritual healing, and in many cases this has seemed so. At the same time, we have on record the overcoming of mongoloid tendencies when they have not been too pronounced especially with the healing having commenced soon after the child's birth.

Treatment for General Psychosomatic Disharmonies

Some people inherit sensitive natures, others are "born worriers". Then there are those whose mental equilibrium has been severely upset by circumstances, possibly a bad fright in childhood; the loss of a very dear one; a sense of personal slight or injury, and so on. All these are frustrations which can be the forerunner of disease.

It has already been shown that mind disharmonies need to be corrected on the same plane as they exist, and we can go a little further to see the way in which the spirit thought influencing reaches the conscious mind.

If we accept that the pineal gland is the doorway between the conscious mind and Spirit, the probability is that this gland may be capable of receiving and transmitting thought impressions and directives from Spirit and the healing intelligences.

We know that thought impulses travel along the nerves to instruct the muscles to act in a definite way. They do so, through characterised vibrations transmitted through the nerve cells. However, a different procedure occurs when the bodily intelligence is called into activity by a mental experience.

In the act of healing there is established a state of affinity between the healer and the spirit doctors as well as the healer's spirit mind with that of the patient. In the healing of psychosomatic disorders it becomes necessary for corrective thought to be directed from the spirit doctor through the healer to the patient, especially when a direct approach from Spirit cannot be received on the patient's conscious mind to influence and overcome the cause of the unrest.

The patient will tell the healer he is suffering from "nerves" and be well aware of his trouble. His mind has been over-burdened and occupied with some continual worry. He cannot sleep; he is short-tempered and has lost incentive and cannot concentrate. He cannot get his mind **free.**

As a rule, the patient will talk freely about his various troubles which the healer listens to attentively and with compassion. With experience, the healer soon becomes able to form an opinion as to the best approach to adopt in calming and soothing the troubled mind. There is no one way to do this. Every case is individual, but there are some general directives worth considering, and perhaps the first of these is that of the healer-patient relationship.

Relationship Between Healer and Patient

The patient has come to the healer for help. Therefore he has confidence in the healer to help him. He is looking for practical help, some positive treatment, his mind is so troubled that he is anxious to gain the feeling of security, of companionship, and a rebuilding of self-assurance. The healer has to convey the impression that he can help the patient, that he fully understands the problem, and will be able to show the patient the way to master it.

There are a number of different approaches. One, is to avoid discussing the symptoms **in detail,** dealing with the trouble in a general affirmative way by urging the patient to let the past remain in the past and that through the good healing influencing from Spirit, he will find the tangle in his mind progressively unravel as the days pass by. Where there are a number of contributory factors, it is best to avoid discussing any one aspect in detail, for this is likely to lead towards more confusion in the patient's mind.

If the issue is more simple, such as domestic trouble, the healer, whilst showing every sympathy, should avoid taking sides, but seek through good influencing to reach all concerned for that which is best.

The healer will probably wish to express his sympathy and understanding by placing his hands close to, or on, the patient's head, and seek to soothe away tensions, quieten angry thoughts, calm down mental unease (possibly with soothing words) and so promote a more contented outlook. Half the battle is often won if the healer can get the patient to smile.

Sometimes, a condition seemingly unrelated to mental unrest is being dealt with, such as arthritis, and then it is far more difficult for the healer to ascertain the psychosomatic cause of the trouble. It may, for instance, lie in an unfulfilled ambition. Obviously, it is not advisable for the healer to question the patient closely to try and find what it is—possibly the patient may have no idea either—in which case, it is best left to the healing guide to deal with.

While we have been dealing with the healer's manner in treating a patient, we must never overlook the fundamental truth that it is the spirit doctor who brings about the beneficial change within a patient. This does not minimise the efforts of the healer, for if his words are wise and based upon healing motives, which become registered on the patient's conscious mind, then, blended as he is with the patient, a worthy contribution can be made in helping the sufferer to throw off the mental stress which has become so burdensome.

Spiritual Healing as a Preventative of Disease

Spiritual healing has built up its vital strength in the homes of countless people who have been healed of disease, often when the doctors could do no more. It has served, and will continue to serve, the noblest of all functions, that of restoring happiness and cleansing minds, bodies and souls of disorders. It serves a greater purpose in demonstrating in this matter-of-fact age, the truth **that living creation is akin to Spirit in this earthly phase of life. From this it is inevitable that there must develop a more spiritual code of values to govern our concepts of life, both national and international, bringing into being the out-lawing of war, poverty, animal cruelties, and all those other ignoble tendencies which have shamed our civilisation.**

With this emancipation comes a new directive and a more important role for spiritual healing for the future. Scientifically advanced as we are in this generation, we are only at the beginning of the understanding of our **real** selves. The evolution of man has a long way to go. It is in this evolving state of change that healership has to play an ever more important role as the science of spirit healing unfolds.

This vision rests upon a two-pronged factor. It is accepted by all medical authorities and spiritual healers that the primary causation of almost all our diseases lies in psychosomatic disharmony; and that our cellular diseases are the physical ill-effects of life's frustrations. So it is, that apart from purely physical conditions, such as broken limbs, burns, infections, dislocations and so on, we can appreciate the basic origin of our ill-health states.

There are, of course, other factors which influence perfect health such as lack of fresh air, incorrect food, insufficient exercise, etc. These are not serious, but do promote minor ill-effects on occasion.

We know, now, that the primary cause of cancer is frustration, mainly through the prevention of carrying out the natural purposes of life. **If these frustrations**

can be recognised early, then through the remedial influencing of spiritual healing they can be overcome and other directives in life can replace them. In this way we shall prevent the onset of cancer. Prevention of disease is spiritual healing's ultimate purpose.

Who can doubt, knowing of the ability of Spirit to overcome mental disharmonies, that through spiritual healing many people have been saved from contracting cancer already? We cannot prove this by statistics, but logic supports it and the author will go further that within his experience he does not recall any instance of a patient subsequently contracting cancer after he, or she, has received spiritual healing for some other kind of sickness.

It may be that some future research is needed to study more deeply human emotional and anxiety states, to find out the **character** of those frustrations which can directly induce diseases like cancer, gastric ulcers, skin complaints, etc. For example, we already know that frustration concerned with the furtherance of life's functions is a major factor in the cause of carcinoma; and such things as business worries, responsibilities, can cause gastric ulcers. Give the business executive or professional man a holiday to soothe his anxiety state and he will lose his ulcer. Medical treatment for gastric troubles is a "holiday in a hospital". Similarly, there may well be a character of frustration which will prevent the bloodstream from functioning as it should, and so be responsible for the family of rheumatic and arthritic complaints.

Future Role of the Healer

This book has endeavoured to establish the connection between spiritual healing and the chemical composition of healing forces; the use of spirit energies; that we possess a number of intelligence systems, capable of being influenced from Spirit, and with this the association of cellular intelligence; the causes of psychosomatic unrest and the influence of all these things upon the health. In addition, we have seen that there is a superior spirit intelligence which can influence and instruct the mind and bodily intelligences to direct dispersive, constructive, strengthening and nutritive energies for our well-being.

Healers who possess knowledge of all the above factors become active collaborators with the healing purpose, even though at times they may not be conscious of it. Today, the average healer tends to be a passive instrument through whom the healing energies flow, but as his understanding of the healing potentials improves, as his attunement becomes stronger and more natural, so he will consciously receive thought directives to enable him to fulfil a greater part in the healing act.

To healers who have been able to gain experience in healing, the art of attunement comes easily—as "second nature". With this, the ability to receive and impart intuitive thought direction from Spirit makes them conscious collaborators with the healing directive and so they are able to influence the patient's spirit and physical mind, as well as his bodily intelligence, to respond in ways, which otherwise, they could not do.

Let us take a final example to explain this. A patient has a growth, it may be a cyst, a goitre, or a tumour. In Contact Healing the healer will place his hand over the growth and his healing intention will be for the guide to use him for the act of dispersal. The healer's mental intention is focused on the purpose. The healer is conscious of this; the patient is aware of the healing objective and thereby becomes receptive. There is a **unity of purpose,** the healer being aware of the guide's direction of characterised molecular energies to bring about a state of chemical change in the structure of the growth; and then, through the patient's conscious mind, the bodily intelligence will co-operate by directing additional leucocytes to the area to carry away the harmful matter which has been changed in its form. Once the process has been instituted, then it should continue until the growth has been dispersed.

We have said that healings can only take place within the scope of the physical and spirit laws, but within this range so much can be done. The difficulty is that healers do not know what condition is likely to yield and what is not. Diagnosis is the responsibility of the spirit guide or doctor, and therefore the healer should never decide himself what can or cannot be achieved but make the effort to seek healing for whatever condition he is confronted with.

In the same respect, no healer can give an assurance or promise in advance that any ill-condition will be healed, even though it appears to be a simple one. Neither should he give any approximation of time for the healing to take place. All sorts of circumstances can interfere with the smooth progress of a healing, for which neither the guide nor the healer is responsible.

So we learn not to blame ourselves, the patient, or the spirit guide, if we do not see all the progress we wish to see.

Summary of Postulates

This book has set out a number of postulates, some of which are factual, the others based on logic and probability. All these postulates are associated with spiritual healing, and the attuned healer is used as the instrument to bring these factors into the healing task on hand. They are as follows:

No change takes place in the state of matter unless there is a reasoned law-governed process responsible for the change.

To purposefully bring about a change, an intelligence is needed to direct the law-governed processes to produce that change.

This intelligence must have the knowledge to use the processes to produce the planned result.

With the healing of medically incurable conditions, we recognise that if the healing intelligence is not human, it must come from a non-human source, namely that of Spirit.

Etheric energy is the basic substance of the universe, and in a characterised form produces the elemental atoms comprising all matter.

An atom is characterised energy in a precisely organised system which has purpose and "personality".

All matter—liquids, solids and gases—is composed of atoms, and two or more atoms together combine to form a molecule.

When two or more molecules are associated together, the energies within the atoms intermix, producing a compound substance.

To produce a chemical state of change in an afflicted part of the human body needs the introduction of specially constructed molecules to counteract the disease molecules and so promote the chemical change for the better.

The healing intelligence must therefore be able to diagnose a patient's trouble down to the harmful molecular structure of the affliction.

The healing intelligence must be so knowledgeable of the manipulation of energies and their potentials, that it can build up counter energies to form healing molecules and then be able to direct them to the precise area in which they are needed to bring about a state of change in the disease.

We possess a physical mind and a spirit mind intimate with each other, and the brain is the computer servant of both minds.

All forms of thought and sensation are mind experiences.

There is a bodily intelligence which acts independently of the brain.

The pituitary and pineal glands possess an intelligence, independent of, but co-operative with, the mind.

All the intelligence systems can be influenced by the physical and spirit mind.

We can receive thought directives from the spirit intelligence which can influence our mental appreciations and give instruction to all the bodily intelligence systems.

The cell is a complete living organism. It possesses an intelligence.

The cell has a definite purpose to perform in life and if frustrated can become insane, i.e. cancerous cells.

The genes are the seeds of inheritance and provide the means of evolution. The genes are the mind of the cell.

An individual thought has a precise energy form.

Like the molecule, one thought energy structure can influence the structure of another thought energy structure.

The conscious mind can be influenced by thought structures arising from physical experiences as well as by thought energies from Spirit.

Thus, in all healing we learn to avoid mechanical processes or techniques and instead to harness the total intelligences to the healing intention. As this more advanced form of co-operation with the healing guides is employed and the patient's intellectual faculties used, so more easily will disharmonies and disease be overcome . . . and eventually prevented.

Only because we are more scientific in our approach to these matters can we become more spiritual. That is to say: only as we increase our real knowledge of the forces of nature and the Spirit can we align moralities and lives to come within the borders of these truths. Only because we have come slowly upwards from deep ignorance can we now understand that the healing miracles in the New Testament were manifestations of the same knowledge in using the power of healing we are witnessing today. Nearly two thousand years have had to elapse since those times before we have been able to learn sufficient to appreciate the nature of matter and the existence and co-operation of Spirit.

INDEX

Compiled by F. D. Buck

Absent Healer, 16, 17, 37, 43,
52, 53, 74, 82, 91, 143,
180, 184, 187, 189, 191,
192, 193, 195, 201, 205,
210, 230, 236, 238, 260,
262, 282, 285–6, 295, 298,
300, 305
  expenses, 68
  opposition and, 66
Absent Healing, 13–70, 97, 103
  conclusion, 68–9
  general observations, 13–16
  joy of, 52–3
  last hope, 47
  limitation, 54–6
  mechanics of, 19
  not casual, 39
  patient contact, 34–7
  qualifications for, 16–17
acne, 285
acromegaly, 272
affliction, 20
allergies, healing of, 282–4
amino acids, 233, 234
anaemia, 92, 182, 186, 234
  pernicious, 232
animals, law and, 212–13
animals, treatment of, 136
arthritic adhesions, 226
arthritic deposit, 230
arthritic substance, 226
arthritis, 21, 63, 92, 130, 147,

198, 225, 229, 232
  healing of, 154–60
asthma, 167, 171, 283–4
atom, the, 219–20
attunement, 27, 75, 76, 91
  ability, 77
  art of, 78–87
  experience, 79
  guide and, 91, 150
  meaning, 79
  mind and Spirit, 23
  seeking of, 23–4
  spirit doctor and, 104
  spirit guide and, 104
  way of, 25–31
attunement with Spirit, 13–70,
123, 203
  establishing, 25
auditory senses, 198
aura:
  cleansing, 141, 173
  healing passes and, 141
  split, 172, 216

Bacteria, harmful, 243, 245
bed wetting, 286–7
belt of pain, 153
blood and circulatory
  conditions, healing of,
  181–5
blood cells, 232, 268
blood pressure, 242

control and communication,
271–2
correspondence, 47, 48
cosmic breathing, 31–4
cosmic energy, 32
cosmic forces, 33
cosmic strength, 284
cysts, 182

Deafness, catarrhal, 198
deafness, healing of, 197–200
deep heat, 262
deep-ray therapies, 228
dentistry, 213
deoxyribonucleic acid (DNA),
223, 233
dermatitis, 190, 285
development, preliminary, 25
diabetes, 213
diagnosis, 37–8, 88–93, 103,
239, 287
clairvoyant, 92
digestive system, 232
digestive troubles, 284–5
disease, prevention of, 308
disharmony, 55, 60, 131, 268
mental, 173, 293, 310
psychosomatic, 306–7
cause of, 291, 309
disseminated sclerosis, 146
Distant Healing, 13
Divine Healing, 13
Divine Plan to Healership, 71,
72, 77, 133
DNA (see deoxyribonucleic
acid)
donations, 67–8
drink, 121
drugs, advice concerning,
111—112

Ears, conditions associated
with, 200–1

ears that do not hear, 200–1
earthly realm, 18
eczema, 190
emergencies, treatment in, 137
emotional states, 292
emotional stresses, 250
emotions, 18
emphysema, 167, 284
endocrine glandular system,
281
enzymes, 234
epilepsy, 213
etheric bodies, 216
etheric mind, the, 278
exhaustion, 167
eyesight, weakening, 20
eye troubles, 194

Failures, 62
faith, 255–6
have I enough?, 129–33
fears, 173
healing of, 292–4
moveable, 175
skin trouble and, 286
fibrin, 242
fibroblast, 243
fibrositic deposits, 239
fibrositis, 253
healing, 154–60
firmness, 296–8
fits, 213
forces, law-governed, 20
free-will, 67
frustration factor, the, 269–71
functional troubles, 181–5

Gall bladder, stones in, 92, 182
gastric ulcers, 92, 130, 284–5,
310
genes, 223, 267—9, 273
frustration of, 275
giddiness, 61

symptoms and, 91
patient-healer relationship, 307
peace within, 32
pecuniary rewards, 67
penances, 30
phagocytes, 242, 260
physical debility, 232
physical laws, 21, 312
  spirit, difference between, 78
physical mind, 18, 19, 277-8
physical reaction, 41
physical realm, 21, 98
physical thought, 38
pituitary control, 272
pituitary endocrine system, 281
plasma, 242
platelets, 242, 243
poliomyelitis, 161
  healing of, 298
possession, healing of, 298-9
power, giving of, 99-102
power water, 142
prayer(s), 27, 81, 123, 137, 203
Prayer Healing, 13
press, dealing with the, 117
prognosis, 90
proteins, 233
protoplasm, 268
psoriasis, 190, 285
psyche, the, 278
psychic gifts, 33
psychic gland, the, 135, 138
psychological approach, 53-54
psychosomatic conditions:
  mental healing and, 277
  mental healing introduction,
    277
psychosomatic diseases, 94, 172,
  179, 180
psychosomatic disharmonies, 279
  treatment for, 306-7
psychosomatic disorders, 250
psychosomatic unrest, 311

Questions, 93

Radiation, deep, 203
radiation, frequency of, 289
rays, 94, 216
reception, 116
relaxing, 121
rescue circle, 298
respiratory diseases, 284
  healing of 167-71
respond, those who fail to, 56
responsibility, sense of, 174
rheumatism, 230
  healing of, 154-60
ribonucleic acid (RNA), 223,
  233
RNA (see ribonucleic acid)

Safeguards, 212
schizophrenia, 298
sclerosis, 253
senility, 20, 62
sensation, 89, 91
sensitive natures, 306
serenity, 119
shingles, 285
sickness:
  extreme, 48
  mental, 269
  physical, 269
sight, healing of, 193-6
sight, restoration of, 21
sittings, 29
skin afflictions, 182, 183, 285-6,
  310
  fears and, 286
skin cells, 268
skin diseases, healing of, 190-2
sleep, 121
slipped discs, 152-3
smallpox, 246
soothing process, 175
soul sickness, 281